Praise for 'Maestro' J(

'Sir John Monash was an outstanding military commander, Australia's greatest. He was the product of a militia system that produced first rate generals not only in Australia but also in Canada, where Sir Arthur Currie was the only other non regular soldier to rise to the heights of a corps commander and become, effectively, commanders of their respective national armies. In this passionate advocacy of Monash's claim to greatness amongst all the Allied commanders, Tim Fischer shows how, despite being a Jew, he surmounted prejudice and earned respect and recognition from his military peers and superiors as well as his sovereign. In a telling chapter, something as innocuous as the victory banquet at Buckingham Palace in 1919 illustrates clearly the conflicts with a jealous home political establishment that bedevilled the postwar careers of both Currie and Monash.'

Rev Nigel Cave IC MA, editor, Battleground Europe series

'This book is an excellent examination, based on new material, of the contribution of John Monash, warts and all, to Australia and the world. Monash very much deserves posthumous promotion to the rank of field marshal and this should be a decision made in the next year or so by the Commonwealth of Australia, the democracy that Monash gave so much to, throughout his civil and military endeavours.'

Rex Lipman, World War Two commando in East Timor,
Reserve Regimental Commander, Lidell Hart confidante,
businessman and author

'Former deputy prime minister Tim Fischer brings his army and political experience into tackling the General Monash story. His flowing and digestible style draws into sharp relief the many internal forces arraigned against Monash, commander-in-chief of the First AIF. First there was Charles Bean the official war historian who intellectualised his dislike of an "outsider", someone with German-Jewish parents, running the Australian Army. Second, Fischer shows how Labor PM Billy Hughes felt so inferior to Monash that he made sure he could never run for high political office. And third, this book demonstrates how the British governor-general Munro Ferguson resented the huge respect shown to Monash by visiting Royals (two future kings—Edward VIII and George VI) to Australia postwar. They knew who had done much to preserve the British Empire, and it wasn't a GG sitting in his vice regal office in Melbourne. Fischer's rendition lucidly explains how these three "pygmies" (in comparison to Monash) did as much as the German Army to bring down the most outstanding general of the Great War. Like the enemy, they failed.'

Professor Roland Perry of Melbourne,
author of *Monash: The Outsider Who Won a War*

'The nation needs to focus more on John Monash, our greatest World War One general, we need to focus on his many achievements and attributes. The nation should consider how best to elevate and salute his genius and greatness that did so much for boosting the fabric of Australia.'

General Sir Phillip Bennett AC KBE DSO KStJ: Ex CO 1 RAR and CDF, former governor of Tasmania; Canberra, Remembrance Day, 2013

'John Monash was the greatest general of World War I by far. His grip of situations silenced all doubters and compelled the admiration of even the most critical professional soldiers.'

Sir Basil Liddell Hart, senior British journalist and world war historian of renown

'It was Billy Hughes' extreme dislike for John Monash that caused Hughes to say of me that I was "the greatest Australian" and of course Billy Hughes was wrong.'

Sir Donald Bradman, Australian cricket legend, in interview with Professor Roland Perry, 1995

'I would name Sir John Monash as the best general on the Western Front in Europe, he possessed real creative originality.'

Field Marshal and first Viscount Montgomery of Alamein, 1968

MAESTRO JOHN MONASH

ABOUT THE AUTHOR

The Honourable Tim Fischer AC is the former deputy prime minister of Australia and was the Australian ambassador to the Holy See for three years until January 2012. A former Australian Army officer, NSW state parliamentarian, leader of the National Party and minister for trade, Tim Fischer is also a consultant, company director, author, broadcaster, and multiple patron.

His previous publications include *Seven Days in East Timor: Ballot and Bullets* (2000), *Tim Fischer's Outback Heroes: and Communities that Count* (2002), *Transcontinental Train Odyssey: The Ghan, the Khyber, the Globe* (2004), *Asia & Australia: Tango in Trade, Tourism and Transport* (2005), *Trains Unlimited in the 21st Century* (2011) and *Holy See, Unholy Me! 1000 Days in Rome* (2013).

Melbourne, Jerilderie, Gallipoli,
Amiens and beyond

MAESTRO JOHN MONASH

AUSTRALIA'S GREATEST CITIZEN GENERAL

TIM FISCHER

MONASH University
Publishing

Third printing, 2014.

Monash University Publishing
Building 4, Monash University
Clayton, Victoria 3800, Australia
www.publishing.monash.edu

Monash University Publishing brings to the world publications which advance the best traditions of humane and enlightened thought.

Monash University Publishing titles pass through a rigorous process of independent peer review.

www.publishing.monash.edu/books/mjm-9781922235596.html

Series: Australian History

Design: Les Thomas

Front cover image: General Sir John Monash mounted on a dappled grey charger leading an Anzac Day march, 25 April 1931. Australian War Memorial photo AO3451.

Back cover image: Prime Minister WM Hughes (centre) steps out with Lieutenant General Sir John Monash (on his left), on the Western Front, 1918. On far left: Brigadier General Edwin Tivey; on far right: UK Daily Mail Editor Thomas Marlowe. Australian War Memorial photo E03851.

National Library of Australia Cataloguing-in-Publication entry:
Author: Fischer, Tim, 1946- author.
Title: Maestro John Monash : Australia's greatest citizen general/Tim Fischer.
ISBN: 9781922235596 (paperback).
Notes: Includes bibliographical references and index.
Subjects: Monash, John, Sir, 1865-1931;
Australia. Army--Officers--Biography;
Generals--Australia--Biography;
World War, 1914-1918--Campaigns;
Engineers--Australia--Biography;
Australia--History--20th century.
Dewey Number: 355.0092

Printed in Australia by Griffin Press an Accredited ISO AS/NZS 14001:2004 Environmental Management System printer.

FSC
www.fsc.org
MIX
Paper from responsible sources
FSC® C009448

The paper this book is printed on is certified against the Forest Stewardship Council ® Standards. Griffin Press holds FSC chain of custody certification SGS-COC-005088. FSC promotes environmentally responsible, socially beneficial and economically viable management of the world's forests.

DEDICATION

This book is dedicated to the 414 chaplains of the Australian Imperial Force who served in World War One and who made a huge contribution to the wellbeing of members of the Australian Imperial Force (AIF). They helped in many ways, from digging steps up the steep slopes out of Anzac Cove to stretcher bearing on the Western Front, providing spiritual support and friendship. This is especially so of the five extraordinary Australians highlighted here:

Anglican chaplain William Dexter MC, the longest serving chaplain of World War One, departed Melbourne on the 12,000 tonne troop carrier HMAT *Orvieto* on 21 October 1914. He served in Gallipoli and (at the front of) the Western Front, including at the Somme; he then served with the John Monash demobilisation staff through 1919 in and around London, before returning to Australia.

Jewish chaplain Rabbi Jacob Danglow, who served on the Western Front and went on to be rabbi at the St Kilda Synagogue in Melbourne and an important Australian Jewish leader for decades. In 1921 in Melbourne he married Bertha, the only child of John and Vic Monash, to Gershon Bennett.

Presbyterian chaplain Frank Rolland MC of South Australia and Victoria started out as a Uniting Church – Flynn of the Inland – minister at Beltana in South Australia, in what was tough going but turned out to be good training. He was an outstanding chaplain who served on no-man's-land at the Battle of Hamel, bravely going forward of the start line and ahead of zero hour at 3:10 A.M. to help establish a Regimental Aid Post. He served in many locations and during many battles on the Western Front. Later he was headmaster of Geelong

College for twenty-five years, helping to build the magnificent main campus, complete with cloister, in Geelong. Later again he was the moderator general of the Presbyterian Church of Australia.

Roman Catholic chaplain Father John Fahey served in Gallipoli and went on to put in the hard yards as a chaplain on the Western Front. He wrote of the Somme: 'It just beggars description.' Later he was a Church leader in Western Australia where he also was one of the founders and creators of the RSL in that state. His funeral in Perth drew thousands, from all faiths.

Salvation Army chaplain Major William McKenzie MC served at Gallipoli and later on the Western Front, where he was awarded the Military Cross and was held in high esteem by the diggers. His enormous popularity amongst the diggers was due to a giving, practical and supportive approach. They nicknamed him 'Fighting Mac'. Some 7,000 Melburnians turned out to welcome him home.

CONTENTS

FOREWORD

Tim Fischer has written a fascinating and important book. *Maestro John Monash* is more than a valuable history lesson, it is a tour de force in advocacy, a call to arms on behalf of Australia's greatest citizen-soldier, Sir John Monash.

While many scholars and historians have recounted Monash's heroic exploits on the battlefield and beyond, none have taken up the cause to have Monash posthumously promoted to field marshal with the vigour and purpose Tim Fischer has now done.

In doing so, this much admired former deputy prime minister of Australia and Vietnam veteran has done us all a service.

With comprehensive research and a practical roadmap for attaining posthumous recognition, this fine book provides us, the broader community, with the wherewithal to right a historical wrong.

Fischer persuasively documents how Monash, despite his exceptional talents and achievements, was continuously the subject of anti-Semitism and discrimination.

The son of migrant Prussian Jews, Monash came through the ranks of the militia rather than the more traditional path of the officer corps.

His troubled relationship with CEW Bean at Gallipoli and later during the war with Keith Murdoch was to dog him for many years. These two powerful and well-connected men worked against Monash, lobbying Prime Minister Billy Hughes to thwart his promotion.

These efforts were compounded by Hughes' own insecurities, conscious as he was that Monash was more popular than he.

With the first postwar Australian federal election looming in 1919, Hughes was not in any mood to promote the then victorious lieutenant general to full general, fearful that Monash may have moved into politics where he would have proved to be a formidable rival.

Fischer argues rightly that were Monash to have been promoted postwar to general, it would have been possible that King George V would have promoted him to field marshal in July 1919 when he promoted four others, Allenby, Plumer, Wilson and the Frenchman Ferdinand Foch.

Monash of course was a favourite of the king, having being knighted at Bertangles, France, on 12 August 1918, just after the Battle of Amiens.

What makes this book so enjoyable are the many insights and anecdotes that spring from the rich canvas of Monash's life.

From his childhood years in Jerilderie where he encountered the legendary Ned Kelly, to his prominent seat at King George and Queen Mary's postwar victory banquet at Buckingham Palace alongside five sitting prime ministers and the American president Woodrow Wilson, Monash's story is re-told with sensitivity and aplomb.

By no means a hagiography, this book looks at Monash's life in its entirety, mistresses and all, but after turning the last page the reader can be left in little doubt about the greatness of this man.

Out of the darkness and brutality of the Western Front, Monash represents a shining light, caring for his troops, meticulously preparing for battle and brilliantly outsmarting the enemy.

Fischer brings his soldier's eye to the many World War One campaigns, including Gallipoli, the Somme, Hamel and Amiens, and compares the performances of the various generals in the context of the challenges they faced. Monash he concludes was in a league of his own.

With the centenary of Anzac soon upon us, the timing of *Maestro John Monash* could not be better as it is a book that delivers a powerful case.

It will prompt us to reassess the events of that time and build momentum for Monash's posthumous promotion.

Such an act by the Australian Parliament, bipartisan it will need to be, will not change history per se but rather complete it, preserving in our nation's memory the rightful place of one very special man.

Acknowledging Field Marshal Monash would also be a fitting tribute to the hundreds of thousands of Australian men and women who served in the Great War with bravery and distinction.

The Hon Josh Frydenberg MP, Parliamentary Secretary to the Prime Minister, Federal Member for Kooyong

INSPIRATION

There are many Australians who served at Gallipoli and who post World War One went on to achieve and contribute much to the fabric of the Australian nation. The list is never able to be completed but forty or more spring to mind. Each of them was an inspiration to me and all of them were appropriately recognised, except one, who was kept one step in rank under what he should have been promoted to after the war. The postwar jealousy of WM Hughes and possibly the anti-Semitism of CEW Bean helped ensure a downplaying of the contribution of this person, namely General Sir John Monash of Jerilderie and Melbourne, Gallipoli and Hamel. Monash was in many ways the 'Maestro General'.

Here is my list of very capable and committed Australians who 'graduated' from Gallipoli, survived World War One and in some cases World War Two and who greatly inspired the writing of this book. They also contributed an enormous amount to the growth and wellbeing of Australia and Great Britain, going on to hold key positions as detailed here:

Hubert Lawrence Anthony:	Federal minister, including postmaster-general
CEW Bean:	Official World War One historian and AWM co-founding chairman
Henry Gordon Bennett:	Eighth Division commander in World War Two during the fall of Singapore
Arthur Blackburn VC:	Co-founder RSL South Australia and state MP

Sir Thomas Blamey:	Victorian Police commissioner and World War Two leader
William Kinsey Bolton:	RSL leader and senator
Albert Borella VC:	Dundas activist and Albury community anchor
Stanley Melbourne Bruce:	Prime minister after World War One and Australian high commissioner in London during World War Two
Lord Richard Casey:	Last governor of Bengal, federal minister and governor-general
Sir Arthur Coles:	Melbourne lord mayor, federal MP and co-founder of Coles stores
Sir Harry Chauvel:	Inspector general of the Army
Sir Albert Coates:	Leading surgeon
William Dunstan VC:	General manager *Herald* and *Weekly Times*
Pompey Elliott:	Senator
Chaplain Father John Fahey:	Co-founder Western Australia RSL
Harry Foll:	Long-serving senator for Queensland and federal minister
Sir Hudson Fysh:	Co-founder of QANTAS
Sir John Gellibrand:	Victorian Police commissioner and federal MP
Cardinal Norman Gilroy:	Bishop of Port Pirie and later of Sydney
Sir Thomas Glasgow:	Defence minister and later high commissioner to Canada
John Hamilton VC:	World War Two captain in Papua New Guinea
Neville Howse VC:	Federal minister

Ion Idriess:	Leading author of, among other works, *Flynn of the Inland*
Albert Jacka VC:	Mayor of St Kilda in Melbourne
Sir George Jones:	Head of the RAAF in World War Two
Sir Charles Kingsford Smith:	Air commodore in the RAAF
Sir Ray Leane:	South Australian chief police commissioner and Police Academy founder
WKS Mackenzie:	Lawyer and leading Sydney-based legal writer
Sir Ross MacPherson Smith:	Pioneer aviator who was the first to fly from the UK to Darwin
Sir John Monash:	Founding chairman of SEC Victoria and driving force behind the creation of the Melbourne Shrine of Remembrance
Leslie Morshead:	Led an important early defeat of the Nazis at Tobruk in World War Two
Sir Keith Murdoch:	Media giant was a letter carrier at Gallipoli
Henry Murray VC:	Most decorated World War One soldier, and CO in World War Two
Sir Thomas Playford:	SA state MP and SA premier for 27 years (1938–1965)
Sir Charles Rosenthal:	NSW state MP and head of Institute of Architects of NSW
Sir Granville Ryrie:	State and federal MP, later high commissioner to London
Sir Stanley Savige:	Co-founder of Legacy

Geoffrey Street MC:	Federal minister for defence, minister for the army and minister of Repatriation
Hugo Throssell VC:	Northam (WA) leader and anti-war campaigner
Charles Ulm:	Pioneer aviator with Charles Kingsford Smith
Sir Cyril Brudenell White:	CGS, Australian Army, and later chairman of the Commonwealth Public Service Board
Matron Grace Margaret Wilson:	Matron in chief, Australian Army, in World War Two

Again I observe this list can never be completed but it points to the fact that those who served in World War One, especially at Gallipoli, were determined not to waste their lives and went on to achieve in many ways. For many it was their way of saluting the fallen. Collectively they made a huge contribution to the progress of Australia after the end of the World War One.

ACKNOWLEDGEMENTS

At the outset I express my sincere thanks to the Buckingham Palace staff who uncovered details relating to the special banquet held there on 27 December 1918. Further I thank Her Majesty Queen Elizabeth II, for granting permission to publish this material. In this I was greatly assisted by the prompt action of diplomat Mike Rann and also throughout the project by other diplomats, including the then ambassador of France to Australia, Stéphane Romatet.

On the research front I was greatly helped by Greig Tillotson, former NSW State Parliamentary librarian, who efficiently found source information, including various details relating to Monash in London and the Buckingham Palace special banquet. Likewise former clerk of the House of Representatives, Lyn Barlin AM, provided guidance and assistance with regard to the contents of federal Hansard of yesteryear.

I wish to express appreciation and to salute the works of CEW Bean including the twelve-volume *Official History of Australia in the War of 1914–1918*. Further I salute the biography of Monash by Geoffrey Serle, the first biography completed after the release of the Monash personal papers. In some ways the Serle biography was like a guiding light, opening up many research leads.

In particular the guidance and writings of both Peter Pedersen, formerly of the AWM, and Professor Roland Perry, are fully acknowledged and greatly appreciated. This work has helped in researching different aspects of the life and military work of Monash, and in turn pointed the way towards the source documents such as contained within the massive correspondence and personal papers created by

Monash himself. The assistance from the AWM and the National Library in Canberra with their treasure trove of Monash documents is also acknowledged.

Relevant permissions have been obtained from the AWM, the Australian Army History Unit and other organisations, including from the Hansard of the federal parliament, to use some WM Hughes quotes and highlight various sins of omission by WM Hughes. In this regard I thank Karen Greening of the Content Management Branch of the Parliament of Australia and note that under relatively new provisions, Hansard comes under the creative commons license provisions, including in relation to republishing parts of Hansard.

Likewise State librarian Alex Byrne and the NSW State Library in Sydney greatly assisted, especially with access to their treasure trove of over one thousand World War One diaries. The Mitchell World War One Diary Project, in conjunction with News Limited, is to be strongly commended. The NSW State Parliamentary Library and the Victorian State Library in Melbourne were both very helpful as well; the latter itself assisted by the Monash designed 'Central Dome'.

Laurie Henery the outstanding Jerilderie local historian greatly assisted with chapter one in particular and remains a great source of information regarding both the early years of Monash at Jerilderie and Ned Kelly's Jerilderie visits. The Bryce family kindly showed me the residence in which the Monash family lived at 30 Jerilderie Street and the location of the stables at the rear.

Mary Brewer played a critical role in reviewing all spelling and syntax of the manuscript before submission to formal editing and publication. Also my wife Judy Brewer gave invaluable support throughout the long process of creating this book, as did my sons

Harrison and Dominic. I especially thank Dominic for doing the illustrations.

Among so many others I appreciate and acknowledge the review contribution of both Charles Bright and Sean Ryan of Melbourne, Fiona White of Adelaide, Garth Strong of Boree Creek, Hazel Watson of Sydney and Peter Whitelaw of Melbourne and Woodend. David and Margaret Richardson of Rome and Melbourne and others I thank for the supply of World War One letters and information.

I was greatly helped by Les Terrett of Myrtleford and the Army History Unit, especially with military rank insignia. Andrew Condon, as a former Australian Army officer, who underwent training in the USA, helpfully and quickly provided an extra dimension relating to the standing of Monash and the Battle of Hamel. The two feature maps of the key battles of Hamel and Amiens were prepared by Keith Mitchell of Canberra. This was much appreciated and the latter map highlights why this was the Black Day for the German Army but the biggest day for the Allies.

The extraordinary Rex Lipman of Adelaide was a very practical help, including providing access to a set of military history books, especially a collection by his friend Sir Basil Lidell Hart. Rex, now in his nineties, is as fit as ever with a near perfect memory on all matters military. Likewise, Ken Brimmaud of Rome was of great help.

Brother Nigel Cave is the padre of the UK Western Front Association. He is a masterful archivist and historian, based for many years in Northern Italy, and I express my appreciation for his detailed guidance in checking assertions in the manuscript. Likewise Vic Puik who lives on the Western Front and acts as a guide, was very helpful.

To Michael Bennett of Melbourne who is a direct descendant of John Monash, and to his father, my sincere thanks, especially for checking references to the Monash family. To Richard Chauvel and Honor Auchinleck, grandchildren of Sir Harry Chauvel, my thanks for facilitating access and guidance to the Chauvel Papers at the AWM, and likewise to the Bean family through Ian Carroll.

The Honourable Josh Frydenberg MP, parliamentary secretary to the prime minister and member for Kooyong, has kindly written the foreword. To Josh my sincere thanks. Likewise Peter Rees, author of many successful books including *Lancaster*, as always remains a guiding light.

The RSL and many veteran organisations have assisted in a number of ways, along with other organisations such as the Jerilderie Shire Council. (The newly located Jerilderie Cenotaph on the side of the lake in the main street of Jerilderie is one of the oldest in Australia and well worth a visit.)

On the photography side many helped, including the AWM and Scotch College but especially the very capable Nick Anchen of Sierra Publishing, taking modern photos of the legacy of John Monash in and around Melbourne.

Finally my thanks to Monash University Publishing, Dr Nathan Hollier and team, for completing the considerable tasks of editing and producing this book in the lead up to the centenary of Anzac. I greatly appreciate their huge efforts.

The General Sir John Monash Scholarship Foundation will receive one half of the author's net proceeds, as a further intergenerational gesture of salute to the positive legacy of John Monash.

ABBREVIATIONS

AIF	Australian Imperial Force
AWM	Australian War Memorial
AWOL	Absent Without Leave
BEF	British Expeditionary Force
CDF	Chief of the Defence Force
CDS	Chief of the Defence Staff
CEF	Canadian Expeditionary Force
CGS	Chief of the General Staff
CIGS	Chief of the Imperial General Staff
CO	Commanding Officer
DCM	Distinguished Conduct Medal (British and Commonwealth)
DSO	Distinguished Service Order (British and Commonwealth)
GI	US serviceman
GOC	General Officer Commanding
HMAT	His Majesty's Australian Transports
HQ	Headquarters
IWM	Imperial War Museum
KIA	Killed in Action
MC	Military Cross
MIA	Missing in Action
MDMP	Military Decision Making Process
PTSD	Post-traumatic stress disorder
RAAF	Royal Australian Air Force
RSL	Returned Serviceman's League
SEC	State Electricity Commission
VC	Victoria Cross
VRC	Victorian Racing Club
WIA	Wounded in Action

INTRODUCTION

> 'A perfected modern battle plan is like nothing so much as a score for an orchestral composition, where the various arms and units are the instruments, and the tasks they perform are their respective musical phrases. Every individual unit must make its entry precisely at the proper moment and play its phrase in the general harmony.'
>
> (John Monash)

On 4 July 1918, 1000 men of the Thirty-Third Illinois Division joined the ranks of the Australian Army Corps and successfully launched the Battle of Hamel, capturing the village of Hamel and all surrounding objectives. In command was Lieutenant General John Monash with his comprehensive Battle Orders and overall plan for capturing Hamel. He had allowed for ninety minutes, if all went well.

History records that the Battle of Hamel took exactly ninety-three minutes, two thousand metres were gained eastward, and over 1,500 prisoners were captured, bringing about a small but decisive rout of the German Army at that location.

Hamel exemplified the turning tide on the Western Front. At long last a new and still evolving holistic approach could capture a dramatic quantity of enemy personnel and weapons, and the bonus: Allied casualties were minimised. The holistic Monash strategy was not unique but it was an embellishment of all that went before and it made a difference.

As Major AC Fidge has noted, Monash's 'command philosophy was the same at brigade, divisional and corps level. The recurrent themes are an emphasis on training, technology, the human element of warfare and, above all, comprehensive planning'. And of this battle Serle summarises, 'Monash's greatest claim to military fame may lie in the model example he gave at Hamel of the concerted use of infantry, artillery, tanks and aircraft and its subsequent application by the British Army'.

When considered on a square-kilometre-per-hour rate of defensive fortifications captured, Monash at Hamel pulled off the fastest rate ever to that time in the war, with minimum Allied casualties and huge numbers of prisoners and weapons captured. After months of retreat and stalemate, the Allies thrust forward, captured key high ground and easily repelled counter attacks launched by the German forces on the same day. Vaire Wood and the village of Le Hamel and immediate surrounds would never be occupied by the German Army in World War One again.

Hamel was for the Allied soldiers the safest and fastest battle of World War One. The holistic template was rapidly shared around the Western Front commanders.

The speed of the battle at Hamel was due to the meticulous planning of John Monash from go to whoa. It may have helped that it was the first battle where Monash had outright command of an Army Corps consisting of several divisions and various support units. Utilising varied Allied resources as well, he was able to be innovative on a range of fronts.

Yet never has a general who did so much to help win a world war, with the Battle of Hamel but more so the Battle of Amiens, and who went on to cement democracy in place during times of economic turmoil, been so unacknowledged, when he is owed so much by so many. It is something very amazing but very 'Australian' that for various reasons, the life and achievements of Australia's greatest general have been downplayed and under-recognised. The naming of a university and a freeway after him in Melbourne have done little to bring about a deep knowledge across Australia of the trailblazing life and work of this man.

Monash was one of the very last leaders of World War One to be the subject of a detailed biography. His personal papers and perspectives were kept under lock and key for several critical decades after his death. For various reasons, the family of Monash, including his daughter Bertha, were not able to assemble, collate and release the huge volume of relevant documentary material, including personal papers, the family had come to possess, until well after World War Two. This meant the first big biographies came many years after John Monash's death in 1931 and, more particularly, after another and longer world war. In a way, Monash's massive record of achievement for the nation and the Allied cause then ended up playing second fiddle to the many leaders from World War Two and their achievements, which were also, of course, in many cases outstanding.

All of this was a great pity.

The comprehensive Geoffrey Serle biography was first published in 1982, five decades after Monash's passing; the different and in its own way superb Roland Perry biography appeared in 2004, with personal memories of the First World War long faded.

It is not only the feats of Monash that are downplayed and under-recognised from World War One but also the feats of the various Australian units both on the Western Front and in Palestine and the Middle East. New Zealand has also been massively downplayed.

Why is this so? Essentially because history writing is dominated by the dominant country on the side of the victorious. Thus, much is credited to Lloyd George, Woodrow Wilson and even Georges Clemenceau, at the political level, and to Ferdinand Foch and Edmund Allenby at the military.

Australian prime minister WM Hughes had to battle for a hearing at Versailles. Australian victories were sometimes reported initially, in the press of the day, as British victories, without any mention of Australia, even in Australia! In numerical terms the losses of Britain, France and the USA were much more than those of Canada, India, New Zealand, South Africa or Australia, but of course in comparative or per capita terms, the situation was different, and devastating for the less populous nations.

A recent major tome on World War One, *100 Days to Victory*, by Saul David, mentions Monash by name twice, both mentions relating to Monash allegedly getting lost on 8 August 1915 at Gallipoli. Later on David discusses 8 August 1918 as the Black Day for the German Army, with only a brief mention of Australian and Canadian forces and zero mention of either Monash or the Canadian leader in the Battle of Amiens, Arthur Currie.

The *Cambridge History of The First World War*, published in 2013 in three large volumes, contains not one mention of John Monash and barely a mention of Canadian Arthur Currie.

This book does not seek to repeat the detail or excellent contextual overview of the Serle and Perry biographies. Rather it focuses on John Monash's contribution to the building of the Australian nation in its first three decades of existence, from 1901 to 1931, the vital three decades of this man at his zenith. It asks the question of whether or not the contribution of Monash was then and is now properly recognised and, suggesting the answer to this question is broadly 'no', considers how Monash's contribution might be most properly respected now.

Let it be clearly stated that John Monash was not perfect, either as a general or in civilian street as a businessman, lawyer and engineer. He made mistakes, most notably at Gallipoli.

But he learnt from those mistakes and, to the extent possible, made amends. He showed true leadership by admitting to errors, analysing them, detailing the lessons learnt and changing strategy accordingly. (As the Australian prime minister Tony Abbott has observed, there is an under-recognised genius about Monash.)

So this is about John Monash, warts and all, Monash the military maestro who developed an ingeniously holistic approach to warfare, and who adopted a mistress while on leave in London: Liz Bentwitch.

To examine the contribution of Monash in military matters it is necessary to examine the leadership matrix in which he worked at critical stages, the importance of Ferdinand Foch, who was ultimately supreme Allied commander, through to those down the chain below him, as well as the various political masters, notably Prime Minister WM Hughes and the defence minister George Pearce.

Again in military matters it has to be said – rank matters. It is greatly prized over the centuries and to this day. The first promotion of a digger or private soldier to lance corporal means a great deal; equally a young subaltern officer being promoted from second lieutenant to first lieutenant and then captain.

In the twentieth and twenty-first century, at officer level, a five star system dominates; and in terms of the Army these are easily laid out, for understanding by civilian and military people alike.

Below the rank of brigadier you are sub one star, so captain, major, lieutenant colonel and colonel (which comes with a red cap) are below the five star ranking. Of course second lieutenant and first lieutenant are called subalterns, and in a sense (dare I observe with a smile?), beneath contempt. It is after all the lowest form of officer rank there is, with just one or two pips worn on the uniform. I was proudly a one pipper, on active service in Australia and Vietnam from 1966 to 1969.[1]

Brigadier was once known as brigadier general and equals one star rank, and the next up is major general or two star and then lieutenant general or three star. Curiously, this kind of reverse order pertains in the nomenclature of higher ranks.

Then come the two big ones. The rank of general or to be clear 'full general' is known as four star and after that there is just one more, the rank of field marshal or five star, and it was introduced by the British as a rank in the sixteenth century.

The great or perhaps not so great Napoleon once asked of a new general, 'Is he one that has luck on his side?' Rank, and luck, do matter on both sides of the English Channel and right around the world.

In the Navy, the rank of five star is known as admiral of the Fleet. In the RAAF the five star rank is known as marshal of the RAAF. Of course Prince Philip, the Duke of Edinburgh, has been a field marshal for over fifty years and from time to time wears the fully fledged field marshal uniform.

---

1 I should add that on graduating from OTU Scheyville back in 1966 I was made a second lieutenant and was posted to the First Battalion, Royal Australian Regiment (1 RAR) and, for the record, I was never promoted above this lowest of ranks and took an honourable discharge in 1969. This was after serving in Australia and nigh on twelve months in Vietnam. I was then and remain now content with the rank I obtained in my brief military career.

During the Blair years at Number 10 Downing Street a suggestion was made that the rank of field marshal should be formally abolished. It is understood Buckingham Palace reacted swiftly by simply saying: 'Have you not forgotten something?' Downing Street officials had to be reminded there was still a very much alive field marshal in the palace and one or two others retired in civilian street.

In the USA the five star rank is depicted as 'General of the Armies' and in 1976, 200 years after the independence battles and 176 years after the death of General George Washington, he was promoted general of the armies posthumously by the White House.

The rank continues to exist worldwide today. The most recent field marshal of the Indian Army passed away in 2011, after a very distinguished career. The most recent British appointment to field marshal was in 2012, officially as an honorary field marshal.

To date Australia has had only one field marshal, the World War One chief of staff to Sir John Monash, namely Sir Thomas Blamey. His Army career saw distinguished service in two world wars, not without some controversy. In between these world wars Blamey was head of the Victorian State Police Force.

Sir Robert Menzies, late in 1949, moved to promote Blamey by having him deemed to be on active service for one day, as Blamey by then had long retired from active service and was on his sick bed. King George VI announced the promotion in June 1950 but in a significant twist it was backdated until 1 January 1950, the day that Blamey was deemed to be on active service.

Near the end of the book I will ask the question I put here in bald terms: 'Given every aspect of the contribution of John Monash to State and Nation in his lifetime, should he be posthumously promoted one step in rank, from general to field marshal, backdated to 11 November 1930, a date one year after he was finally promoted from lieutenant general to general?'

We live in a democracy and so the delivery of this promotion is to a large extent in your hands. Please be advised it is an idea hated by some military historians and I accept there will be many opposed for various reasons. Equally there are and will be many in favour, again for various reasons, particularly those keen to rectify a gross discrimination. Let the debate be informed and let the debate begin in earnest.

So 'all aboard' for a different and unique look at the great maestro general, Sir John Monash, of Jerilderie and Melbourne, Gallipoli and Hamel.

Let us also salute all Allied forces in World War One but focus here on those who turned the German tide in the first half of 1918 in the Battle of Anzac Amiens and then pushed forward to and through the Hindenburg Line.

In the process of researching both core documents and various secondary sources I discovered another dimension relating to the Western Front and 1918, worth noting now. This was the truly significant extent of the month long fighting just east of Amiens, from 25 March to 25 April 1918, the month long battle of what might be termed the Battle of Anzac Amiens or even 'Le mois des Anzac'.

This period is increasingly recognised as the turning point on the Western Front but it is less understood that it was a month of especially fierce fighting, back and forth, before the Anzacs gained the superiority. It led to the Battle of Hamel on 4 July 1918 and the Battle of Amiens, which might be better termed the Battle of Greater Amiens, on 8 August 1918. Both of these were successful Monash-led battles that helped build the necessary momentum, with the help of Allied forces, to ultimate victory in November 1918, and not in 1919 as some Allied generals envisaged.

It goes without saying that Monash did not do the fighting. He was not on the frontline except at Gallipoli. But he did do his allocated job of commanding a brigade, then a division and ultimately a corps, brilliantly; the Australian Army Corps. In this he was greatly helped by his senior officers and the stamina and fighting spirit of the diggers throughout four long years.

Yes you can say what a hide I have to challenge established histories and decades of the downplaying of John Monash, especially his magnificent contributions at Messines, Hamel, and even more so in the Battle of Amiens on 8 August 1918. It was the black day of the German Army that, as German general Erich Ludendorff observed, helped break the back of the German Army in France. I simply invite you to read on and reach your own conclusions about the boy who grew up in Jerilderie and Melbourne and who delivered so much on so many fronts.

SECTION ONE

BEFORE THE GREAT WAR

Chapter 1

EARLY YEARS IN JERILDERIE AND MELBOURNE

'I had always grave fears that you were having too much study.'

(William Elliott, Teacher in Charge, Jerilderie Public School and later Editor, *Jerilderie and Urana Gazette*, writing to his 12-year-old student John Monash in 1877. At the time Monash was studying French, German, Hebrew and Music as extra subjects, plus mathematics with a slide rule.)

Louis Monasch arrived in Australia from Prussia in 1854, attracted by the reports of huge pickings to be obtained with the gold rush. He immediately set about attempting to make a fortune, an objective that he never achieved. The quest for financial success led to many changes of residence in Victoria and across the border in New South Wales around several Riverina towns, as he tried different locations for his horse trading and general stores, selling useful items for country living and farming.

After an initial nine years getting on top of the language and trying out various business activities in and around Melbourne, Louis decided to return to his home region in Europe to find a bride and persuade her to migrate to Australia. It was less than 100 years since the First

Fleet had landed at Circular Quay in Port Jackson and less than fifty years since John Batman had crossed over from Tasmania to establish Melbourne. Yet the young and bold Louis thought nothing of sailing back to the old land to regroup and, in a sense, migrate again.

He married Bertha Manesse in Prussia and together they ventured back down under, arriving in Melbourne in 1864 and setting up home. In June 1865 Louis and Bertha Monash celebrated the arrival of their first and only son, who they named John. He was born at a cottage in Richhill Terrace on the north side of the Flagstaff Gardens in West Melbourne.

After the birth of John Monash in 1865, two sisters were to follow; Mathilde in 1869 and Louise in 1873. But the family found making a living hard going. There had been a split with a key business partner, and the initial economic surge from the gold rush of the 1850s was coming to an end. Gold was becoming more costly to find and refine, and some banks had gone bust. Louis decided to head bush to the north and with reluctance Bertha followed with the three children.

After a stint at Narrandera, where his brother Max had a general store business, and visiting other Riverina locations, Louis settled on Jerilderie, and a house in the main street, in fact next to the Jerilderie newsagency of today. The family moved up from Melbourne and John was enrolled in the small Jerilderie Public School, located on Bolton Street. Bolton Street heads direct to the Billabong Creek and to what was a ford and later bridge crossing, opened in 1902, allowing traffic to head due north out of town.

Jerilderie was a small town on a key junction of several tracks that were later to become arterial roads and in the case of one, the main highway direct between Melbourne and Brisbane: the Newell Highway. The town had a small bank, a post office and hotels from the very early days, and later a railway connection when the regional standard gauge line, from Tocumwal on the Victorian-New South Wales state border, to Narrandera and on to Junee Junction, was completed. Junee Junction is on the Sydney-Melbourne mainline at the halfway mark.

There are just 140 steps between the Monash house at Jerilderie and the Bank of New South Wales Annex, as it was known, the bank that Ned Kelly raided during his occupation of the town of Jerilderie. The Monash House and store had a large set of stables in the rear. It was well built and today graces the central section of the main street of Jerilderie.[1]

As mentioned, Louis made the journey to Australia twice, the second time with his wife who, to speed up disembarking at Melbourne, was hoisted over the side of the ship onto a smaller boat. Station Wharf or Pier was a congested area connected by the first short railway line to Flinders Street in the CBD. This had only just been completed in 1856.

Louis was years ahead of that great businessman and trader Sidney Myer, who arrived in 1899 from Russia and set up in Bendigo initially and then, in 1911, on Bourke Street in the centre of Melbourne. But sadly for Louis, who was dedicated enough it seems, he was not very good at his business and trading endeavours and certainly not as clever as Myer. Extended periods of crippling drought in the Riverina would also certainly not have helped.

Rainfall records for the decade of the 1870s at Jerilderie show some years with half the annual average rainfall or even less. At the time major and minor dam construction was in its infancy in the

---

1 It is meticulously maintained by John Bryce and his wife, Jerilderie councillor Faith Bryce.

Riverina and worse still the rabbit had arrived from the south after being brought into Victoria by the Austin family. Trading times were tough and the wool boom years had yet to arrive.

Young John Monash was not afraid to venture around the town and up and down Billabong Creek. He knew how to study hard and soak up all that school had to offer but he was also quick to learn some bushcraft skills that helped him throughout his whole life. Fishing along the waters of the creek was a special delight and added variety to the standard salted beef that dominated the cuisine of the era.

It was the luck of John to have a particularly dedicated teacher in William Elliott, who allowed him to learn and study ahead, diving into the next year's subject matter and beyond. Elliott, it became legend, stated that this brilliant multi-lingual student should go on to schooling in Melbourne for he had taught him all he could and could teach him no more. John was fluent from an early age in English and German and had been taught Hebrew. He also played the piano with vigour and promise.

From time to time various colourful and sometimes unsavoury people would come through Jerilderie, a crossroads channelling traffic from Melbourne and many parts of Victoria towards Narrandera, which was to become the major Riverina gateway to Sydney, Adelaide, Melbourne and Brisbane.

Ned Kelly and his gang came to Jerilderie from Glenrowan and north-east Victoria to trade horses with Louis Monash and, later, to raid the Bank of New South Wales and tender his famous 'Jerilderie letter', a political manifesto of careful construction with a loaded set of messages against the establishment of the time.

Laurie Henery, a local historian who has lived for many years at Jerilderie, contends that John Monash did meet Ned Kelly during one of Ned Kelly's horse trading visits, although not during the famous bank raid visit of February 1879. By that time John was at Scotch College in Melbourne. John attended South Yarra College in Melbourne for six weeks in 1876 and, in the spring of 1877, Bertha and the three children moved to Melbourne, especially to facilitate improved schooling for the children.

The local consensus, supported by Roland Perry in his biography of Monash, is that … yes … John Monash as a boy most likely met the young bush ranger Ned Kelly. Many relate that Ned Kelly gave John Monash a coin for holding his horse during one of the horse trading visits, and just after World War One, Monash stated that he *had* met Kelly '41 years' earlier; in other words, in the year or so before the 1879 bank robbery. This precise recalling of time was an example of the meticulous memory of Monash, a diary keeper of renown.

While it is possible Monash was embellishing this tale of meeting Ned Kelly, in the wake of his famous World War One exploits he had no particular reason to do this. The chances are that in fact he was accurately recalling a moment of his life. Famous people met or brushed past or seen in close proximity always register with motivated, memory-blessed people. So after a splendid banquet at Buckingham Palace on 27 December 1918, dining with King George V of England, the president of the USA and five prime ministers – the banquet of all banquets dealt with in detail in a later chapter – John Monash cast back to recall the Kelly meeting in the little town of Jerilderie.

In 1897 an accomplished Monash returned to Jerilderie. By then he had been equal dux of Scotch College (in 1881) and graduated from Melbourne University with degrees in arts, engineering and law. He had established a healthy bridge-building and concrete business but had also stumbled into a role as an expert witness in cases relating to various engineering jobs and resolving the issue of costs and payments with big contracts.

Jerilderie was suffering from the action of the McCaughey brothers, David and Samuel, who owned the mighty Coonong station that stretched from Lake Urana to and beyond the Morundah Jerilderie railway line. The McCaugheys had developed a system of weirs and mini dams to facilitate irrigation of Coonong from the Colombo Creek, that then impacted on the flow of water further downstream.

Jerilderie's livelihood was being arbitrarily restricted by the over-exploitation and diversion of waters upstream. It was a case of upstream entrepreneurs versus hard-pressed downstream water users in an even drier part of the Riverina.

The real economic agony was plain to behold in the eyes of experienced John Monash, now in his early thirties.

A former long-serving and dedicated mayor of nearby Urana, Councillor Ian Coghill, has strongly stated the view that this lengthy case of upstream versus downstream decided a great deal about the future of several Riverina towns, notably Urana and Jerilderie but also Conargo and Deniliquin and even Moulamein further to the west.

Monash went in to bat for the down-streamers. He inspected the full length of the creek system from Morundah right through to Moulamein and then presented at the Land Board hearing at the Urana Court House.

The Urana Land Board sitting ruled in favour of a loaded compromise that would tend to support the continued activities of the up-streamers, the powerful and well-connected McCaugheys.

Monash saw through this compromise and in a fine example of his careful and analytic approach – evident in his dealings large and small – he pointed out the realities to the down-streamers and helped them lodge an appeal.

In December 1897 the Land Appeal Court in Sydney heard the case, and Monash was at his persuasive best, securing an outright victory for the down-streamers, mostly based around Jerilderie. The litigation continued until a final Supreme Court ruling locked in victory for the down-streamers.

As it was just before Christmas, on the evening of the victory the defeated McCaugheys invited all litigants present, the down-streamers and the up-streamers, to their Sydney residence for drinks and a party.

The McCaugheys continued on with their irrigation activities. They kept Coonong station but also bought along the Darling and developed large-scale irrigation at Tralee station, now a National Park still containing some of the classic McCaughey embankments and weirs of 100 years standing. Some environmental purists argue they should be removed (at the cost of millions of dollars), but they have created micro environments of advantage and beauty, ultimately, it can be said, due to the successful advocacy of Monash, effectively forcing the McCaugheys' irrigation operations north.

For Monash the links with Jerilderie were now to become remote, but nonetheless remain; maintained primarily by an active correspondence with his old school teacher and later newspaper editor, Elliott. (Elliott's *Jerilderie and Urana Gazette* survived in various incarnations until 1972, when Jerilderie adopted as its local newspaper the *Southern Riverina News*, based out of nearby Finley.)

As a curious postscript, years later Monash as Melbourne University vice-chancellor raised funds for the Melbourne University Medical Library named after Sir Anthony Colling Brownless, father of William Hamilton Brownless (and great-great grandfather of the star AFL footballer Billy), who was president of the shire that surrounded Jerilderie. Today the enlarged Jerilderie Council, which replaced that earlier Shire of Wunnamarra, hosts a very successful Annual Monash Lecture.

In the twenty-first century the Monash connection has been more fully recognised by the burghers and good people of Jerilderie. Still, the town remains more famous for the Ned Kelly bank raid than for the fact that for vital years of his development, John Monash grew up and went to school here. It was here that John, this son of migrants, became truly steeped in the Australia of the bush and, thanks to the extra step taken by his father, in changing the family's name, even more accepted as Australian.

The Urana Court House is now a magnificent heritage building, fully restored, but there is little mention of the Monash appearances and the historic case of 1897, that played so crucial a role in the region's development. A suggestion that the main street of the town, currently named Jerilderie Street, be renamed John Monash Parade, Jerilderie, fell on deaf ears when I formally raised it in 2008. The suggestion (along with the suggester) were attacked quite strongly and the idea lapsed as I headed overseas on posting as the Australian ambassador to the Holy See.

All I can observe in response to this is summarised in one word, 'damnation'. It is a lost opportunity for a town that owes John Monash a great deal.

Ned Kelly and young John Monash meet up in the main street of Jerilderie, the year before the famous Ned Kelly gang's raid of the Bank of New South Wales Annex, some 140 metres from the Monash family house.

Chapter 2

OF MARRIAGE, BRIDGES AND CONCRETE

> 'I will have to choose, sooner or later, between my military work and my business career.'
>
> (John Monash writing to his wife Vic, 1898.)

John Monash never stood still. He was determined not to waste a minute or an hour of his life on earth. In terms of richness of experience and ground covered in the first twenty-five years of life, he was up there with the great Winston Churchill or the South African giant – general, field marshal and prime minister – Jan Smuts.

In the boom times of the 1880s in Melbourne, opportunities abounded for a still very young John Monash, even before completing his degrees in arts, engineering and law. The intensity of this highly intelligent, very motivated, fit and handsome 'man about town' was noticed by many.

Simultaneously he conducted a busy social life, an embryonic military career with the Melbourne University Regiment, a heavy load of studies, and held down dangerous construction jobs as a supervisor.

On top of all of this he was inventing improvements for rifles, giving popular lectures on modern munitions and playing the piano at concerts and hotels, while also performing on the piano for his dying mother Bertha.

Monash's biographers Serle and then Perry have been able to reveal many details of their subject's private, as well as public life, including from when he was a young man. In this they were aided by the diaries and lists that Monash kept with characteristic discipline. He kept a list of early girlfriends and noted his first serious affair, and was generally an unabashed hoarder of information. After he discovered his parents were reading his diaries, he kept a separate personal diary in code, or at least in a form of shorthand, along with his more formal diary.

It was the beautiful Princes Bridge carrying Swanston Street traffic over the Yarra River onto St Kilda Road that saw young John Monash land his first employment of substance. This was the bridge designed to anchor the superb Turin-style CBD grid of Melbourne to the southern suburbs and Port Phillip Bay, at a time when major infrastructure in Melbourne was paid for by the gold rush and constructed with an eye to Melbourne becoming accepted as the first national capital and hub of Australia.

David Munro, who ran a large engineering firm, had the job of building this key gateway bridge. He engaged the young John Monash and Monash was quickly given extra tasks such as opening up quarries on the edge of Melbourne for the necessary bluestone for the bridge.

Monash was paid a pittance for the work, given his responsibilities, which included completing complex calculations relating to the fundamental design of various parts of this bridge that remains in good shape to this day and that retains an unmistakable gracefulness. He was not the overall project manager or engineer in charge but he was the up-and-coming 'Mr Fixit'. Further he was often down in the mud leading by very direct example.

From the Princes Bridge project, Monash moved on to win employment with Graham and Wadick to build the Outer Circle railway on the east and north of the city of Melbourne. This was to provide for Gippsland freight trains to bypass the busy Flinders Street and Spencer Street stations in the city and proceed through Camberwell East around to the Dynon freight yards, passing to the north of the city. A limited passenger service was provided but, due to insufficient demand existing at the time, this was discontinued and the Outer Circle abruptly closed. Remnants of the corridor can be seen today in Camberwell and Kew.

Today part of the Outer Circle is a magnificent bike trail, another part is still in use as the Alamein train line.

Then came a stint by Monash with the Port of Melbourne Harbour Trust and, with it, regular paid employment, though in the rather suffocating setting of a government department. The security of this employment was a blessing for Monash when the financial crash of 1891 descended on Melbourne, but eventually the axe fell even on him, and he was retrenched.

Monash then teamed up with Joshua Anderson, opening the engineering and advocacy firm of Monash and Anderson, with an office in Elizabeth Street in the city. After a very difficult set of start-up years, eventually, despite the hard times, this team built a strong business.

In the meantime, Monash's advocacy work attracted good pay. As an expert witness he appeared in libel cases, perhaps most notably helping to successfully defend the Syme family and the *Age* newspaper against a damages claim in Melbourne. He was also a leading recognised expert in disputes over the costing of big railway construction projects in Queensland and Western Australia.

Various new bridge and concrete-manufacturing techniques were emerging, including the breakthrough by Frenchman Joseph Monier involving the placing of steel rods in concrete to boost strength and ability to absorb shock force. The Monier technique bridges were spreading around the world and this led to Monash and Anderson trying them out with success in Melbourne and Geelong.

The Morell Anderson Street Bridge across the Yarra further upstream from Melbourne is another fine example of the Monash influence (and is today a revamped glorious pedestrian bridge).

In general terms these bridges were stronger and more flexible in span length, though not without danger to produce, as was soon to be discovered in Bendigo. The Bendigo creek and other watercourses were disruptive to the CBD of Bendigo and so the Bendigo Council went for a major revamp that included the plan to expand drainage and put in several bridges, including a key bridge with a planned skew, known as the King's Bridge. The first test of this bridge was satisfactory but repeated tests on the same day, maximising weight at the very centre of the large span, resulted in disaster, as the bridge collapsed, killing one and causing many to have a near miss as concrete and spans fell into the water.

Monash persevered and rebuilt the bridge, again using the radical Monier design but this time with a middle pylon. The second lot of tests were all satisfactory.

Joshua Anderson in 1902 departed the firm for New Zealand and Monash was now in sole control of the business. Unfortunately much of his time was involved with litigation to get tardy councils to pay the bills for their bridges and other structures. On one occasion a minor case went all the way to the Privy Council, with the Hawthorn litigant represented by Monash beating the Hawthorn Council represented by Isaac Isaacs, Australia's first Australian born-and-bred governor-general.

After four good years of trading Monash and his fortunes were for the first time in good shape, with most debts repaid, but it had been a long, hard haul, requiring careful leadership and attention to detail.

Monash played an even bigger role in building the original Hume Highway Bridge at Benalla, carrying all local traffic and most Melbourne-Sydney traffic for decades, until eventually the Benalla bypass was opened in the last quarter of the twentieth century. Today this is a particularly attractive and graceful bridge across a water course and lake, with the structure being best viewed from the superb Benalla Art Gallery nearby.

In March 1913 the Victorian Country Roads Board was formed and work commenced on upgrading many key roads, including that from Lilydale to Healesville. Monash won the tender for the bridge across the Yeringberg Creek – perhaps the first ever bridge of the Board – with a price of 424 pounds. He also won the tender for the nearby Stringybark Creek bridge.

Today both the 11 metre Yeringberg and 17.6 metre Stringybark bridges give good service, having been in use since around the time when the first AIF convoys were arriving in Egypt.

On the personal front, at age twenty-five Monash made a big decision. He proposed marriage to Victoria Moss, a lady of some standing around Melbourne, but did so harbouring secret reservations. In the autumn of 1891 in Melbourne, John Monash married Victoria, an independent-minded woman who was never going to be a neat fit in a household role, in the shadow of an illustrious and dominating husband. It was in some ways a marriage built on clay foundations rather than hard rock.

The opening weeks of wedded life were not made more blissful by Monash maintaining a correspondence with Annie Gabriel, with whom he had experienced a burst of young love and with whom he had had an on-again off-again affair for many years. In the interim, the hard done-by husband Fred Gabriel had moved the family to Sydney to try to ensure his wife broke off with Monash.

Nevertheless Monash rather cheekily wrote to Annie Gabriel to advise that he and Victoria were coming to Sydney on their honeymoon by train and he hoped they might meet up at some stage. What on earth, one might ask, was he thinking?

Unbeknown to Monash, the cuckolded husband intercepted the communication and in a scene belonging to an Italian grand opera by Giuseppe Verdi, Fred Gabriel sauntered down to Platform One at Sydney Central Station, where the Melbourne Express was due to arrive mid-morning.

Victoria and John Monash had changed trains near midnight at the famous or infamous Albury (Break of Gauge) platform, a change which Mark Twain endured five years later and drew on to ask which 'paralysis of Parliamentary intellect' dreamt up the Australian break of gauge saga. Australia at its rail zenith had twenty-two different rail gauges, with six still operating today.

Over the decades everybody from prime ministers to ambassadors to General Douglas MacArthur to Dame Nellie Melba and even the (later) Saint Mary MacKillop changed at Albury, until 1963 when the standard gauge was extended from Albury to Melbourne to allow the through running of trains.

The changing of trains meant a major disruption and a weary couple arriving at Sydney Central for the not-by-chance encounter with one Fred Gabriel. He had not only moved to Sydney from Melbourne with his wife and children to break up the affair between Monash and his wife but was now presented with a chance to get even with Monash.

Was Fred Gabriel going to confront Monash? Was he carrying a knife or revolver and going to lash out? Was he going to challenge Monash to a gentleman's duel, still a common practise in the nineteenth century? Did Monash sense danger, having been nearly killed on various bridge and viaduct construction sites? Was this going to be the death of the young engineer by cupid misadventure at Platform One, old Sydney Central Station, on Devonshire Street?

As the long overnight steam train eased to a halt, passengers soon emerged along the platform and Gabriel sauntered along in the mix of greeters and those arriving. He pointedly made his presence known to Monash as the passengers came along the platform but avoided any confrontation.

The Monash diaries point to two weeks of bliss for the newlyweds spent around Sydney and up in the Blue Mountains. They returned to Melbourne by train again, changing at breakfast time at Albury for that final leg back to Melbourne.

Over the two decades of the marriage there was much turmoil and there were even periods of separation. Victoria sailed to London for a few months leaving their young daughter Bertha behind. John had a lengthy affair with Liz Bentwitch in London during and after World War One and probably other relationships during this period.

Generals of the era (and afterwards) were renowned for having mistresses: Dwight Eisenhower, Douglas MacArthur, Jan Smuts.

After the death of Victoria in 1921 from cancer, Liz appeared again and stayed at the Windsor Hotel in Spring street Melbourne. Monash wanted to marry her but by then daughter Bertha held some sway and managed to 'block' any marriage. So for the last ten years of his life John Monash lived at his house 'Iona' in Toorak, which he purchased in 1912, with his daughter and her husband Gershon Bennett. Later their children lived there as well. Liz remained in the background.

Had Monash for some reason not lived long enough to serve in World War One, the legacy he would have left behind would still have been a very noteworthy one.

Today the Princes Bridge carries thousands of people by car and tram from the city to the southern suburbs of Melbourne, and vice versa. There are his bridges in Bendigo, Benalla, Yeringberg Creek, Stringybark Creek and elsewhere.

He pioneered the radical Monier reinforced-concrete building technique in Australia. And the Outer Circle rail line he helped to construct in Melbourne could today have been the route for fast east-west metro train linkages, extending onto Tullamarine and with another arm heading to Geelong. Trains on these lines would surely beat all current comparable transport alternatives.

The traits that Monash was to demonstrate in World War One to such palpable effect were already strongly evident within this earlier phase of his life: a capacity for handling big projects, a willingness to perform humble and if necessary dirty tasks, perseverance, a constant concern for detail, a strong interest in new ideas and techniques. For

Monash, vision and practical, technical, know-how and ability co-existed without any apparent tension.

Which is not to say he was able to find the secret of resolving all tensions in his personal, private life. In that he was, and is, far from alone, whatever we might come to make of his personal behaviour.

When prompted (by me) Benalla Council decided to rename its bridge the Benalla Monash Bridge, though rejecting any stronger alternative such as the 'John Monash Bridge'. This I thought was unfortunate. And it is more unfortunate still that there is no signage on or around the Princes Bridge to remind people this is where Monash at the age of twenty-two was calling many shots and helping to complete a bridge of great renown. A new plaque could be erected, associated with a major anniversary of the bridge, that might read: 'The first creation to which young engineer John Monash contributed, working under David Munro.'

Chapter 3

THE SECOND AIF CONVOY

From Melbourne via Albany and Colombo, to Egypt

'The fleet at sea is a truly magnificent and impressive sight, we left Albany in a single column over twenty miles long ... [T]oday we are cruising in three columns line ahead. I can see the whole fleet spread out in regular formation and responsive to every signal as to course, speed, distance and interval. I feel it is something to have lived for, to be entrusted by one's country with so magnificent a responsibility.'

(John Monash in command, on board the flagship *Ulysses* with the second AIF convoy at sea, December 1914.)

You could not start a military career at a lower level than Monash did, in July 1884, as a part-time reservist in a Citizen Military Force unit of the Melbourne University Regiment. No rank was lower and, additionally, the first unit Monash joined, known as D Company of the Fourth Battalion, was disbanded, due to a lack of interest it would seem. But equally you could barely finish a military career higher than the rank of general, eventually conferred on Monash on 11 November 1929.

The first promotion of Monash, in October 1884, was to the rank of corporal. Twenty years later he sailed as a colonel and Fourth Brigade commander in the AIF second convoy. He had to wait till the middle of the Gallipoli campaign to be promoted brigadier. Fifteen years later again he received his final promotion to four star general in *Government Gazette* no. 105, effective 11 November 1929. He earned every single promotion the hard way and on absolute merit.

Heavy losses across all ranks at Gallipoli and on the Western Front meant opportunities availed for fast track promotion. The Great War was like no other and the impact on individuals often involved promotions from base level to senior officer over not a lifetime but just a couple of years.

As we start to examine the military aspects of Monash's contribution in detail we should be aware that there were many others who achieved against the odds from inauspicious beginnings. It was the kind of war that upended decades of hereditary officer selection and promotion, that broke down class and educated-elite barriers. The drive, sacrifice and achievement of Anzac soldiers may have assisted this process.

A young lad from Gippsland with no formal secondary education was in many ways an example even greater than Monash in this regard. Stan Savige rose from private to major general and even fought in 1919 with the 'White Russians' against the Bolsheviks in and around Baku, east of Turkey. He went on to be co-founder of the Legacy movement. In World War Two he gained promotion to lieutenant general and served in Greece and Lebanon and later in Papua New Guinea.

Monash, though, faced multi-level discrimination right throughout his military career: some minor and some withering and of a major dimension. He withstood all and had a record of 'on duty service' second to none.

Being equal dux of Scotch College may have smoothed the path for Monash to think about military involvement but, almost immediately upon his commencement with D Company of the Fourth Battalion of the Victorian Rifles at Melbourne University, he began sorting out the good instructors and the good leaders and commanders from the bad.

Monash's personal attention to detail was to the fore, together with a preparedness to read widely and digest modern theories and techniques and to break the mould if there were any indications this would constitute a better way forward. There was little time for malingerers, for ill-discipline or a lack of motivation. In short, every hour on operation or parade mattered.

After the disbanding of the Fourth Battalion, Monash moved on to the North Melbourne Battery of the Militia Garrison Artillery as a probationary lieutenant and in April 1887, after passing the relevant military exams, he became a full lieutenant.

He enjoyed the exercises involving firing the battery guns that guarded Point Lonsdale, Queenscliff and Portsea, the entrance of Port Phillip Bay. The first shots in anger in the whole of World War One were fired from the battery at Fort Nepean near the mouth of Port Phillip Bay, to intercept the German merchant cargo ship SS *Pfalz*, as it tried to escape in the aftermath of the British Declaration of War, effective 11:00 P.M., on 4 August 1914. The advent of the telegraph cable from London in 1872 meant remote Australia knew of the declaration and was at war as of 9:00 A.M. on Tuesday 5 August. After inspections early that morning, the *Pfalz* was allowed to sail on towards the Heads of Port Phillip Bay but as soon as the news came through to the Queenscliff Fort of the declaration of war, the orders went out by telephone and heliograph to stop this German ship.

A shot was fired across the bows of the *Pfalz* at 12:45 P.M. Tuesday 5 August 1914 by the Fort Nepean Battery, a 100 pound shell from Gun Emplacement No 6. And it was effective, as the ship soon came to a halt and was taken into custody. Later the *Pfalz* was used as a troop carrier in the second AIF convoy commanded by Monash.

A committee now exists in Victoria to build knowledge and salute this twist of World War One history, simply called 'The First Shot'. The capture of the first German ship in World War One, albeit a merchant navy ship, was an example of good training and good readiness.

One week after the Declaration of War, the SS *Hobart* was likewise apprehended off Fort Nepean and valiant action by Captain JT Richardson, who led the boarding party, ensured that the code books were obtained before they could be thrown overboard. They were sent immediately to the admiralty in London and gave the Allies an advantage in the early phases of the naval World War One engagements.

Step by step Monash became 'noticed' at very senior levels in the Military. He was promoted to captain in October 1885 and after more hard studies and exams he was promoted to major in April 1887.

Then came a long lull, as business affairs and marriage and other dynamics intervened. On exercises large or small, Monash was unrelenting and, despite a few setbacks, in 1908 he was appointed commander of the Victorian section of the Australian Intelligence Corps, with the rank of lieutenant colonel.

It had been a long haul and it was always against a background in which Monash, as a Jew, was in the eyes of some never to be fully trusted and was to be where possible held back. Jealousy of the successful modus operandi of Jews and the notion that Jews were pushing forward at every opportunity were rampant at the time. Moreover, anti-Semitism was part of polite Anglo society in both Australia and Great Britain, especially during periods of economic downturn.

Though Monash himself claimed not to have suffered discrimination as a Jew, this assessment may have been partly tactical. As John Levi argues in his book about Rabbi Jacob Dangalow, in the early part of the twentieth century:

> Discreet social ostracism confronted the Jew, whether he was a schoolboy, a judge or a parliamentarian. No Jew was permitted to sit at the board table of any Victorian Bank. Fifty years would pass after Sir Isaac Isaacs became a Federal Judge before another Victorian Jew would be appointed to the judiciary, although candidates were not lacking. The Jews of Melbourne formed a fragile, nervous and self conscious community.

Monash was not only Jewish but of Prussian German background. Occasionally reminders went out that his 'real' name was 'John Monasch' – although his father Louis had dropped the 'c' before John was born – as if this cast doubt on his capacity for loyalty.

Monash could speak near-perfect German, as well as Hebrew and a smattering of French, and again this language proficiency was tossed around as a big 'no no'. Reportedly he once conferred with another German speaker of renown in 'High German', namely George Saxe-Coburg-Gotha (with an element of Battenburg), otherwise known as the commander in chief, King George V. Presumably they did this well out of earshot of frontline soldiers.

The Jewish aspect clearly weighed heavily against Monash in the eyes of journalist CEW Bean and will be examined in more detail as the Bean-Monash relationship developed at Gallipoli and on the Western Front. Suffice to say here it was a brittle and at times destructive relationship.

Monash's Germanic heritage was a factor allowing for cheap shots from many who should have known better, including not only Bean but later Sir Keith Murdoch, another very influential journalist and writer.

Both had well-known views against Monash and at critical times within earshot of senior Australian government leaders did not hesitate to heavily criticise him.

I communicated with Rupert Murdoch on this subject, in 2012, and Rupert responded quickly and with pinpoint accuracy: 'My father (Sir Keith Murdoch) often spoke to me about Gallipoli but not much about John Monash. However I formed the view that in respect of Monash my father's views "moderated considerably" from his original position of being opposed to Monash having senior command'.

In 2009 I had a brief opportunity to ask Sir Keith Murdoch's widow, Dame Elizabeth Murdoch, about John Monash, during a reception at Government House, Melbourne, on Australia Day eve. I asked if she had met Monash as a young girl around Melbourne decades ago and her reply came quickly, as follows: 'No I never met John Monash but you know something Mr Fischer, Monash had a mistress'.

Indeed he did; and more than one.

This too was an issue held against Monash, though perhaps not to the extent it might have been in the Victorian era, both before the end of World War One and also in the years after victory. People knew about the Monash mistress after 1918, around Collins Street, Melbourne, and in polite Melburnian society more generally. There is no doubt that the prime ministers of the day, all headquartered in Melbourne as the then nation's capital, knew that Monash had a mistress. Prime Minister Billy Hughes, who held sway for seven years in the top job during and after World War One, certainly knew.

As mentioned in chapter one, there was Annie Gabriel and then during and after World War One there was Liz Bentwitch, who Monash wanted to marry after Victoria died of cancer in 1920. Until the end Liz was installed in the Hotel Windsor and dined regularly with Monash and she even travelled with him on his last journey overseas, in 1931 to India for the giant New Delhi Durbar. They then went to the western portal of the Khyber Pass into Afghanistan. Later they travelled home via Kandy in Ceylon, now Sri Lanka.

A further factor weighing against Monash's advance was that he was a Reservist or part-time officer. He was not from the full-time professional Army; so he was militia not regular. He had not graduated from Sandhurst in Britain or Duntroon, the new Army officer training college established in Australia in 1911 at Canberra.

Step by step he moved up the ranks, but the regular officers from Great Britain, in some cases with Boer War experience, were, as late as mid-1914, not readily persuaded of the capability of somebody from civilian street. British generals Sir Hubert Gough, Sir Ian Hamilton and Sir Henry Rawlinson had all been together at Ladysmith in the Boer War and were members of the senior Boer War veterans circle.

At the start of the Gallipoli campaign, John Monash had been less than nine months full-time in the Army but he was already commanding a brigade in fierce attack and counter attack. It was a case of battle after battle against a hardened Turkish Army, with the brilliant Kemal Atatürk in charge, helped by overall commander and advisor – a smart German officer – Otto Von Sanders.

What made a difference for most of the militia officers was that they brought a more open mindset, new ideas and new tactics, as they were in the habit of thinking outside the square and left behind set-piece battle techniques of the nineteenth century. In a sense it infuriated some of the old and bold brigade that these upstarts challenged existing long-held battle strategies and as the Great War rolled on, this was to be more and more the case.

The next factor was that of age discrimination. Monash sailed as convoy commander in his fiftieth year and was actually described as being too old for senior battle command. He soon lost weight at Gallipoli and on the Western Front but again Bean had him in the gun as being too old and a few smirked about the portly ancient commanding officer.

These five factors of firstly Jewishness, secondly being of Prussian German descent, thirdly being known to have mistresses, fourth, his being a militia or part-time officer for a majority of his career, and fifth, his being apparently 'too old' for the position, were hurdles for Monash to overcome. This the maestro did by dint of determination and dedication and above all else, repeated success in the field.

As the lieutenant colonel heading up the Victorian section of the Army Intelligence Corps in 1908, there was much to do and specifically much mapping of the newly federated lands of Victoria and Australia to complete. Accurate maps were essential tools of defence and attack, together with an ability to read a map and envisage sight unseen the advantages and disadvantages of the terrain under consideration for movement of troops.

While my platoon seemed to follow me out of a benevolent curiosity just to see where they might end up, usually some distance from the grid point laid out as the objective of the day, Monash could look at a map of ground ahead and quickly detail a course of most tactical advantage and least physical agony and effort.

He became the key person to go to for writing complex military exercise scenarios. Several large-scale exercises took place with the Monash templates and exercise reviews, which delivered real training progress, though not without ruffling some feathers.

All of this was helpful but as with any contested ladder climb an element of luck was required in addition to the successful performance.

General Hamilton, a former chief of staff to Earl Kitchener of Khartoum during the Boer War, who like Monash spoke a number of languages (in Hamilton's case four, including Hindi), turned up in Melbourne and took the opportunity to meet Monash and observe a harsh Monash-orchestrated exercise at Lilydale. Hamilton and other VIPs were impressed by the performance of Monash and of course Hamilton was to become overall commander at the Dardanelles and the Gallipoli campaign.

Then came Herbert Horatio Kitchener himself. He made a famous visit to Australia in late 1909 and early 1910. To this day, Earl Kitchener of Khartoum has a reputation for being a man in a military cocoon. He never married and was capable of harsh judgements and large-scale brutality but – in fairness – in order to get the job done.

Should he be the face on every dartboard of every Australian officers' mess? And that of other ranks? He was the Boer War commander in chief after Lord Roberts. Given the guerrilla phase of the Boer War, Kitchener took steps to build an irregular capacity to match commando versus guerrilla with no prisoners to be taken.

This led to a fine grey line with Boers being shot when coming in to surrender. Eventually this went too far. Lutheran Pastor Daniel Hesse was murdered near Pietersburg and also his native driver, with the news going worldwide. Noted Boer War historian Charles Leach contends that Kaiser Wilhelm contacted King Edward VII to complain bitterly and request retribution.

In turn Kitchener had to find two culprits to satisfy the requirements from London. Kitchener finessed the execution of Australian Bushveldt Carbineers Harry 'The Breaker' Morant and Peter Handcock in 1902 near Pretoria, albeit after a kind of Court Martial at Pietersburg. In the middle of the Court Martial the Boers attacked at night and the prisoners on trial were ordered up on the roof to shoot Boers – while on trial for shooting Boers.

Morant burst into laughter at being told of this order, as he highlighted the incongruity of the situation. The cell doors were unlocked and weapons issued to the prisoners. Morant, Handcock and Witton fought valiantly, helping to turn the tide as they fired from behind chimneys at the circling Boer raiders. Eventually after taking heavy losses from the rifles along the fort wall and the rooftop, the Boers broke off the raid and withdrew. The next morning, the defending lawyer J Thomas, originally from Tenterfield, lodged a plea for the dropping of the charges under the legal rule and established concept of condonation but it was an inconvenient plea and dismissed outright. Kitchener had intimated a required result from the Court Martial: 'Two will do'.

Morant and Handcock were guilty of murdering Boer War prisoners and one of them may have shot dead Pastor Hesse but they took action within the expected operational requirements laid down at the time by Kitchener. Kitchener had moved into the centre of Pretoria at beautiful Melrose House in December 1900 and ordered a stepped-up scorched earth policy that eventually saw a peace treaty signed in the Melrose House dining room in May 1902. Kitchener delivered victory over the Boers once and for all, and now the British had open slather for exploiting the rich minerals of South Africa.

Kitchener was then sent as commander in chief to India, hoping this would be a step up for the ultimate position of viceroy of India, a promotion he expected in 1910. Instead he was passed over and given a trip to Australia, as a form of compensation. He also was ordered to conduct a range of inspections before returning to the UK with his reports.

On an infamous visit Kitchener made to Bathurst, he refused to participate in a welcome ceremony because the name of Peter Handcock (executed with Breaker Morant) was on the Boer War memorial in front of the Bathurst Courthouse. In the upshot, a banquet was wasted.

The Handcock name was removed for a period but then restored. Today it can be sighted on a small extra panel at the bottom of the list of other names in the park in front of the Bathurst Court House. Dare I observe the hide of Kitchener? And he was lucky the tabloids of the era did not pick up on his bad manners.

So Monash had to create a major military exercise at brigade level in the presence of the giant from military central casting who had already undertaken action on two continents. In a sense, Kitchener had seen it all.

By now Monash was in business equilibrium but closely following the gathering storm clouds over Europe as the pieces that were to cause war fell into place, due in part to interlocking treaties, especially between the German and Austrian-Hungarian Empires. And the leadership role of Monash stood out as one commander of overall capability, based on a huge attention to detail and to communication at all levels. Even British senior commanders, such as Hamilton, having met Monash, received updated reports on the Monash prowess.

Monash then landed the job of commanding officer of the Thirteenth Brigade and on 13 July 1913 won promotion to full colonel. He began to weld this brigade into shape when World War One was declared in August 1914. For months the momentum had been building towards a massive set-piece war between nations across Europe and beyond.

The spark was the assassination of Archduke Ferdinand of the Austro-Hungarian Empire and his wife on a beautiful street corner alongside the Latin Bridge that crosses the fast-flowing stream in the middle of Sarajevo in the Balkans. It was Sunday 28 June 1914, an early summer Sunday and earlier in the day a grenade bomb had been thrown at their motorcade as it moved from the Sarajevo Railway Station.

It is now known that on 5 July 1914, the kaiser chaired a meeting of the Imperial Council, with all key sectors represented. It was held at Potsdam, just out of Berlin, to help ensure secrecy. The kaiser asked if those representatives were ready for war. The answer was 'Yes' except from a group of bankers. They were granted a fortnight to get certain international borrowings sorted. Some subterfuge followed with the kaiser and others going on summer holidays but the step-by-step march to war was continuing in Germany. The countdown to action and declaration was on in earnest.

German ambassador in London in 1914, Karl 'Max the Prince' Lichnowsky, dutifully sent cables to Berlin with the various last minute peace and mediation offers, to no avail. On 25 July there was a cable offering mediation, on 28 July a cable saying King George V was prepared to convene a special Conference and finally on 29 July there was an extraordinary cable saying France would step back and be a non-combatant if Germany gave an assurance it would not attack France.

In other words, just briefly that weekend there was a live offer of no Western Front. But reflecting the momentum of the mobilisation, with trains already rolling across Germany to the east and the west, the kaiser was told by a senior officer: 'We cannot stop now, we are already massively on the move, it would be impossible to change.'

Some contend to this day that it was the fact that the trains were on the move, locking in mobilisation, that ensured no turning back in the northern summer of 1914 by the then militaristic Germany.

Just thirty-seven days after the spark of the assassination, on 4 August 1914, Great Britain declared war on Germany. The German demand for Belgium to allow passage of the German Army across Belgium and on into France was the flashpoint that led to Belgium's mobilisation on 31 July 1914. The unfolding invasion of neutral Belgium tipped the balance to war. During the previous fortnight the German army, complete with their supply trains, had swept on towards the various borders on both the eastern and the western fronts.

As a consequence, as a member of the Empire and with a British governor-general in Government House in Melbourne, Australia was at war and, straight away, as mentioned, a gun was firing at Fort

Nepean, near the mouth of Port Phillip Bay. It was just twenty-one years after a then bachelor prince, Archduke Ferdinand, had visited Australia and New Zealand to, amongst other things, check out the kangaroo. His untimely death had become the spark that lit the fire that was to see millions die in what was called the Great War; the war to end all wars.

On those first critical few days of August 1914, then Opposition frontbencher WM Hughes and Labor leader Andrew Fisher were in Narrandera in the Riverina and, it was reported, they took a stroll in the local park to contemplate and consider the news from Britain that it was war.

Monash in Melbourne did not blink. He was immediately given the awkward role of chief censor, in which he had to terminate all civilian communication with people who lived in Germany, including his own close relatives. His language skills were to the fore but it was not his preferred role, pouring over telegrams, letters and newspapers.

This turned out to be a short stint, ending when he received promotion to command what was to become his beloved Fourth Brigade on 15 September 1914 (though he was not formally promoted to brigadier until July 1915, whilst serving in the theatre of Gallipoli). The promotion was backdated to September 1914. From that month intense preparations were made, with training and pre-embarkation processes.

During this period there was an intense outpouring of patriotism and huge recruitment drives for the Army and Navy, along with the despatch of the first AIF convoy from Melbourne via Albany to Egypt. The misplaced concern was whether or not the Australian soldiers, all volunteers, would get to the frontlines before it was all over and wrapped up. The suggestion was that Germany would be overwhelmed by the Allied effort within months; possibly by Christmas 1914.

As if and if only!

Despite the hectic times, Monash with his daughter Bertha and a small group had a brief sojourn and final weekend away at Mount Buffalo Chalet near Myrtleford. There were just nine hectic weeks before final embarkation.

John Monash had participated in the early exploration of the nearby plateau (as affirmed by his great grandson Michael Bennett), and the area is dear to the Monash descendants to this day. There is a cave on the plateau named after John.

Nonetheless, the family descendants recall a sad postscript to this final pre-embarkation weekend of leave. Bertha told her son Colin Bennett that many of that party of ten or so were in fact killed early on in the war.

By the time of this last little holiday thousands of recruits for the AIF were being processed through various camps, including a big camp at Broadmeadows on the northern outskirts of Melbourne. Water was short in that part of Melbourne, as no main pipelines had been laid, so the Army moved quickly to lay pipes and connect the area to the Melbourne Water Supply. Also water carts had to be used to help with distribution around the rows of tents and the latrine and shower blocks. The Shepparton company J Furphy and Sons was the main supplier, providing their already famous Furphy Farm Water Carts that had a capacity of 180 gallons of water each.

Having these Furphy carts moving all around the camp, with clear-cut wording denoting they were a Furphy cart painted on their sides, in turn led to the AIF developing the use of the word 'furphy' to mean a rumour arising from gossip, often idle talk around the watering points. Time and time again, some battalions were ordered to pack up and entrain to the wharves, only to be sent back to the camp a day later to unpack and rebuild tents. This was due to further delays in the assembling of the two big AIF convoys. The phenomena caused some bemusement and also anger. It led to orders to pack up being denoted as simply another 'furphy', amongst the volunteer recruits, and the term 'furphy' resonates to this day.

However the recruits soon discovered this furphy period was rapidly coming to an end. Huge numbers and equipment were despatched by shuttle steam trains to the Port of Melbourne and large crowds turned out to wave the lads goodbye amongst scenes of great optimism, laced with a sober realisation they were heading to war.

In those final days, Monash packed carefully and conducted a round of farewells. He then embarked at the Port of Melbourne wearing his uniform as a colonel, in his role as the Fourth Brigade commander. In his case there were to be five long years of dangerous, exhausting and intense work before he was to sight Melbourne again, a period longer than almost all others.

The second AIF convoy departed on 22 December. Five of the convoy ships were captured German ships with scratch crews trying to work out how to make propulsion when all levers and taps were marked in German. The quickly assembled crews soon mastered their ex-German merchant navy ships and ensured they maintained convoy direction and speed.

Because the Fourth Brigade was the largest unit on board, Monash was convoy commander with regard to all military matters. He found this role onerous. At Albany several issues needed sorting and improvements needed to be made in the signal system between ships to ensure the convoy was in fact organised with training and exercise for the troops. Across the Indian Ocean, various inoculations were administered and en route there were deaths from pneumonia, necessitating burial at sea.

Monash wrote that in the late afternoons there were French and German language courses, in the evening additional officer training by lecture. As always Monash was keen to see no opportunity lost in preparing for all that lay ahead, including the opportunity to have the ability to interrogate prisoners captured from the German divisions they expected to be up against.

While the second AIF convoy was midway between Albany and Colombo, what some call the 'Broken Hill massacre' or the 'Battle of Broken Hill', took place: the ambush of the Silverton Picnic Train on New Year's Day 1915, just 3 kilometres west of Broken Hill, by two local men with a Turkish flag and an icecream cart. The train was the annual picnic train of the Manchester Unity Order of Oddfellows and was heading north-west out of Broken Hill towards Silverton. The shootout resulted in the killing of four people and the wounding of several others. The two assailants were later cut down by local troopers and buried that night. These killings were the only ones to occur on Australian soil in the Great War. The incident was an ugly reminder that death and destruction could occur right around the world at isolated places a long way from the frontlines, during the first worldwide war.

One war correspondent, the journalist CP Smith, on board the convoy, wrote about Monash and his position as leader (in a way that CEW Bean could never bring himself to) in an article for *The Argus*:

> Colonel J Monash up to the present has had the whole of his time busily occupied … [H]is powerful personality and impregnable sense of justice were however revealed to all ranks during the period of training … [T]here is not a man on board who would not follow him to the ends of the earth with perfect conficence (sic) … [T]his appreciation of their chief finds constant expression on every troop deck.

To establish this level of rapport so early in war-time command points to the capability of Monash. Obviously all on board were as keen as mustard and this helped Monash and the various key officers boost control and training but even so a level of positive discipline had to be imposed.

The convoy made it safely to Ceylon, now Sri Lanka, and to the west coast port of Colombo, where some victualling took place. A small percentage of the soldiers went absent without leave – AWOL – while ashore on the morning of 14 January, because the Ceylon water police had mistakenly allowed local lighters to approach the ships at anchor. It did not help when local ladies came out on canoes and dinghies to entice the soldiers ashore to the bustling colourful city, used to entertaining sailors.

However the dreaded Military Police stepped in and did a roundup and many members of the AIF, with a touch of class about them, were found ensconced in the bars of that grand old lady the Galle Face Hotel. It is located on the large seaside promenade at Colombo, looking west towards Suez, with huge balconies and an ambience of colonial luxury. Twenty soldiers out of 13,000 were to become actual deserters as they were not to be found on board when the convoy departed.

It was a slow two-day passage through the Suez Canal, then just forty years old and under threat from Turkish forces and their skirmishes from the north. Last-minute training was wrapped up and packing completed for disembarkation at Alexandria. The troops were soon in proximity to the pyramids, near Cairo, getting ready for serious battle.

On the first night ashore, Monash was invited to dine with the British generals William Birdwood and Alexander Godley. He was in the loop early on and increasingly well regarded for running a tight ship.

In Alexandria training dominated with divisional exercises and brutal analysis by the supervisors. After one busy exercise, General Godley said of the Fourth Brigade, led by Monash: 'As to our new Australian brigade, all I need to say is that they fell into place, and did what they were ordered to do with a punctuality, precision, steadiness and thoroughness which makes further comment unnecessary'.

High praise indeed, and later Godley told Monash that his brigade was the best Australian brigade in Egypt. Still the absolute test awaited: that of performing under fire in battle conditions.

Harry Chauvel and the AIF's First Light Horse Brigade, that he commanded, were neighbours to Monash and at one stage Chauvel happily lent Monash and his team some horses to assist with training, which was conducted by day and by night and often in extreme temperatures, with all in readiness for the Battle Orders to arrive.

Monash seized one lull to take his first weekend leave and go by train to Luxor with a small group of officers. Two special carriages were added in their honour and they soaked up the beauty of the underground chambers of mummified Pharaohs surrounded by rich carvings. But all knew the clock was ticking down.

The AIF would not have to wait long for their first serious battle orders as Churchill and Kitchener devised a cunning plan, that was to be badly executed, for the nearby Dardanelles.

John Monash leaves Porepunkah by the 6:14 A.M. train for Wangaratta and embarkation.

SECTION TWO
THE WORLD AT WAR

Chapter 4

GALLIPOLI'S BITTER LESSONS LEARNT

> 'He was not a fighting commander, Monash's qualities were of a different order; but in this crisis, he ultimately decided to take personal control and since one staff officer after another sent to the head of the column had failed to return, went forward himself to ascertain the reason of the delay.'
>
> (CEW Bean, *Official History of Australia in the War of 1914–18*, Volume II.)

German colonel Otto von Sanders was the son of a Prussian Jew. Australian brigadier John Monash was the son of a Prussian Jew. Both were fluent in 'High German', both were military masterminds and both influenced the tide of World War One, albeit at different stages. At Gallipoli they were on either side of no-man's-land.

Germany had come late to the business of colonisation and hegemony. It was playing catch up against Britain, France and the Netherlands with their worldwide networks of colonies. Even Belgium had done better in this regard than Germany, up until 1900.

Berlin decided to build, in Stephenson standard gauge, the great Berlin-Baghdad railway, through Turkey to rich places further east. In the thinking of Berlin, Turkey was to be to Germany what Egypt had been to Britain.

Over the decades, the role of Otto von Sanders has been underplayed. As chief tactician from the Ides of March 1915, with command of the Turkish units allocated to the Dardanelles, he moved quickly to build defences along the peninsula.

This giant of best German military practice picked up on the tell-tale signs of increased Allied activity at sea near the Dardanelles and began moving at a furious pace to ensure any invasion could and would be resisted. Turkish mines activity at the mouth of the Straits leading to Istanbul resulted in a delay of around four weeks and this was enough to frustrate First Lord of the Admiralty Winston Churchill, along with Kitchener and the Allied War Council Headquarters in London.

It was a near run thing but by the time the dithering Hamilton gave the go-ahead for the Anzac landing, the Turks were ready and waiting and far better prepared than just a month before.

The AIF units had sailed from Alexandria to Lemnos Island for the final assembly and issue of orders, which Monash noted as having the ANZAC forces land north of Gabe Tepe. History records this was not to be, as for whatever reason the landing was south of Gabe Tepe, leading to early confusion. In went the Anzacs and on day one, 25 April 1915, in the late afternoon, they made it to the high ground and, in the case of one New Zealand unit, to right on top, where the ocean on the other side of the Gallipoli Peninsula could be sighted. Initial Turkish resistance was patchy.

Alas for the Allies this bold dash was undone by one of the many mistakes made early on what was to become Anzac Day: the decision of Major General Ewen Sinclair-MacLagan, with his

Third Brigade, to stop on the second ridge and dig in that Anzac Day morning, rather than push on as the orders instructed and capture the vital and higher third ridge, overlooking most of the contested land right back to what would become Anzac Cove.[1]

There is evidence – hotly debated to this day – that the hesitation of Sinclair-MacLagan undid the success of the Anzac landings. Joan Beaumont in her important book *Broken Nation* highlights how critical the timings were that morning. Around 5:30 A.M. Sinclair-MacLagan pauses and stops on the second ridge line; at 7:20 Generals William Bridges and Cyril Brudenell White land at Anzac Cove but do not order Sinclair-MacLagan and the Third Brigade to push on and capture the then lightly defended third ridge. At 10:00 A.M. the dynamic changed as a young Turkish colonel arrived on the third ridge.

Enter one Mustafa Kemal who worked out what to do in a few minutes and, even without contacting overall commander Otto von Sanders, ordered a charge in the knowledge that if the Anzacs dug in on the first night on the high ground they would be difficult if not impossible to dislodge.

Later Mustafa Kemal added the name Atatürk and justifiably so as he went on to become the founder of modern Turkey and president for a decade and a half between the world wars. His words to his troops were blunt: 'I order you to die for your country'. Within an hour many had but they achieved the objective of routing the Anzacs from their early vital gains.

---

1 The name 'Anzac Cove', for the original landing site, was suggested by General Birdwood on 29 April. This name for the cove was officially recognised by the Turkish government on Anzac Day 1985.

And so the scene was set for a battle of attrition, for a few metres here and a few metres there.

Monash sensed things were not going well as the reports came in and he prepared to send his Fourth Brigade ashore. Late into the night of the 25th, Hamilton and senior staff officers wrestled with the prospect of an immediate withdrawal, but that was never really an option.

Instead Hamilton sent an order to hold on, fortify and, famously, 'dig, dig, dig', but for over two thousand Anzacs this was to mean nothing as they were already dead or severely injured. Monash made it ashore on the morning of 26 April and proceeded to pull his scattered units together and establish a command post and brigade headquarters.

Monash was faced with shelling and bullets heading in all directions. In addition there were the usual ingredients of battle chaos, absolute danger, awful communication capabilities and the added spice of crazy orders from headquarters in a distant location on board the command ship. Monash was headquartered in a bunker about one hundred yards from the firing line, as he recorded on 14 May 1915 in a letter home, his first from Gallipoli after a long, intense period of fighting during the first twenty days of the campaign.

All ranks were up front and in danger; indeed General Bridges, who was first commandant of Duntroon College of officer training, was cut down by a Turkish sniper on 15 May and bled to death. Private Simpson Kilpatrick used a donkey to bring down wounded to the beach. He was killed by flying shrapnel on 19 May. The casualties mounted in their thousands. Every day more were killed and injured on both sides, involving all ranks.

For the Riverina, one of the first casualties was a simple farmer's son from the Moffat family who lived on the left bank of the Boree Creek on the property named Aloeburn. The cold brief formal notification of these early Gallipoli battle casualties was the usual telegram from defence headquarters in Melbourne. The more valuable letter from a mate, that must have been bitter-sweet for the family to read and absorb, arrived weeks later:

> Dear Mr Moffat,
>
> I've been thinking of writing for some time as I am in D Troop and was with Ernie on the night of the 19th. Mother said she had written to you about Ernie's illness here before we left. He was just beginning to look well again when we went over to Gallipoli.
>
> We went into the trenches the day after landing and had been there nine days when the big attack came on the morning of the 19th of May. Our squadron held the left position and got rather badly cut up but we felt the loss of Ernie more than any. He was a favourite right through the regiment, always in good spirits and nothing seemed to put him out. I am.
>
> Yours Sincerely,
> E. Lionel Bigg.

So this young man Ernie had gone by horse and buggy with his parents down the country lane and into Boree Creek to the local station platform, farewelled his family and departed by train like so many thousands did for the final training, embarkation, convoy and then into battle. 'Killed in action' (KIA) and 'missing in action' (MIA) statistics tell one side of the story of loss in World War One but for each family who lost a son it was a huge wrench. In the case of the Moffatt family this was a double wrench, as brother Gordon had already died of pneumonia on the convoy to the Middle East, and been buried at sea.

The Moffat family had a third son, John Moffat, who was able to take on the farm in place of his two brothers who were never to return from the Great War; however for many families there were no other children to step up.

There were four key moments in the saga of Gallipoli for Monash, which each helped to lay the foundations for what lay ahead on the Western Front. Each reflected the ugliness but also the many contrasts to ugliness, of full-on battle on a large scale. For Monash each was a new experience a long way from home and accompanied by enormous personal danger.

The first of these transformational moments for Monash was the realisation of the huge gap between the Australian military modus operandi – to protect as much as possible the lives of soldiers of all ranks – versus the prevailing British senior ranks' view that the average low-rank soldier was expendable and simple cannon fodder. Further, blind discipline was expected from these soldiers as they were ordered over the top to their death.

Roland Perry and for that matter, in a more roundabout way, CEW Bean, in their respective histories, highlight the wanton, counterproductive and outright crazy orders by too many British generals.

Monash could resist orders. He could argue for amendments. But ultimately, until he became a three star general, he was not in a position to impose his improved tactics and holistic strategic approach.

His divisional commander General Godley, acting under the overall orders of General Hamilton, ordered the Fourth Brigade at short notice to attack and capture 'Baby 700' hill, a very strategic hill but one able to be covered by heavy support fire from the nearby Turks. To quote Roland Perry, Godley was 'a leader who planned on the basis of assumptions rather than clear information'. He insisted on a foolhardy sortie that quickly led to disaster.

The Godley orders given to Monash on the afternoon of 2 May were some of the worst given during the whole of the Gallipoli campaign and decimated the Fourth Brigade for zero gain. The orders were late – just five hours before actual battle – based on a false set of premises, and didn't allow a comprehensive support barrage to be developed.

It was as if Boer War veteran Hamilton and his key divisional commanders had learnt nothing from that South African war or the intervening years with regard to modern warfare and armament capability, and nothing either about appreciating the value of human life of all ranks in the units under control.

Lieutenant Richard Casey wrote about a platoon-sized raiding party ordered to their death in that same dreadful month, May 1915. As they plunged forward on an inadequate scale they were soon slaughtered by the Turks, each and every one of them.

Monash soldiered on, not lowering his guard, and maintaining stoic confidence and a brave face. It was Monash, acting within his brigade command remit, that showed great promise, sighting support machineguns and building defences at the top of what was to become Monash Valley. A huge attack by the Turks on 19 May, with numbers more than double the Anzacs, was repulsed, due in part to the Monash approach.

In a quiet aside written on 30 May, Monash records how a group of Turks – around sixteen or seventeen – were caught in the middle of a trench that the Australians held both ends of, after a local scrap.

Despite the adrenaline flowing to bring it all to an end, an interpreter was sent for and the Turks surrendered and were soon offered water and biscuits by the Anzacs. All of this took place while wounded diggers were being carried on stretchers away from the scene. So the Geneva Convention and the practical and humane approach of the still standing diggers was to the fore, as Monash wrote: 'Gallantry can surely touch no higher pinnacle'.

The second transformational moment was the realisation by Monash that he made mistakes at Gallipoli. These were mistakes of varying degrees from which he vowed to learn from and never repeat. It was the action of 6–8 August 1915, the disastrous 'hook' to the left with the objective of capturing Hill 971, that underlined the need to complete adequate fire support plans involving detailed reconnaissance and absolute accuracy. More generally the need existed to be very much in control of every stage of a major offensive.

While it was not entirely the fault of Monash, on two critical occasions he was in a location in the middle of his brigade as it swept around to the north when he should have been near the head sections of the brigade to give much needed direction and help maintain momentum. Later he moved forward to apply direction and there was considerable confusion, with the local guides providing wrong directions.

Perhaps the most critical writing against Monash on military matters relates to the 'left hook' and attempt on Hill 971 and flows from the pen of Major CJL Allanson who was commanding the Sixth Ghurkha Battalion. Allanson said: 'I discovered him hopelessly tied up … What upset me most was that Monash himself seemed to have temporarily lost his head, he was running about saying: "I thought I could command men"'.

Many have challenged whether this report, given some twenty years after the event and contradicted by Allanson's own evidence presented to the Dardanelles Commission in 1917, is an accurate report on Monash. The consensus seems to be that Monash on the morning of 8 August 1915 was very frustrated and perhaps briefly unhinged by the long night's manoeuvres, lack of real progress and growing number of casualties.

He may have had a brain snap but he soon was back on top of things.

Whatever the real situation, Monash was in coherent command throughout the Gallipoli campaign, holding in his own feelings to present a confident and calming profile to his men. He did not have one day of sick leave at Gallipoli, or one extra day off, other than unit stand down and for his visit to the rear headquarters on board ship, as we will see. Further, he was renewed in his recognition of the need to give perfect clarity to complex battle orders at his brigade level.

As Serle has noted, 'Against all of (his superiors at Gallipoli) charges of incompetence could be laid much more easily than against Monash.'

Monash was still however not in a position to ensure that the orders were well thought out and contained a balanced, fully detailed, comprehensive approach. He needed to work with strategies that were within his overall orders, the orders from divisional HQs down to his brigade.

As mentioned, the bigger issue was the huge gap between British military thinking and Australian military thinking relating to the core resource of the private soldiers or Anzac diggers. Were they simply expendable cannon fodder to be mowed down by machinegun fire or valuable assets to be protected to maximise fighting capabilities. In a specific analysis, Monash wrote that much of the fault lies in the British leadership, where the officers did not mix with the men as the Australians did, but kept aloof. Clearly there were many brilliant British leaders in the field but many others were not very practical and were very class- and structure-orientated.

Monash was tortured by the issue, as he sought to improve on early mistakes and correct for mistakes by others. Could he do more to resist confused and ultimately destructive orders that led to the unnecessary deaths of his men, short of outright resignation? One outcome of all of this was that when he eventually reached outright command of the Australian Army Corps, he adopted holistic tactics that saved Allied lives and also maximised enemy defeat.

The third transformational factor was a very simple one but a reminder that rank does matter. In July Monash was promoted to the rank of brigadier, at that time known as brigadier general and often shortened to just general. This came shortly after his fiftieth birthday, celebrated near the beach of Anzac Cove, in his HQ dugout.

After a ten month delay Monash held the rank that was appropriate to the unit he commanded and a raft of rumours about him being a German spy and a German collaborator were finally put to rest, at least for a time. These had swept around the pyramids of Cairo from time to time, having started right back in the salons and saloons of Melbourne. It should be noted that Melbourne society throughout the first three decades of Federation was a mixture of powerful people of strong will and wealth, with upfront opinions and the odd bias. Monash was not ever regarded as being part of the centrum of Melbourne society in the nation's then capital city.

Once again the accusations had centred on his Prussian background. The idea he changed his name was wrongfully bandied around, particularly by a certain Major McInerny in a campaign directed at the minister for defence George Pearce, whereas it was his father who had changed the family name from Monasch to Monash. Fluency in German was another matter, especially when later in the war he interrogated German prisoners in their language.

Monash had deserved his promotion. He now had real status and he also had received his 'Mention in Despatches' award for conspicuous service and bravery. He had done as well as any of the other commanders at brigade level at Gallipoli during the first four months and he had maintained his personal fitness levels. Even Bean, who suggested in the *Official History* that there was some complaint against Monash for being 'seldom seen in the front line', praised Monash's articulation of complex orders and his capacity to, in the process, motivate the troops one more time, many more times.

The fourth transformational element was more subtle. It was an ability of Monash to maintain his equilibrium, hold his nerve as he prepared to go into battle, after battle, and then hold it also and not go to pieces in periods of furlough and leave from the frontlines. This was often an occurrence for soldiers when the pressure was off. Some fell apart and could not face going back into the frontline. Except for approved leave, Monash was on deck every day from embarkation to the eleventh hour of the eleventh day of the eleventh month of 1918, Armistice Day.

Again Monash held his nerve in the most difficult period of them all – going back ashore after leave, going back into harness after a period of rest and safety, good food and good beds. This was always a very critical period, a crunch time when those returning to battle knew exactly what to expect: the sheer exhausting routine, the brutality, the chance of instant death by a millimetre here and a grenade there.

Some officers and soldiers excel in the actual battle. Albert Jacka won a VC by single-handedly clearing a vital trench of Turks near the Monash bunker HQ at Gallipoli, with the adrenalin flowing. The last hour before a stunt or attack was another period of acute tension. Was it going to be the one attack too many? For Monash the last hour before battle was not so tense as he had done all the hard yards, as a general commanding officer, by then: the recce, planning and formulation of orders and their issue and dissemination. He would not personally be likely to be facing death. However the overall responsibility would always weigh heavily.

Monash enjoyed four extraordinary breaks from battle, the first two in May 1915. First, an incredible ceasefire was agreed for one day – 24 May – to bury the dead from both sides in no-man's-land. It was the initiative of Monash that brought it about. As he records, this started on 22 May with calls for a doctor out in no-man's-land. Two doctors were sent out by Monash under a Red Cross flag. Suddenly many small groups of Turks appeared waving white flags and asking for an armistice.

There had been a precedent of sorts with the now famous one off Christmas Day truce on the Western Front in 1914.

Monash asked for a Turkish staff officer to come forward and they conferred in French, Monash saying he had no power to make a treaty but if tomorrow at 4:30 P.M. a group clearly identified came along the beach from Gabe Tepe, the Allies would send a party along to meet and agree terms. It was agreed that the ceasefire would be from 8:00 A.M. to 5:00 P.M. on 24 May and it was conducted with total honour and no breach on that day.

Monash and many officers were able to walk up what would become Monash Valley and out the top past Courtney's and Quinn's Posts and beyond the wire into elevated lands in front of the Turkish trenches while both sides were burying badly decaying bodies.

As the bodies were buried there was even an exchange of some rations between the opposing troops but this was frowned upon by Monash who believed you needed to maintain hate levels to continue to go out and kill the enemy. With a sweep of the eyes in all directions, the generals were able to see where the next breakout attempts might best take place.

It was a fleeting ceasefire and by nightfall the conflict was resumed with the usual exchange of grenade, artillery shells and bursts of gunfire.

Monash's handling of the initial Turkish approach was brave, decisive and correct, allowing for a negotiation to be completed and the day of curfew to work.

His second break in May came when Monash was invited by Sir Ian Hamilton on board the British navy command ship for a two-day rest and pep talk from the general. From the dust and mud – not to mention the flying shrapnel – suddenly it was silver service, hot showers and soft bed plus pleasant conversation in the Wardroom of HMS *Arcadian*.

It was a sharp contrast and as for all who enjoyed brief bursts of rest and recreation it would soon be over and Monash would have to saddle up again. This he did at the end of May, coming ashore at Anzac Cove and immediately throwing himself at the constant workload.

Later there was a longer break about 50 miles away at Lemnos island and later again in the Dardanelles campaign there was an even longer break back to Cairo, incredible in the circumstances but helping to restore health and morale, so long as there was no nervous breakdown generated by the contrasts out of the firing line.

In a prescient way, Monash also wrote that when peace returns, no doubt the tourist of the future will come to inspect these parts, stating that: 'The Catacombs of Rome will be a baby compared to the extraordinary amount of digging and trenching and tunnelling that we have done … [O]n some high plateau overlooking ANZAC beach, there will be a noble memorial erected by the people of Australia, to honour the memory of their fallen dead.'

A couple of years before the war Monash had made a grand tour of the USA and Europe, incuding Berlin and Rome, with his family. Clearly he visited one of the many sets of catacombs of Rome in a whirlwind few days in the eternal city.

Monash was back in the thick of it when who should turn up on 13 November 1915 but Lord Kitchener, British Secretary of State for War, for a two-hour inspection of Anzac Cove and nearby trenches. Kitchener met Monash with a message from the king conveying congratulations to the Australians. He then walked with Monash up what would become Monash Valley and climbed Walker's Ridge.

Kitchener was to have been accompanied by Winston Churchill, who was busting to make an inspection of his disastrous handiwork. Political machinations back in London prevented this visit by Churchill, perhaps just as well as he would have found it hard not to second guess the generals. All of them. At once.

Kitchener saw nothing to dissuade him of the need to pull out, before the bitter winter weather and while it could be done in an organised way and not as a chaotic retreat and rout. It was a wise call by Kitchener who went on to be lost at sea later in World War One, while on a secret mission to Russia, when the ship he was travelling on was sunk by a German mine.

Just as winter loomed across the Dardanelles, the orders came to evacuate, and Monash was one of the last to leave the land where so much death had befallen the Allies, including the British and Indian forces as well as the Anzacs, for ultimately zero gain in terms of territory or the destruction of Ottoman Turkish morale. It was no doubt with mixed feelings that Monash and his brigade prepared to sail away, leaving a few guns firing on delay to keep the Turks at bay until the cove had been cleared.

It was a brilliant withdrawal, a complete evacuation of thousands of exhausted Allied soldiers, along with guns and equipment, completed on 19 December 1915, without the Turks realising the enemy had physically gone. General Brudenell White carried the key role in planning and organising the huge evacuation with complete secrecy.

This resulted in no casualties throughout the precious final hours of Gallipoli when estimates had been for up to 40 per cent of the Allied landed force facing wipe-out during the withdrawal. If only the landing had been so smoothly conducted less than nine months before; for many what seemed an eternity ago.

The news of the withdrawal was greeted with much celebration by the Turks, at least those who survived the delayed explosions and retreating naval fire. Kemal Atatürk was in Istanbul at that time and rejoiced in a victory he had largely brought about. Otto von Sanders also had a very happy 1915 Christmas.

writing to Kitchener: 'Keep Haig in the right line. Haig is one of the strongest supporters of the sword [and lance] and charging. You will have to be very firm with him. Instead of the firearm being adjunct to the sword, the sword must henceforth be adjunct to the rifle.'

Think about this: the British army was well into the twentieth century and one of its key leaders was still pushing the use of the sword and the bayonet against modern rifles and very powerful machineguns. Haig and Monash were to bring their different approaches to the Western Front, as we shall see.

Meanwhile it was a case of 'back to Egypt' for Monash and the AIF, to regather and help train new recruits from Australia. Also, on 25 April 1916, Monash devised and conducted the first in-the-field Anzac Day service near the Suez Canal. It was a hot day and after the parade and service the Anzacs were allowed to head off for a deserved swim in the Suez Canal.

The first ever Anzac Day service was held in New Zealand, owing to its earlier time zone, but Monash created the first service in the field. It was of course to remember many mates; to remember the fallen and injured. Officers might have been thinking about General Bridges. All ranks would have been thinking about the likes of Private Simpson and his donkey and thousands of other individuals.

Their loss and the whole effort in the Dardanelles had seemingly been for no military gain whatsoever. The battle conditions had been horrific from dawn on day one, 25 April 1915, until dawn on 19 December that year.

But worse was to come. Five times more Anzacs were to be killed in action through 1916, 1917 and 1918 on the Western Front than were killed at Gallipoli.

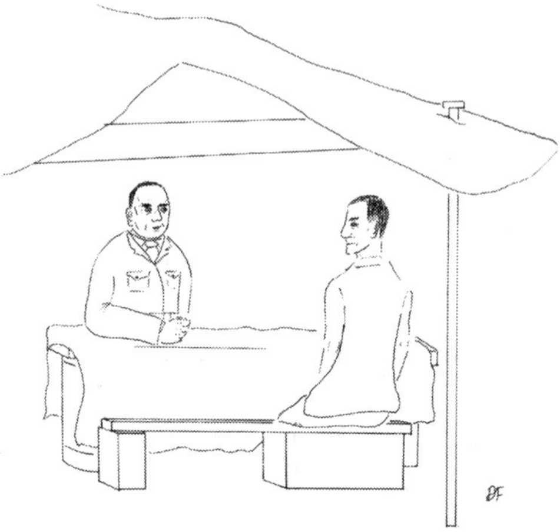

John Monash and CEW Bean have another terse meeting at the Monash bunker at Gallipoli. Their relationship was strained from the outset.

Chapter 5

MONASH ON THE WESTERN FRONT

'I hate the business of war and soldiering with a loathing that I cannot describe – the awful horror of it, the waste, the destruction and the inefficiency. My only consolation has been the sense of faithfully doing my duty to my country.'

(John Monash writing to his wife Vic, March 1917.)

After some minor manoeuvres near the Suez Canal, ensuring there would be no Turkish push through the Sinai to attack Cairo, Monash and the regrouped and replenished Fourth Brigade sailed for France, arriving at Marseilles on 7 June 1916. This was just three weeks ahead of the battle of the Somme. An overnight train soon saw Monash in Paris with some free time. He took in the usual sights but key museums and the Eiffel Tower were closed. At night he managed to attend the Folies Bergère, but due to the curfew on the serving of alcohol, the streets soon emptied.

This was another brief break before heading to the frontline locations on the Western Front not far from Amiens, about a four-hour train ride from Gare du Nord then and about a one-hour train ride today. Already staff officers were setting up the Fourth Brigade

HQs with a composition normally of over 100 men all up, all in readiness for the next round of battle orders.

Two men steeped in British military methodology of the nineteenth century were about to issue orders for the 1916 Battle of the Somme, a rigid attack in the worst location, for the Allies, along the frontline. The Germans held the high ground where the battle was set to begin along the axis of the Somme River, thus forcing the Allies to advance uphill. The British commander in chief Field Marshal Douglas Haig and General Sir Henry Rawlinson were determined to try and punch a hole through the German frontline but then gave a huge hint to the German High Command of exactly where the punch was coming.

In early July northern France can be hot and dry, broadly useful conditions for attack. However the start time was fixed at 7:30 A.M. on Saturday 1 July, by which time there was broad daylight. Haig and Rawlinson had actually wanted a true dawn attack but the Battle of the Somme involved French divisions and the French wanted a later kick-off hour. When Monash finally had the chance two years later to fix the start time for a battle at that time of the year in that area – near Hamel – he chose 3:10 A.M. (on 4 July 1918).

It could be said there was a difference of over four hours in key planning and attack methodology between Haig and Rawlinson – taking account of French demands – on the one hand, and Currie and Monash on the other. More accurately it could be said there were four million light years between the old guard from the centrum and a new guard of Army leaders, many militia promoted through the ranks, who were from the colonies.

Haig and his contribution must be weighed carefully. He supported the introduction of the tank and radio or wireless, so was not completely anti-modern, but he was still urging a cavalry role involving horses up front, well into 1918, when modern versions of the tank had arrived.

In the dreadful middle years of the war there were massive communication and logistic problems behind the Allied frontline. Haig spotted talent in the form of Eric Campbell Geddes, a former railway manager in Baltimore and Ohio as well as in the UK, who Lloyd George had asked to step in to British-government service to untangle munitions production and supply. In 1916 Geddes was made a major general immediately and quickly got to work to untangle the logjams with the dual gauge railways on the Western Front.

Interestingly, Haig the quintessential regular officer did not hesitate to turn to civilians and promote them to get the job done, if he thought they were competent. In a sense he repeated this approach in later backing the appointments of pre-war civilians Currie (as the Canadian commander) and Monash (as Australian corps commander).

These are positives for Haig. Now for the negatives …

At precisely 7:30 A.M. on that wretched Saturday morning, the five days of sporadic bombardment ended and of course this bombardment had removed the element of surprise. Then there was a lull, an excruciating, devastating lull. The lull alerted the Germans to the next phase and allowed them to quickly man their machinegun nests, mostly in well concealed and well protected bunkers.

The German machinegun teams did not have to wait long. Four perfect straight lines or waves of Allied soldiers stood up and were presented to the German gunners on a silver plate (of the kind first Earl Haig was perhaps used to eating from). By lunch time 20,000

Allied soldiers lay dead; 20,000 killed in one inglorious morning. Another 40,000 were wounded and out of action.

That morning was only the beginning of a five-month wrestle before the generals woke up and gave up on this particular disaster.

Rawlinson knew of the horrific losses by early afternoon on the fateful first of July 1916 but did little to adjust or respond. It was as if he was frozen in mind and action because of the enormity of the disaster. French divisions made more progress on this day but the losses were a crushing body blow to the Allied efforts.

This first day of the battle was a disaster on a scale never before reached or endured by the British in hundreds of years of fighting. The level of loss has never been encountered since; nor is it ever likely to be, short of a nuclear war. It was such a disaster that the logic was advanced that General Rawlinson could not be sacked as this would fully expose the size of the defeat and the extent of casualties.

'Almost imperceptibly', Sergeant JE Yates of the West Yorkshire Regiment was to write, in a stark account, 'the first day merged with the second when we held grimly to a battered trench and watched each other grow old under the day long storm of shelling. For hours, sweating, praying, swearing we worked on the heaps of chalk and the mangled bodies. Men did astonishing things … [A]t dawn next morning we were back in a wood. There were flowers among the ferns, and my last thought was a dull wonder that there could still be flowers in the world.'

On the first evening of the Somme, Monash stepped up for a limited role in the battle. On the night of 1–2 July, his orders were to mount a raiding party through a gap in the wire, take a trench or two, collect information, destroy trenches and machinegun nests and where possible kill Germans, then scamper back. He nominated the Fourteenth Battalion for the task but it was not a brilliant success due to bad communications and difficulty in getting through the wire across no-man's-land.

With raiding activity, the hope always was not to be shot by friendly fire on return to the Allied trenches, as sometimes those returning were mistaken for enemy. Of the eighty-nine that set out on this patrol, just fifty-one returned in fit shape. Some trenches were entered and held briefly but it was a very high price to pay for one raid. It was Monash operating at the smaller level of the Battalion and it rather justified the statement that the bigger the command the better Monash was.

Monash wrote of this raid concisely, almost too concisely, as if playing down what was a very ordinary outcome: 'Last night I carried out my first raid. We disposed of over fifty enemy'.

On all accounts this first Monash raid had been workmanlike but not a brilliant success. Personally, he was lucky at the Somme and during his first few weeks on the Western Front. Long distance shelling by the big guns of the German heavy artillery reached far into Allied lines to rear echelons and well past brigade and divisional HQs. Random death and destruction did not respect rank.

Later in July that year – 1916 – Monash was pulled out of the Fourth Brigade. He had to say farewell after two long years of battle endeavour, and was sent to England.

It was a good time to be out of the Western Front, with Australian divisions being cut up at Pozières and later at Le Mouquet Farm. The Canadians eventually captured Le Mouquet Farm, after Australian divisions had tried and failed, and held it against all counter attacks.

The following letter by a soldier to the father of a close mate is an example of the sheer determination and dedication during this dreadful period of the ongoing Battle of the Somme:

2058 L. Cpl J. Doggett
'D' Coy, 47th Batt.,
1st Southern General Hospital,
Birmingham, England

11/9/16

Dear Mr Becker,

I am quite a stranger to you, but feel I must write you a few lines. Your son Jim was one of my section and it is in reference to him that I am sending this letter. No doubt you will have had the news that poor Jim met his death on the battlefield last month. I know written sympathy can be but poor solace to such a blow, but you and Mrs Becker have a soldier's honest sympathy in the grief which we his old comrades share too ...... After a few weeks we came south, & were billeted back of the Somme front. Early in August, we moved up toward Albert, & in course of time found ourselves in reserve trenches. Am sorry I cannot remember the exact date we went up into the front line, but both Jim and George were hit on the first day we were in. We had to occupy a front trench beyond Pozieres.

This trench had been captured just a short time before, by other Australian troops, & the task of our Division was to hold the new line, and repel any counterattacks. Our 'D' Company went up in the afternoon, & struck the place at a bad time for the enemy were shelling from three directions. Casualties were heavy & poor Jim had not been in the trench long before he fell mortally wounded. I did not see him myself for I was farther along the trench but other boys of the section tended to him. Poor lad, he was gone too far & his release came soon.

Your son died like a soldier right in the foremost line fighting for what we are sure is a Right cause, against an enemy who if he had his way would turn the fair lands of the British Empire into countries devoid of freedom & ruled on the terrible blood & iron principle. Jim could not have died for a better cause & those of us which are still spared will not forget or fail to see that the sacrifices which have been made shall not be made in vain. A great price has been, & is still being paid, but I feel sure history will show results which will as far as possible console the Allied Nations for the loss of the boys who have gone. I do not know what you think about this life & the hereafter, Mr Becker. Such a lot is a mystery to me but whatever our beliefs I think we are all united in the feeling that those brave boys who are gone are now in a far happier sphere, & if we think of the matter in this light we must be cheered.

A day or so before we went into the first line, Jim was one of a party which went digging a communication trench. They were shelled there & Jim was close to one shell when it exploded. It gave him a shaking, & he was not better when we were ready to go up to firing line. I went to him & advised him to see the Doctor & get permission to stay behind until he felt better, but although I did my best to persuade him, he would not hear of it & came up with the rest of us. Most men would have jumped at the chance of a rest if they had it, & the fact that Jim absolutely refused it though he knew he was going to the front line, shows plainly in my opinion what a fine character was his. I lost many pals while I was on Gallipoli but I confess Jim's going upset me more than any.

Regarding myself, I took sick on coming out from trenches last time, & had the good fortune to be sent to Eng. Am grateful to be alive. May the war soon end. I think it must before long. To see what has been done by our boys on the Somme is marvellous. It is only the Huns artillery & machine guns which keep him going.

I do not know what you will think of this letter, Mr Becker. I realize it is a strange one. Please forgive all that is wrong. Would you mind sending me a card if you receive this safely. Anything I can do or answer for you, will be only too pleased. Would you address me c/o Mrs Doggett, Flaunden, Chesham, Bucks, England.

Now to close, with renewed sympathy, I remain,

Yours sincerely
John Doggett

This letter is one of many writings by the diggers of the AIF that shows immense calm, courage and grace. In this case it may have been longer than usual as Corporal Doggett was in hospital in the safety of England, in every way a long distance from the Western Front. It shows a glimpse of the camaraderie of the men of the AIF at about the middle point of the Great War.

In England Monash was promoted to major general to take command of the formation of the Third Division of the AIF. At last he had his own division of several thousand men and they embarked on training on Salisbury Plain, around the moors near Dartmoor and Stonehenge, in southern England.

He soon had the division in good shape and ready for an inspection by King George V himself. This was a kind of grand durbar with the presentation of arms, march past salute, and then the king passing by horse along the lines, unit after unit.

Monash was chatting readily with the commander in chief and a warm relationship developed. They shared a Prussian background and a love of the military and were even born in the same month of the same year. 'Apart from being the biggest and most splendid', Monash wrote to Vic, 'it was much the most successful Review I have ever been present at'. He went on to report that the king 'made one remark commencing "If we win this war ..." and I smiled and said "If we win?" and he threw back his head and laughed a full laugh and said "Oh yes! We'll win right enough, nobody need make any mistake about that"'.

The king subsequently related his confidence in Monash as a field commander to British High Command, which then began to take notice of this detail-driven tactician.

The weather held for the duration of the royal inspection, a lucky break in a part of England known for downpours. Monash escorted the king back to the royal train waiting at a nearby station. As soon as the train departed down came the rain and the soldiers were all drenched on the way back to their tents and billets.

In all these activities, Monash found time to nurture public relations and press coverage of his units as, in a far-sighted way, he knew his diggers wanted to see their exploits (even a royal inspection) well covered back at home. After all it was good for morale. Back in Gallipoli, Monash had remonstrated with Bean on the amount of coverage, or non-coverage, that the Fourth Brigade had been receiving.

To this day a debate continues about whether or not Monash was excessive in publicity hunting and was actually seeking self-aggrandisement. On balance Monash's interest in publicity was an element of his comprehensive use of all that a modern commander had at his disposal to advance morale and performance. Monash, once tackled on this score, replied: 'What if it is advertising, we need to attract recruits'.

Despite the work of censors, in 1916 and 1917 Monash succeeded in bringing about some improvement in the coverage of the work of his units. But alas on 11 November 1918 he was in a car sweeping across France towards Germany to take up an occupying role, so there was no iconic photo of him on that day throwing his cap up into the air.

After the training in England the Third Division now readied for action in the mud and trenches of mid-winter, somewhere near the middle of the Western Front. However, firstly they had to vote in a non-binding Australian conscription referendum. Prime Minister Hughes was determined to have the AIF vote early and then post the results to boost momentum at home for a 'Yes' vote.

The campaign around the referendum saw a massive debate unfold across Australia with a split in various Labor governments at state and federal level and huge rallies for and against. Ultimately Hughes was expelled from the Labor Party but while adroitly moving to form a Nationalist Labor Government and later a National Liberal-Conservative government with the support of conservatives, so that he remained as prime minister for a seven-year term.

The Trade Union movement from which Hughes had launched his federal career was bitterly opposed to conscription and he could not persuade them otherwise. The Catholic Church remained officially neutral but the Irish Catholics would not have a bar of conscription. The powerful long-serving archbishop Daniel Mannix of Melbourne swung into action in leading elements of the 'No' campaign.

Hughes sought to make contact with the Vatican to have Mannix sent back to Ireland or simply sent on to somewhere beyond Australia. At the time Australia did not have an ambassador to the Holy See and nothing came of this request. In the previous decade, Australia's first prime minister Edmund Barton had called on the then Pope Leo XIII and chatted with the Pope in Latin. Australian-Holy See relations were cordial but the transfer of bishops and archbishops to this day is regarded as a matter internal to the Church.

The Irish Easter uprising of 1916 had created its own momentum and divisive dynamic. Even a former British diplomat, Sir Roger Casement, sought German weapons for the Irish rebellion and went fund-raising in the US. In late 1914 Casement had actually travelled to Germany via Norway and sought and obtained a statement from on high, issued in November, that Germany would never invade Ireland: 'The Imperial Government formally declares that under no circumstances would Germany invade Ireland'.

Casement was conveyed by German U Boat to Ireland just before the 1916 Easter rebellion but almost immediately he was caught and arrested and taken to the Tower of London, found guilty of treason and later sentenced to death by hanging. Not even pleas by Sir Arthur Conan Doyle and George Bernard Shaw for clemency held sway and in August 1916 Casement, who had returned his knighthood, was hanged, to remain a curious example of a diplomat who played hard and paid with his life.

It was also an example of the efforts some were prepared to go to for the Irish cause and a pointer to the bitterness – especially sectarian bitterness – that emerged even in Australia, during the dreadful middle years of the Great War. It was another headache for Haig who had some Irish units on the Western Front and he may have wondered about their loyalty, though they proved themselves to be as determined and loyal as the British units.

Generals are not meant to buy into political fights but Birdwood was asked to make a statement in favour of a 'Yes' vote and for that to be widely distributed through the AIF.

Eventually the soldiers voted, in October 1916, and back in Australia the vote was held later that month. The overall result was a narrow loss for Hughes, by a margin of 72,476 votes: Yes 1,087,557 (48.39 per cent) and No 1,160,033 (51.61 per cent). A repeat exercise in December 1917 saw the No vote margin more than double to 166,588 votes. The official results for the 20 December 1917 referendum was: Yes 1,015,159 (46.21 per cent), No 1,181,747 (53.79 per cent). So the first referendum loss margin was 3.22 per cent and the second referendum more than double that, at 7.58 per cent. In both cases, though, the margins were not huge.

Joan Beaumont in her recent book on the Great War, *Broken Nation*, highlights the Keith Murdoch observation that the Third Division in training on the Salisbury Plain had voted yes, counterbalancing the margin from the trenches. Contrary to Hughes' expectation, there was not a resounding vote for 'Yes' amongst the diggers.

Maybe the Third Division soldiers voting were thinking about extra recruits to maintain their manpower near full strength before they went to the Western Front. It was not to be but soon enough in late 1916, the under-strength division had its equipment and its embarkation orders. Had Monash, as leader, been a further factor in this 'Yes' vote? The answer is maybe.

Simply to move the Third Division anywhere was a huge logistical effort. Monash recorded the movement to the wharves at

Southampton took eighty-seven full train loads. He crossed the Channel on 24 November without any mishap, though writing, on 26 November, that it had been a rather rough crossing with a wetting involved.

Monash set up HQ at Château de la Motte. The Third Division had to hold five of the ninety-two miles of the British section of the Western Front. Even away from large-scale battles, intricate re-supply logistics had to be executed to ensure the supply of ammunition and all range of necessary victuals to maintain the first, second and third line of trenches, as well as the communication trenches.

Having reached the rank of major general, Monash had the luxury of being able to wangle short leave breaks and on occasions long leave breaks of up to a fortnight. On top of a pile of theatre programs in the Monash archives at the National Library in Canberra is a splendid copy of the war-time program from the Folies Bergère cabaret in Paris. Monash also dashed up to London and caught up with old family friend Liz Bentwitch. He soon found that she was supportive and understanding. In turn she helped distract the general from the pressure of war with a round of theatre and restaurant visits.

For now, after a long absence from his beloved home 'Iona' in Toorak, and from his own wife and family, the London affair waxed and waned but never distracted Monash from the many tasks to hand in his role as a divisional commander, fighting for country and Empire. Again the heavy weight of battle planning was on his shoulders as the division prepared to step up from patrolling and raiding to mounting a formal attack.

Monash had the luck of finding or being allocated superb headquarters in French Châteaus, with one extraordinary exception later in 1917. Typically the French Château had thick walls and a couple of floors so that the occasional enemy shell or embryonic aerial bombing rarely brought about total destruction.

In this setting Monash was to maximise his planning and writing of detailed orders, on occasions right down to platoon level. This is where Monash sifted through aerial photos, studied reports of enemy movements and thought through his evolving central strategy: apply holistic comprehensive tactics to all military action with achievable objectives and the maximum protection of troops of all ranks at all times.

In short it was the Monash Australian way to bring about results and two full years into the Great War both Monash and his distinctive strategic approach were becoming known, despite being given little attention by CEW Bean. This was the case at both the highest levels, of King George V and the prime ministers Lloyd George and Billy Hughes, right down to corporals and even private soldiers.

There was always a regular stream of VIP visitors to the Monash HQs as his reputation grew. This was time consuming but Monash could see the use of getting better known, building contacts and above all else spreading the knowledge of his holistic strategic approach, which would save lives and help to win the war.

It is worth examining the core template of the Monash strategic approach further and this we are able to do as he wrote much on the subject and gave some definitive speeches on this topic, including one to the Beefsteak Club in Melbourne on 30 March 1926. It is possible to distil a lot from this well prepared and deeply reflective speech. The overall axiom of Monash can be paraphrased as follows:

> The best form of defence is offense. The mounting of an attack should be done on the basis of a comprehensive holistic battle plan aimed at applying an overwhelming concentration of resources involving rested and well prepared troops with all necessary supporting arms, against a limited, finite, calibrated objective. This must be done with provision to hold captured objectives against inevitable and swift counter attack.

This was Monash the ever careful deep thinker, laying down the elements that had made him a general to be noticed, with the Monash battles being closely followed in the closing 100 days of the Great War.

The four key principles embraced as part of the Monash strategic approach were laid out in some detail in the speech: firstly the absolute emphasis on selecting the right objective with the related criteria that it be achievable by assembling the right amount of resources to overwhelm the enemy at the time and place selected.

Equally once the objective was captured, it must be readily able to be strongly defended against counter attack.

In other words you do not select an objective at the bottom of a hill with swampy ground and exposed in all forward directions to enemy fire from on high. To quote Monash directly from his spell-binding speech: 'This, translated into the circumstances of the late war meant, simply, that one merely had to choose an objective which, in magnitude, lay well within the capacity of the military resources at one's disposal, in order to make practically certain of success'.

Of course Monash did not mind where extra top-up resources came from, as highlighted by the example of the Battle of Hamel, in which the troops were mainly from within the Australian Army

Corps but with 2000 – reduced to 1000 – from the Thirty-Third Division of Illinois, commanded by American general George Bell, also involved. With the Battle of Amiens or Greater Amiens, huge extra numbers and resources were borrowed or allocated, including four brigades of tanks, sixteen extra brigades of artillery, and twenty extra air force squadrons, blowing out numbers to three times the normal size of the Australian Army Corps.

Secondly Monash hammered away at the need to have 'fixity of plans', as last minute changes created massive confusion and often caused a huge boost to the Allied death toll. On occasions this involved friendly artillery fire due to targeting errors as a consequence of confusion, and killing our best and bravest who had moved forward. An example was at Passchendaele when Field Marshal Haig insisted on deploying exhausted troops in impossible conditions, with the result of a massive set of casualties, thousands upon thousands wounded and killed in action.

Thirdly Monash believed in using rested and well trained troops, well briefed for the particular set of tasks within the denoted battle. In his meticulous planning he factored in the condition and repair of his units that were going to be utilised. Further there was an unwritten rule that fast evacuation of wounded would be provided on the Western Front, a factor that helped morale.

Monash rotated units to areas behind the lines for rest and recovery, and was in touch even as a corps commander with the fitness and morale of the men. He addressed them directly ahead of big battles, if not physically then issuing these addresses by letter to be read out to all ranks. Notably he insisted where possible that a hot meal be served before any battle, reflecting practical concerns for the fitness of the soldiers. He wanted the best from his men and he knew he had to give them the best in available rest and sustenance before a big stunt or huge battle.

Finally Monash believed in maintaining discrete reserves, units held back and ready to move forward to fill gaps and complete other unexpected or suddenly arising tasks. Inevitably the enemy would mount counterattacks and so Monash often planned on the attacking units to pause at a given line, to allow other units from the rear to step up and either move through to secure a new line or assist in holding that which had been captured.

He contended further that you had to anticipate and know what your superiors were thinking at all times but also develop a sixth sense, an automatic set of reflexes in battle to help bring about victory.

It really was a case of a maestro being required and Monash was a maestro in so many ways, the equivalent of an orchestra conductor.

Andrew Condon, current CEO of Sydney Legacy, recalls that his History lecturer in the United States Army Command and General Staff College he attended in Fort Leavenworth, Kansas, from 1996 to 1997, identified the first known use and best early example of a staff planning process as being by Monash at the Battle of Hamel.

The US Army was using and teaching the Military Decision Making Process (MDMP). Here, the emphasis is on the commander using all his different staff advisers (artillery, armour, intelligence, aviation, logistics, engineers, public relations, etcetera) to make decisions and formulate a plan.

Before Monash's example at the Battle of Hamel, Condon analyses,

> the military decision making and planning was the commander's prerogative, and a process that was predominately limited to the commander, who may have used a small number of trusted

> advisers. Monash and the MDMP fully engaged all the specialist expertise and thinking of all the staff before decisions were made, and continued to do so in the planning process. Once the decision making and planning process was complete, orders were produced/issued, and Monash ensured there were no subsequent changes to the plan (that often happened in WWI).

Condon also suggests the particular cultural and occupational bases facilitating Monash's development and application of this new approach:

> British generals of the day (career soldiers) did not have the background experience, nor inclination to consult openly with their subordinates, and nor did their subordinates expect to be consulted (they would have been anxious about giving advice above their position). On the battlefields of earlier centuries the commander's role was to motivate and lead with strength. Asking subordinates for advice would have been seen as a lack of strength in a commander. Monash being a militia officer (Army Reserve), was not constrained by past military culture and practices, and more importantly his engineering background gave him a great insight in[to] how to make decisions and plan in complex matters.

Monash's application of his strategic approach required a certain practical modus operandi, which he detailed in forthright style near the beginning of his Beefsteak 'tour de force':

> A successful leader must be unemotional to the extent of being callous to the external issues that evoke joy or sorrow, elation or despondency; he must be indifferent to praise or blame; he must have the capacity to persevere calmly and dispassionately with

> the business in hand, undisturbed by the menace of imminent calamity, or by the exultation of success.
>
> He must be patient to a degree. He must have determination and steadfastness of purpose of a very high order. He must have an exulted confidence in himself and in the correctness of his judgement, amounting to an intellectual arrogance. His capacity to appreciate the workings of the minds of others must be automatic and swift.
>
> His personality must be of a kind which inspires confidence in others and which dominates their instinct to exercise independent judgement. He should be, in short, temperamentally a paragon of excellence, which I fear none of us, in spite of earnest aspirations, ever completely reached.

One thing irked Monash a great deal: being referred to as an amateur, in 1918. Monash was scathing of these comments by the London based media highlighting those who had not been to a Duntroon or a Sandhurst-type officers academy. He maintained that no matter how a commanding officer started out in 1914, by 1918 if still alive and in enhanced roles then nigh on five years' very active training and experience had been obtained.

Monash asked if you would call a student in his fifth year in any professional curriculum 'a mere amateur'. This was a fair question and he highlighted how many Australian militia officers had started out in 1914 commanding 1000 or less, to end up in 1918 commanding 20,000 or in one case over 100,000, and the truth is that militia officers did very well in World War One. Indeed some Australian and Canadian militia officers did a whole lot better than regular army personnel.

Monash was no shrinking violet but he had an overall set of strategies and a performance record that meant his template should have been revered and studied in detail. It attracted support from all levels, from staff officers working in close proximity at HQs right down through the ranks. Monash was, warts and all, greatly respected. He was not deeply popular and did not seek cheap popularity but he gained immense respect.

In 1917 Haig was under the pump. He was under pressure to bring about breakthroughs and Lloyd George was having doubts about this doyen of the British military establishment from the previous century. Whole villages in the UK were becoming aware that hundreds of their menfolk would never be coming home as the dreaded letters giving official notification of death arrived.

Local newspapers from the Riverina to Yorkshire were carrying lists of the war dead and injured on their front pages. Since the dreadful morning of 1 July 1916, when 20,000 were killed at the Somme, the lists had become dramatically longer and longer. Initially shock and disbelief turned to deep despair and stoic mourning.

Lloyd George was considering replacing Haig and after the war observed, though he also said much the same about the Canadian leader Lieutenant General Arthur Currie, that had Monash replaced Haig in 1917, the Great War would have ended months earlier.

During the war years Monash was criticised for his use of headquarters some distance from the action. Yet he was quick to move forward and was right up front with the Fourth Brigade raiding party on the night of 1 July 1916 at the Somme. Yes, then Brigadier General Monash was shepherding eighty-eight diggers right up and through the wire to undertake a raid.

In the mind of Monash was the usual belief of all diggers, that there was no bullet going to hit him. Although as the war rolled on, battle after battle, the chances were narrowing, and certainly shrapnel and bullets did not respect rank. His personal courage was as strong as anyone's but, consistent with his careful nature, he always endeavoured to minimise unnecessary risks.

After weeks of raiding, the Third Division was given orders to mount a divisional attack at Messines, near Ypres. Monash examined all the available maps in detail and wrote a huge set of orders, nominating 3:10 A.M. on 7 June 1917 for the attack to physically begin. It was a huge effort, linked with Allied units on both sides, and victory was obtained.

The use of artillery creeping barrages was emerging but gas attacks had to be contended with by both sides. Monash was a bit player at Messines but showed resolve and careful planning, and the Third Division emerged enhanced.

Here was Monash at last commanding a division in battle and producing successful results, under General Herbert Plumer but with a chance to lay out divisional battle orders in great detail. Overall Commander Haig wrote, after a visit to examine preparations for Messines: 'Monash is a clear headed determined commander, every detail has been thought of'.

At zero hour, 3:10 on 7 June 1917, the Monash led Third Division swung into action, but only after nineteen huge mines, created by the Royal Engineer tunnelling companies, had erupted, wiping out a large chunk of the German trench system and killing hundreds of German soldiers before they could fire a shot in this particular battle. Hill 60 was obliterated and the Third Division, with the Twenty-Fifth

British and the New Zealand division, swept forward, later assisted by another AIF division. The targeted Green line was reached and the handiwork of Plumer as the Second Army overall commander for this Battle of Messines, helped greatly by the inaugural performance of Monash and his new Third Division, worked a treat.

After Messines there was a break well behind the lines for the division, and some lighter activities were permitted, such as a 'Dinner Concert' by the Fifth Field Company of Australian Engineers. Gladstone Robert McGowan from Melbourne was one of the ring leaders for this function, which had a glorious printed program. It denoted the venue as being 'Somewhere in France'. There was a choice of roast beef, veal cutlets or pork chops and a huge range of vegetables.

The morale boosting function was for all ranks and included an overture or in fact two overtures and a jolly night was had by all a long way from home, though their minds were no doubt not far from 'The folks at home', for whom there was a last toast before interval.

McGowan survived the Great War, went on to survive serving in World War Two, despite having the dangerous job at one stage of creeping forward with tapes in the dark to show attacking units the way forward. His diaries show how he could be at the Moulin Rouge cabaret in Paris one night and the very next night creeping out into no-man's-land a long way from safety and the Can Can girls.

For the Third Division it was onto Broodseeinde and Windmill Ridge in early October 1917, near the dreaded Passchendaele Ridge and the historic Belgium town of Ypres. On 1 October Monash had moved into new headquarters located in the old city walls of Ypres, damp and not without the odd rat or two but reasonably sheltered from shelling.

Today this location is dominated by the giant Menin Gates and Memorial with thousands of names of the Allied fallen listed on the inside walls. This was completed between the world wars and survived the Nazi occupation of World War Two. Each evening at 8:00 P.M. a short ode ceremony is held and in recent years this has been frequently attended by the Australian NATO and EU ambassador, a practise initiated by Dr Brendan Nelson.

Once again there is no noticeable plaque recording that this was the location of the Monash Third Division headquarters. Yes he was part of a huge team effort and yes he gave great leadership like so many others but often Australian leaders are diminished by the failure of Australians to give credit to their fellow Australians where it is due, let alone by the failure of the British to praise Australian leaders.

The Monash strategic approach was to come to the fore again from within the giant 'Walls of Ypres'. He and the Third Division succeeded again, despite some initial confusion, and the set of objectives was obtained and counter attacks fiercely repelled. The almost impregnable Windmill Ridge was captured, and casualties minimised. The Third Division of the Anzac Corps of the Second Army was at its zenith.

By now Monash had a deep understanding of the weaknesses of his direct superiors Godley and Haig and of the relative strengths of Plumer and later the French commander Foch. The inflexibility of Haig and the complicatedness of Godley were now going to lead to a complete disaster and defeat at Passchendaele.

As one walks in the early evening along the city walls of Ypres and attends the Menin Gates Ode ceremony, the dimension of the costly stubbornness, bordering on criminal neglect, from the senior British generals, bears reflecting on. It was on a grand scale. In 1915 it may have cost the Allies victory at Gallipoli. In 1917 it nearly cost the Allies victory completely.

After the victories at Broodsiende and Windmill Ridge in the first week of October, Haig developed a passion to take Passchendaele and to do so on 9 October, come rain or shine. It had started raining around 6 October and this turned to a downpour on 8 October. To attack in heavy rain may be a good tactic but only if forward movement can be physically obtained.

Haig was at his murderous worst and in one of the dumbest and most defining moves of the Great War, he would not relent and ordered the Battle for Passchendaele to proceed on 9 October regardless of the conditions. Monash's pleas for a delay were over-ruled.

Thousands were sent into waist-deep mud, to their death, from direct wounds or drowning in the slush.

Nothing was gained and by sunset most units had withdrawn behind or back to the original start line. The Third Division was decimated although in the strict meaning of the word they were more than decimated as they lost over 60 per cent of the men who went over the top.

Monash had to keep a stiff upper lip. He was a member of the senior inner-circle of Allied military leaders on the Western front. But he was furious at this wanton waste of life on a scale that was totally unacceptable and also he knew it was totally injurious to the overall war effort. The pure pig-headedness of Haig should have resulted in him being sacked by 1 November 1917. Alas this was not to be.

Godley for his part was also to blame. He survived the Great War and lived until 1957, playing a role in the Home Guard in World War Two (think Captain Mainwaring from the BBC TV series *Dad's Army*). Soon after, Monash was to no longer be under Godley but was to remain under Haig as the Australian Army Corps was formed and the Third Division moved into this new corps.

As the New Year rolled in, spirits were mixed in London and along the Western front, and there were two new factors in play: the slow but sure entry of the USA into the Great War, with a huge contingent led by General Pershing, and the exit of Russia from the war, in a deal with Germany devised by the new rulers in Russia, the Bolsheviks.

This in turn led to a huge push by Germany, one last lunge to do over the Allies, using extra divisions transferred from the now relatively peaceful Eastern Front. As predicted by British intelligence, a prediction widely ignored, on 21 March 1918 the Germans attacked westward, in a concentrated way along the axis of the Somme. Within a week they had gone a long way west by dint of superior numbers and sheer force and pushed the Allies back and back. They were in sight of the tall steeples of the Amiens Cathedral, at least what was left of it, thanks to new German light machineguns and a tactic in which units of the most skilled fighters smashed through, while leaving the mopping up to lesser units.

'Le mois des Anzacs' – perhaps this could be shortened to just 'the month of L'Anzac' – had arrived on the Western Front. It was the period from 25 March to 25 April 1918 where the Australian divisions stopped dead the huge German push, or lunge, code-named by General Erich Ludendorff as Operation Michael. Some British units played their role in stopping the Bosch, and again New Zealand units were outstanding, but the Australians were a force that greatly helped turn the tide and stabilise the area around Albert and east of Amiens. As Serle assesses: 'The AIF indeed was given pride of place in shoring up the dangerous gap on the Somme, at several places it blunted German attacks and counter attacked brilliantly and this rallied the British on the flanks. The AIF as a whole could not but be proud ... they had nowhere yielded an inch.'

It was what might be renamed the Battle of Anzac Amiens, immediately to the east of Amiens in fact, around Villers-Brettoneux. Monash had quickly come off leave from down south on the French Riviera and his division was brought forward from a rest area near Boulogne, to plug holes in the line and face down the might of the attack forces of the German Army.

Much of the British Fifth Army, led by General Gough, had been wiped out. Badly trained battalions with a raw combination of first timers both at officer level and through the ranks, just fell apart. It was not a case of mutiny, as the French had endured in 1917, leading to soldiers being pulled out of the mutineer ranks and shot dead and the remaining soldiers having to march past the lines of bodies of their colleagues. Still it was a rapid retreat and rout.

Not unlike the Canadians, the motivated and high spirited Anzacs provided the tonic to stabilise the situation on the ground and then push back against the Germans. The Australian officer ranks produced the massive organising and front-foot work that made a huge difference in this part of the Western Front in that critical 'Le mois des Anzacs'. John Monash was to the fore but also key operators such as Pompey Elliott and Les Morshead and many more. Typical of many in the AIF, Sergeant JA Brennan of the Fifty-Seventh Battalion always spoke highly of Pompey Elliott, describing him to his son as a 'Man's man', and he spoke of Monash in similar terms.

In the chaos of many British troops retreating and Australians stepping forward – the two groups at times marching past each other – Monash managed to command a fleet of London buses to rapidly deploy his division. He quickly established his dictum that any sort of plan is better than no plan at all and then he applied a steadying hand across the whole critical section of the frontlines to the east of Amiens and especially around Corbie.

The holding of the line and the development of a set of support trenches to reflect the new frontline was a near-run thing, after the German lunge had been halted. Amiens was in range of the long distance German artillery but it was in Allied hands and would remain so right throughout 1918, due especially to the huge efforts of the Australian units.

As the Third Division pushed forward in late March 1918, on a spring morning, proud Commander Monash wrote: 'The spectacle of that infantry will be memorable to me as one of the most inspiring sights of the whole War. Here was the Third Division … It had come into its own at last, and was called upon to prove its mettle'.

This it did both as an anchor on the line and in contributions to the fighting around Villers-Brettoneux, which changed hands during the period but, in a huge effort on the morning of Anzac Day 1918, was recaptured by the Australians, never to be lost again to the Germans in the Great War. The spirit of Anzac had been renewed just three years to the day after the Gallipoli landing.

It was at the crossroads village of Villers-Brettoneaux that the 1918 Operation Michael, the German 1918 push, reached its westernmost point. In the spring sunshine of April 1918, the hilltops presented the all-conquering Germans views of the tempting target of Amiens itself, now just a few kilometres to the west. Monash knew he had to strike first and push back as soon as possible. In the first weeks of April there were many raids intended in part to straighten and strengthen the Allied line.

With an eye to the date, the third anniversary of Anzac, on the morning of 25 April 1918 a superb counterattack unfolded. Highly motivated Anzacs lunged forward, taking big risks but fighting tenaciously and soon Villers-Brettoneaux, with pockets of vital high ground, was back in the hands of the Allies, who quickly fortified the new line. Pompey Elliott and Les Morshead and their units played their roles magnificently, delivering decisive results against very substantial odds.

British officer G Grogon VC, described this night battle as 'the finest feat of soldiering of the whole war'. The mayor of Villers Bretonneux said in July 1919, 'the first inhabitants of Villers Bretonneux to re-establish themselves in the ruins of what was once a flourishing little town have, by means of donations, shown a desire to thank the valorous Australian armies, who with the spontaneous enthusiasm and characteristic dash of their race, in a few hours chased (away) an enemy ten times their number.'

It had truly been touch and go. At times mistakes on the Allied side nearly delivered victory to the enemy. This would have meant the key hub and railway junction of Amiens falling to the Germans. The Germans were pressing hard in the centre, in the north near Flanders and in the south directly east of Paris. The Germans were delighted with having captured much ground in late March and early April 1918 but equally they had over-extended their supply lines.

Had Amiens itself fallen back into German hands (after they held it briefly in 1914), then World War One might conceivably have been over by 8 August 1918, with Germany extracting huge fines and reparations from a conquered France and a subjugated Britain. Instead, by sunset on Anzac Day 1918, the Germans had been pushed back. The next day they could no longer see Amiens in the distance and the palpable threat from Operation Michael, with its concentrated and very nearly successful lunge, had been largely dealt with. A period of stalemate returned to the new lines of trenches. This was not for long, as once again Monash was planning and thinking ahead.

Monash and many others have contended that this was the real turning point of World War One. Had the Germans captured Amiens, this major hub and key rail junction, Ludendorff would have pivoted south direct to Paris and, further, British resupply would have been cut off. This was just ahead of Pershing's US forces being in the theatre and battle ready. The Yanks were not yet deployed or deployable, needing some in-country training.

Let it be repeated that it was from 25 March till 25 April 1918, at Albert and Villers-Brettoneux, that the Australians took the full brunt of the German push and stopped them in their tracks. It had been touch and go but a new trench line was created, a new frontline that importantly, as will be discussed in the next chapter, included a large indent into Allied-held territory around the village of Hamel.

In May 1918 Monash had been promoted lieutenant general and made Australian Army Corps commander, against continuing static from both Keith Murdoch and CEW Bean, who argued against Monash being given a plum fighting command position. They thought Monash would be better in administration behind the lines in England. Monash politely did not agree.

Prime Minister Billy Hughes was en route to England via the USA at the time and while the promotion of Monash went through, it was not publicly announced. When Hughes reached England he was bombarded with criticisms of Monash by both Bean and Murdoch. They lobbied massively against Monash and in favour of Brudenell White, as covered in more detail in the next chapter.

Suffice to say here that Bean had long had some suspicion of Monash, since they first met at Gallipoli, as an old, initially portly and not your bronzed, hardened, Australian officer, and who was pushy as well and after all a Jew of Prussian descent.

Hughes at the start of July, en route to a crucial conference in Paris, called on Monash and the Australian Army Corps and questioned many senior officers out of earshot of Monash about what they thought of him. He encountered much support for Monash and no criticisms and Monash himself made it clear to Hughes he would not lightly accept removal from command of the Australian Army Corps.

Finally Hughes decided not to overturn the promotion of Monash and affirmed that Monash would continue as corps commander. This mini-campaign against the promotion of Monash had been a massive distraction for busy people, such as Brudenell White and Monash himself, at a critical juncture, but at last Monash was in a position to have real sway and apply the Monash strategic approach. This template was not precisely unique but was a rigorous application of holistic thinking and harmonised timing.

It had been a long haul from a tiny university unit as a private soldier or irregular of no rank, back in Melbourne, over three decades ago, to lieutenant general commanding the Australian Army Corps of five divisions. Many obstacles had been overcome. There had been a degree of luck with both his survival and promotion. On 1 April 1918, at a forward brigade headquarters, Monash had escaped death by shelling by ten minutes, while two staff officers were killed. However Monash had never deviated from the belief the Germans would be defeated and sooner than many people would have expected. The Great War had gone on long enough. Millions had died but there was still to be a twist or three in what was to become the final year of the so called war to end all wars.

Monash carefully planned the next round of implementation of his strategic approach, doing so this time as a lieutenant general and commander of the battle-weary but dynamic Australian Army Corps.

Chapter 6

THE BATTLE OF HAMEL

> 'We knew you would fight a real fight, but we did not know that from the very beginning you would astonish the whole continent with your valour … I shall go back to Paris tomorrow and say to my countryman: I have seen the Australians, I have looked into their eyes. I know that they, men who have fought great battles in the cause of freedom, will fight on alongside us, till the freedom for which we are fighting is guaranteed for us and our future.'
>
> (Prime Minister Georges Clemenceau, addressing Australian soldiers in the aftermath of the successful 93-minute battle of Hamel, Sunday 7 July 1918.)

It was a shining exemplary jewel of a battle, if any battle can be so described. It was a much needed tonic for the hard pressed Australian forces and indeed for the Allied forces overall. It greatly cheered the Allied leadership at the highest levels. Further it was the deployment of every aspect of the holistic Monash strategic approach and while not without precedent, the tactics at Hamel brought cohesion in battle to a new high level. In short it was a standout battle and one of only a couple of offensive battles since the German Operation Michael and the Battle of Anzac Amiens or 'Le mois des Anzac', 25 March to 25 April 1918.

To some extent because of World War One history then and now being written by the biggest player on the winning side (Great Britain) and also according to the fixed formula of some military historians, for nearly 100 years the Battle of Hamel has been downplayed. The ultimate proof of this was the release of the three-volume *Cambridge History of the First World War* in 2014, referred to in the Introduction, with seventy chapters and not one mention of Monash or the Monash role in creating the 93-minute Battle of Hamel.

Further claims that the Hamel tactics were merely copied from *GHQ SS135 Tactical Pamphlet* ignore the fact that even if this was in part true, there is a huge leap of leadership required to convert from a pamphlet on tactics to actual practical battle plans and then implement them to bring about victory.

The Battle of Hamel was a rare set-piece action launched by the Allies as they recovered from the huge lunge of the German Army, launched in March 1918 and not finally stopped until the third Anzac Day, 25 April 1918, at Villers-Brettoneaux, by some very brave and determined Australians. Forces from the other Allied countries were rebuilding and in the case of the Pershing-led US forces, still arriving in France.

Hamel was a clear-cut victory and reversal of fortunes, worthy of reappraisal for the breakthrough it afforded against a German Army that was still not giving in and was always quick to mount vicious counter attacks, especially in mid-1918.

John F Williams, in his illuminating book *Anzacs, the Media and the Great War*, wrote that due to several factors, including the work of the official censor, Hamel was hugely downplayed: 'The Church bells were not ordered rung, great celebrations were not called and Hamel drifted from a popular consciousness'. Indeed it did, then, and the drift continues to this day.

It was not a pretty battle. No battle is, as a diary extract by the chaplain Frank Rolland, describing being way out in no-man's-land before the start hour and in front of the actual start line, reveals:

> It was still almost dark but I noticed a few German shells dropping behind us and towards us, so I crept over to the doctor and advised him to push on further at once. He agreed and as we stood up and moved again, the scene was indescribably apocalyptic. The eye, and not the ear, was receptive, though I remember the machine gun crackle shrilling through the heavy roar. Every kind of gun was at work. It was cloud and fire, lead falling in colossal showers, the hill hidden with smoke, the smoke flashed with flame; all the force of the elements seemed concentrated and hurled.

To step back a little in time and reiterate, there was much for Monash to endure in 1918, which had started with sweeping rumours of a huge German push coming to end the stalemate of trench warfare on the Western Front and bring about a result as quickly as possible. The thinking generals on both sides knew there was a limit in any war of attrition, even with the new dynamics flowing from Russia out and the USA in.

The closing down of the Eastern Front was a reminder to Germany of how much easier it would have been if the kaiser, the German centrum, Hindenburg, and General Erich Ludendorff, had stuck with a one-front world war. There is little doubt that France would have fallen, and within the first six months of the hostilities.

Following the winding up of the Eastern Front, the railways of 'Greater Germany' were cranked up to move the German divisions freed from freezing Russia back to and through Germany, ready to launch a spring time offensive in the first quarter of 1918 in France.

Monash was on leave in the south of France in March when the German offensive began in earnest. Among the thousands involved was young corporal Adolf Hitler who was learning perhaps not so much in the horrific turmoil of battle. Hitler was to repeat the same mistake as Germany in World War One by opening two fronts, indeed multiple fronts to the east, west and south, in World War Two, against Russia, France, the Allies in Africa, and later against Italy when elements there threatened to switch sides in 1943.

One-front wars with a focused effort along the lines recalled by the Reverend Frank Rolland – with all the elements concentrated and hurled – make a lot of sense when war must be conducted. It has been ever thus.

The German Armies swept westward in March. Several British units were decimated. The Fifth British Army, led by General Gough, was broken or routed and in full retreat. And it was a case of maestro Monash, refreshed by a few days' leave, to the rescue. That is once he could find his battalions. Famously he linked up with one or two generals under candlelight in a ruined castle and managed to locate his units and order them to start moving forward into the gaps near Amiens.

The area Monash found himself in on 25 March 1918 was familiar country, just east of Amiens and almost due north of Paris, with gentle rolling farmlands dotted by hilltop villages which in turn were dominated by church steeples. There was chaos and confusion but Monash quickly established a new frontline to be held against the fast advancing German forces, threatening Amiens itself. The objective and prize was the very strategically valuable large railway junction on the vital Allied supply corridor from the coast.

At the same time the British Haig and French Philippe Pétain were shuffling around various divisions, trying to anticipate the next big push under Operation Michael and the nearby Operation Georgette.

It had been a near-run thing. Like a cut snake the German Army was lashing out with fresh, professional panzer divisions opening gaps in the Allied lines, less well trained divisions filling the gaps to expand on the initial breakthroughs. However Ludendorff was inconsistent with his targeting. Just when a huge breakthough was obtained and the advantage seized, with a chance of another surge forward to really crush the opposing Allied units, a sudden halt would be ordered.

As usual Monash was consolidating and planning. He was also once again on the hunt for a new headquarters in the area and settled on the magnificent Château Bertangles. This soon became the noted location for rapidly unfolding events in the middle of 1918.

Sadly, since World War One, part of the inside of Château Bertangles has been destroyed by fire, but externally it is glistening today, standing in formal gardens behind a grand fence but easily visible from the road.

Monash was frustrated that the new line between the Allies and the Germans had a kink in it whereby the village of Le Hamel and the nearby *petite bois* or Vaire wood was held by the Germans, with strong, heavily fortified defensive trench lines. The jutting out of the

German positions gave them the chance to create arcs of enfilade fire straight into the trenches of the Allies.

Monash put up a plan to mount the Battle of Hamel for early July and it went via Rawlinson and on to Haig, now known by many as 'the butcher of the Battle of the Somme', who was looking for breakthroughs and ideas.

Approval was given in late June and the preparations intensified, complete with new tactics involving the new generation of one-man driveable tanks. Joint training commenced a safe distance behind the lines, involving many diggers of all ranks riding the tanks and becoming familiar with and more confident in their capabilities, as earlier versions had been prone to break down and were difficult for infantry to work with.

As the clock ticked over the half-year mark of 1918, the necessary conferences and finalisation of detailed plans took place at Château Bertangles, with the tanks embedded and the artillery barrage planned meticulously. Platoons as small units were now taken back behind the lines to practise movements, especially with the tanks, and so close links were built between infantry and the tank personnel. All was looking good when not one but two interventions out of left field nearly derailed everything. It could be said they were two unexpected salvos from friendly fire on high.

As mentioned Prime Minister Billy Hughes was en route from London to Paris and sought a visit at short notice to the Australian Army Corps. Monash had to say 'Yes' but he had only an inkling as to what the purpose might be. Bean and Murdoch had been mounting a concerted campaign against Monash and his appointment as corps commander, from May that year (1918). They were still seeking the appointment of Brudenell White, a competent

Australian senior officer but one who had not commanded units in large-scale battle.

The great CEW Bean was up to anti-Semite mischief, always critical of Monash and the way that Monash allegedly promoted his units and himself. Back in 1914 Bean had stated that Australians do not want to be represented by Jews '… because of their ability, natural and inborn in Jews, to push themselves.' Bean was by his own admission doubting and critical of Monash right throughout World War One.

Murdoch was doing his own soundings around London but, as Roland Perry and others have observed, these were not comprehensive soundings and were selectively chosen to bolster his bias against Monash and in favour of Brudenell White, who had not only never commanded big units in large-scale battle but was adjudged by many to not be of the right temper to do so. He had brilliantly organised the retreat and evacuation of Gallipoli but this was not necessarily your best item to lead with on a CV in an application for leading the Australian Army Corps in attack mode.

Journalists around London with good connections to the high and mighty, as Murdoch had, were able to wield considerable influence. Wrongly, Murdoch had come to the view that Monash was simply not competent enough; a big call and an erroneous call but he loaded up Prime Minister Billy Hughes and others with this very negative view of Monash.

The added problem was the phenomena of 'easy access to VIPs overseas', or what I always denoted in shorthand as EATVIPS overseas. Ambassadors and high commissioners pride themselves in peace times and war on assembling interesting heavy hitters but, if they are really good, also assembling up and comers, to meet visiting

Australian federal ministers and especially the prime minister. Hughes was at this time resident in London. The praetorian guard protection walls are more easily pierced when the leader is away from the national capital.

This EATVIPS overseas phenomena very nearly destroyed Monash and his command of the Australian Army Corps, during an intense period in which he was preparing for offensive battle after withstanding the huge German push of March and April 1918. Hughes was heading to France with a mindset poisoned against Monash after repeated negativity had been served up to him around London by Bean and Murdoch in particular, but, in fairness, he wanted to see for himself.

At times Bean and Murdoch conspired by indirect means, using very senior generals they encountered to ram home their choice of Brudenell White, or anyone but the Jewish Army Reservist John Monash, channelling all and sundry who they thought could bend Hughes' ear and mindset.

Hughes set off with fellow Nationalist Party of Australia member (and former prime minister) Sir Joseph Cook and a small entourage to visit Château Bertangles near Amiens and see Monash in the field at his headquarters, just ahead of a major battle. For his part Monash provided a full briefing for the prime ministerial party in relation to the battle plans and on the afternoon of 3 July arranged for Hughes to address the troops. This Hughes did in quick time as enemy artillery were firing and landing shells not far away.

In several meetings with senior commanders under Monash, during the visit and as troops started to move forward to the start line, Hughes quickly learnt that they all held Monash in high regard and were happy serving under him. There were five divisional commanders on deck by then, all loyal to Monash. The First Division was commanded by Queenslander and Boer War veteran, Major General Thomas William Glasgow; the Second by Sydney architect Charles Rosenthal; the Third by another Boer War veteran, from Tasmania, who had spent a little time growing up in Frankfurt and also had graduated from Sandhurst, John Gellibrand; the Fourth by a Scottish man with Indian and Boer War experience, Ewen George Sinclair-MacLagan; and the Fifth by a second architect, who worked in Perth, Western Australia, Talbot Hobbs. There was no dissent from these battle hardened warriors, just strong support for their leader.

If Hughes had come to sack Monash and replace him with Brudenell White, now was the time to do so, during their first set of meetings on the Western Front. The political instincts of the shrewd Welsh prime minister took over, after his high-level consultations, and Hughes prepared to wait and see the outcome of the Battle of Hamel.

The very fact that the promotion of Monash to Australian Army Corps commander was implemented but the public announcement was delayed weeks in May and June 1918 points to the extent of the Bean campaign against Monash and the success he and Murdoch had in sewing seeds of doubt that the appointment would stand, once Hughes arrived from Australia via the USA and went to France.

Monash noticed that Hughes was in awe and absolute admiration of the soldiers ahead of the battle, writing later that the prime minister had met with about five per cent of the Australian Army Corps and been sighted by a few more. Word of the Hughes visit rippled through all ranks.

For Monash, the next move was to win his upcoming battle, and in a decisive way, with no stalemate or weeks of trench warfare. To do this he had to resolve another major complication. There had been two thousand US troops embedded from a militia-type US Army division, the Thirty-Third or Prairie Division, mainly from south of Chicago, Illinois. These fit GI soldiers had been spread around the Australian companies and were a real tonic for the war-weary Anzacs. The problem was that nobody had told US supreme commander general JJ Pershing, based back near Paris. Pershing was determined that no US soldiers would go into a set-piece battle under the command of any non-American.

Pershing was keen that as soon as possible the US First Army would enter the frontline as a sizeable unit, crush the Germans in that section of the frontline, and so win an influential place in the postwar carve up for the US and President Woodrow Wilson. Breaking up the steady stream of US arrivals and spreading them thinly around depleted Allied units was not going to happen on his watch.

When told of this, Monash threatened to cancel the Hamel attack, telling Rawlinson that he could pull out about half the Americans but if he had not heard any more about the matter by 1800 or 1900 at the latest on the eve of the Battle of Hamel, the remaining 1000 US soldiers would stay. In other words, he would be proceeding anyhow as it would be too late to turn back the units moving to the start line, along with the tanks and artillery.

For once slow communications favoured Monash as there was no order to pull the US elements out. At the last minute, when finally he had been tracked down, Haig actually stood up and told Rawlinson to allow Monash to proceed with the 1000 Americans. For the first time in World War One, these 1000 US soldiers went into planned offensive battle, and under the command of a non-US officer.

It has been stated by some historians that some of the Yanks amongst the 1000 ordered from the line were so keen that they borrowed some Australian uniforms to ensure they stayed for the big stunt at Hamel. However this story has never been corroborated.

All in all these Americans proved to be sturdy fighters who were soon in close friendship with the Anzacs. Still it rankled with Pershing and most US military historians that Hamel took place with 1000 Yanks mixing freely with 7000 Australians, so much so that it was largely air-brushed out of World War One history.

There was to be no use of nomenclature such as AUSTUSA force from this first-up success at Hamel, no trumpeting of Australian-US early success and victory there. As with the USS *Liberty* saga in 1967, when on the fourth day of the Six-Day War, Israeli forces attacked and killed thirty-four US sailors, and later apologised and paid reparations, this joint operation with the Australians was very inconvenient for the USA, politically, and so it was a case of no publicity applying.

Likewise, in sight of a corner of the White House in Washington there is Pershing Park and a number of plaques tracking through World War One in detail, especially 1918. There are inaccuracies but worse still, there is not a mention of the US participation in the Battle of Hamel. This has even been reported on by Australia's ABC North American Correspondent Ben Knight, I confess at my urging. Recently the Australian Embassy in Washington has made an attempt to bring about a rectification of this with an approach made to the Pershing Park trustees.

In the most comprehensive, holistic approach, nothing is left to chance, and so for several days at Hamel a mixture of gas and smoke was fired by the Allied artillery in pre-dawn shelling to soften up the Germans and, on the day of battle, this was switched to smoke alone. This gave one more advantage to the Allies as the Germans had donned their gas masks expecting gas with the shelling. The Allies up front encountered the Germans still in their vision-restricting gas masks. Also the white tape markers, brave soldiers of stealth, went forward into no-man's-land to lay tapes so that the advancing troops would hold the correct direction and close up on the artillery barrage, as it jumped forward every four minutes. It was a four-minute cycle and not the more usual five-minute creep forward of fire.

The exact start time was 3:10 A.M. on American Independence Day 1918, the Fourth of July. A huge Allied artillery barrage involving over 300 iconic 18 pounder field guns and another 300-plus heavy artillery guns commenced firing in deafening unison and precisely on time. The initial surge was downhill towards the heavily manned German trenches. The ground to be covered in this phase was open farmland, south of the Somme River and just to the north-west of Villers-Brettoneaux. It was now or never for a clean victory to be scored on the Western Front and it was now or never for Monash.

If you stand on the start line and look east, as I did ninety-two years after this battle, in July 2010, one can see almost the whole battlefield in one glance, with a dip then a climb to Hamel village on the left and Vaire Wood on the right. The distance to cover to reach the end line and capture all objectives was not far – about two thousand metres – though it shouldn't be forgotten the soldiers were carrying combat packs, heavy ammunition, and grenade bombs and all. Machinegun ammunition had been loaded onto the backs of tanks and onto the light aircraft that would drop it in the forward zone and so greatly ease the weight burden.

A platoon on the right was killed by 'friendly fire', and there was some stiff opposition from a trench halfway along, which had to be overcome by serious fighting at close range. Bravery generally and individual acts of attack made a big difference. But as daylight emerged the key ground and trenches had been captured. As noted earlier, the battle Monash had figured would take ninety minutes took just three minutes more. Some 1500 prisoners and many weapons were captured and Allied casualties had been minimal.

The new forward line was quickly established and the troops prepared for a counter attack by the Germans. This eventuated later in the afternoon but the ground captured, including the village of Hamel, was not surrendered. Indeed the Germans were never going to get this close to Hamel or Amiens again. At last they were being pushed back.

News of the clear-cut victory travelled quickly up the command ladder and also into Paris, where the Supreme Allied War Council was meeting. Haig sent a message to Prime Minister Hughes, attending the Paris meeting, extending congratulations to Monash and all involved, both Australians and Americans.

Monash built on the tactics of holistic preparation and operation, rapidly evolving from 1917 onwards, and implemented brilliantly by the Canadians at Vimy Ridge under the control of General Currie. In many ways Currie was, like Monash, a general never fully recognised, in his case by the Canadian Government and Canadian people, though as I argue in this book, it is never too late.

Monash began to get a feeling that the German defeat could be hurried along. He was now very well regarded after obtaining a victory for his AIF Corps first up. And he had useful connections in the inner Allied military circles, right up to and including King George V.

A few days after Hamel, that great French leader Clemenceau paid a visit uttering his famous words of praise, in English, direct to the Australian diggers and cabled around the world, placed at the start of this chapter.

The Battle of Hamel is decreed by most military historians as being a tiny battle, involving a pimple of land captured from the Germans. The fact that it was all over in less than two hours and Monash was still under a cloud of sorts over promotion, were possibly reasons for it to be further downplayed.

But it gave the Allied effort a very useful morale boost. It was a big tonic and it helped straighten out and in the process greatly strengthen the line. It also demonstrated that the Americans could fight in unison and harmony with the other Allies. Those who were there on the ground captured the significance of what had been achieved. The tank corps' JF Fuller observed for example, 'In rapidity, brevity and completeness of success, no battle of the war can compare with Hamel; it was the perfect battle'. Monash himself allowed that it was the perfection of team work.

A criticism of Monash that surfaces from time to time is that he spent the entire ninety-three minutes of the battle way behind the lines, pacing up and down at Château Bertangles. It has been argued he should have gone way forward in the planning stages of the battle, to see the land and the features as well as using his legendary study of the maps.

However Bertangles was not that far behind the lines and was still within enemy shelling range. The Monash view, as laid out by many historians, was that he had to be where he could be reached and from where he had good communications, and that this could not be in a moving HQ group surging ahead across no-man's-land. As for whether or not he should have gone forward in the planning stages of the battle, this suggestion will be examined in a later chapter.

The really bitter pill in the aftermath of Hamel was the nature of the first despatches to the newspapers back home. The *Sydney Morning Herald* first report on Hamel on Friday 5 July made no references to the Australian or American successful efforts. It spoke merely of a British forces breakthrough at Hamel, east of Amiens. The headline actually read: 'BRITISH SUCCESS, HAMEL CAPTURED.'

Now had that first ever report highlighted that it was the Australian Army Corps in conjunction with 1000 US soldiers from Illinois, who had captured Hamel, then it is possible to think that the AUSTUSA force may have become, if not as well known as that of the ANZACs, perhaps halfway there.

What deserved a banner headline was left unstated. This primarily reflected the fact that the Australian Army Corps was still so new at the time that it was not fully recognised and so fell into the old labelling as part of the British forces under command of Rawlinson, Haig and ultimately Foch.

This is not good enough, then or now. Of course the headlines should have more accurately portrayed the Battle of Hamel and at least the source of the units involved. On 4 July 2018, if not before, the surviving newspapers from 100 years earlier could take a step towards correcting this fault of the past by leading with the story:

'100 Years ago Australian and American troops smashed through at Hamel with a 93 minute victory'.

Equally the sub-heading should read something like: 'Monash led corps to a precision victory'. It is part of the genesis of this book that at no stage did Monash receive that kind of recognition.

By the end of that first week of July, 1918, the victory at Hamel was increasingly well known in powerful circles in London and Paris. Not only did the French Premier Clemenceau, The Tiger himself, personally deliver his message of gratitude and commendation, other messages poured in, heaping praise on the victorious diggers. The American participants were also praised, though Pershing and even the Thirty-Third Illinois Divisional commander George Ball are not strongly on the record as congratulating their participants in the battle.

Later Corporal Thomas Pope of the Thirty-Third Illinois Division became the first US soldier in World War One to receive the Army Medal of Honour, for brave action at Hamel near the Wolfsberg feature. He was also awarded the Croix de guerre and the British DCM. When he died in 1989 at age ninety-four, he was the last survivor of the war holding the Medal of Honour. He is buried at Arlington, Washington DC. Pope's citations alone should persuade the USA to review and revamp their historical view of the Battle of Hamel and stop airbrushing it from history.

Meanwhile, ever restless Monash was now thinking about and planning the next big push to the east, of course within the orders and remit applied by his immediate superior Rawlinson as head of the British Fourth Army, to which the Australian Army Corps was allocated.

Chapter 7

A SUPREME COMMANDER, AND THE UPPER HAND AT LAST

'I sent ahead a general with a cavalry division to pursue the Germans, he stopped at the first bridge. When I arrived I asked him: What are you still here? Haven't you advanced? The general replied no as they are much too strong for me, I can't sabre them all. I replied but that is not what I am asking you to do, you have guns, you should have used them.'

(Ferdinand Foch recording the exchange just ahead of sacking a French general on the frontline, Battle of the Marne, September 1914. The Foch motto throughout World War One was 'Long, dur, sur', translating roughly as 'long drive on'.)

For nigh on the first four years of the Western Front, there had been no supreme Allied commander. Agreement had been reached on the British being allocated the northern half of the Western Front, with Australia and Canada deemed part of this, and the French occupying the southern half with, from 1918, the Americans taking over the most southern quarter of that French sector.

It was not exactly the smartest set of arrangements, especially as the Allies were up against a unified command for the second half of the war, led by Quartermaster General Erich Ludendorff. Further, the Western Front German forces had been reinforced by troops previously on the Eastern Front. While the kaiser and Hindenburg had their roles, as many historians have concluded it was Ludendorff who was issuing the orders and who was the most powerful director of the German war effort through 1917 and 1918. (Ludendorff resigned late in October 1918, pushed out just before the Armistice.)

Ludendorff came from a Prussian village, Kruszewnia in Posen Province, just 100 kilometres exactly from Krotoschin where Louis, the father of John Monash, grew up. The whole area was originally Polish, then Prussian, then German and after World War One Polish again before becoming German again and after World War Two being returned to Poland.

Ludendorff had excelled at mathematics as a student and this had won him army officer rank. Further promotion came with his early victories in Belgium in August 1914. In spite of retaining the relatively minor title of quartermaster general he was catapulted into the de facto leadership of the German war machine. Curiously he was to eventually reach a view that all the world troubles were created by Free Masons, Jews and Christians, notably the Catholics and Jesuits. If he had added Muslims and Hindus he would have had almost all bases covered.

It was the big lunge by Ludendorff, with the additional forces returned from the Eastern Front in March and April 1918, that had nearly led to a German breakthrough and the fall of Paris. Faced with this lunge, in near panic at a series of key high-level meetings in April 1918, Foch was given overall command and affirmed as supreme general.

Of course the Allied Supreme War Council and related bodies, involving meetings of the Allies political leadership at the highest level, had waxed and waned, but this had not translated to an overall Allied Military Headquarters with just one 'commander in chief'. One month after the appointment of Foch to that role in April 1918, the forces of Italy were added to his jurisdiction. Haig had been generally encouraging of the Foch appointment and certainly Wilson was in favour and helped persuade the Lloyd George led British Cabinet.

There is no evidence that the Australian and Canadian prime ministers were consulted about the creation of the position of supreme commander of all Allied forces and the granting of that position to Ferdinand Foch. As always, at this time in history, it was the British and the French in control with a minimal liaison with the USA legation and General Pershing.

Foch was born in October 1851 at Tarbes in southern France and his education included secondary schooling under the French Jesuits at St Etienne. It can be observed this Jesuitical influence added a lifelong interest and curiosity in all aspects of military history to the modus operandi of Foch. Later his brother was to become a Jesuit, not personally rewarding during the bursts of fierce anti-clericalism often occurring in France then and to this day.

Foch was an early enlistee for the Franco-Prussian or Franco-German War of 1870 and 1871, manufactured by Bismarck to help lock in German unity, and which Germany won easily. After a period of fragile peace, Foch returned to study at the Metz Polytechnique,

Monash (on left) and JP McGlinn prepare to sail with the second AIF convoy, December 1914.

Courtesy of the Australian War Memorial, PB1077.

Awaiting the belated arrival of Kitchener at Gallipoli, 13 November 1915. From left: Brig Gen Johnson of New Zealand Field Artillery Brigade, Brig Gen Russell, Brig Gen Monash, Brig Gen Johnson of New Zealand Light Infantry, Brig Gen Stephenson and Brig Gen JM Antill of 3rd Australian Light Horse.

Courtesy of the Australian War Memorial, G01325.

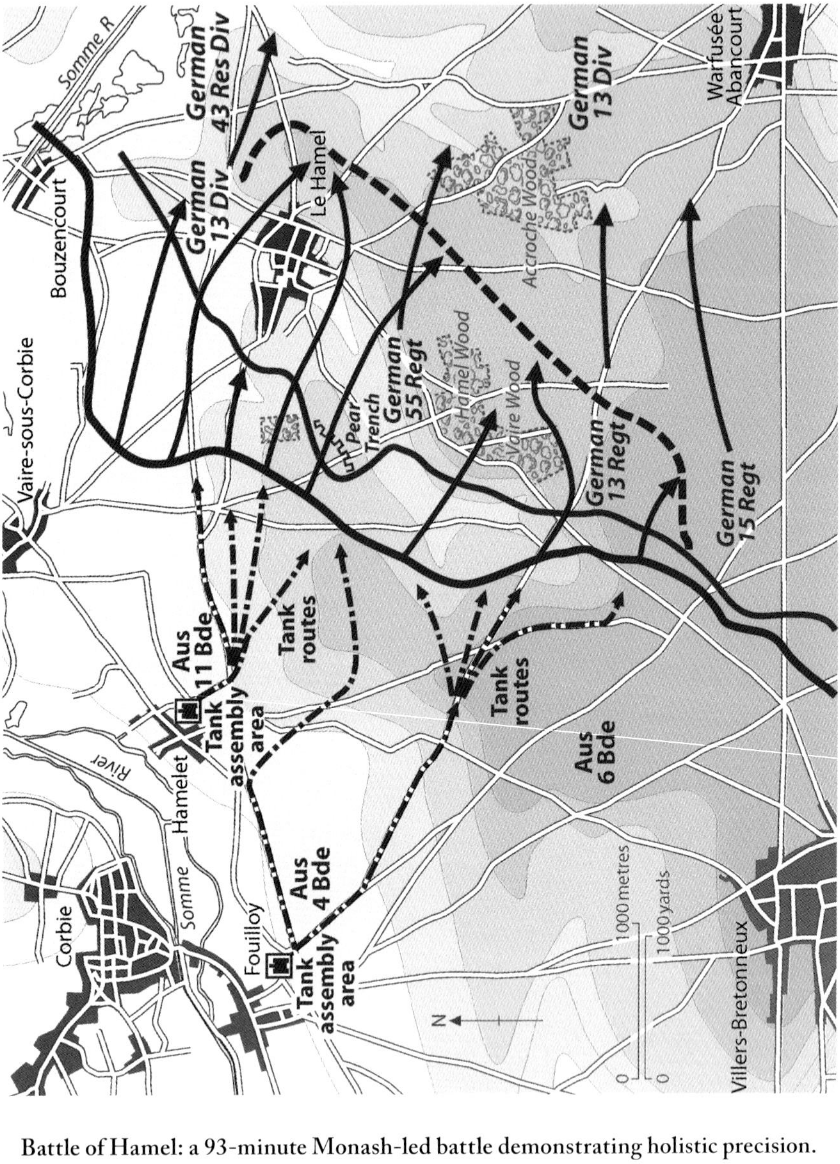

Battle of Hamel: a 93-minute Monash-led battle demonstrating holistic precision.

Courtesy of Keith Mitchell of Canberra.

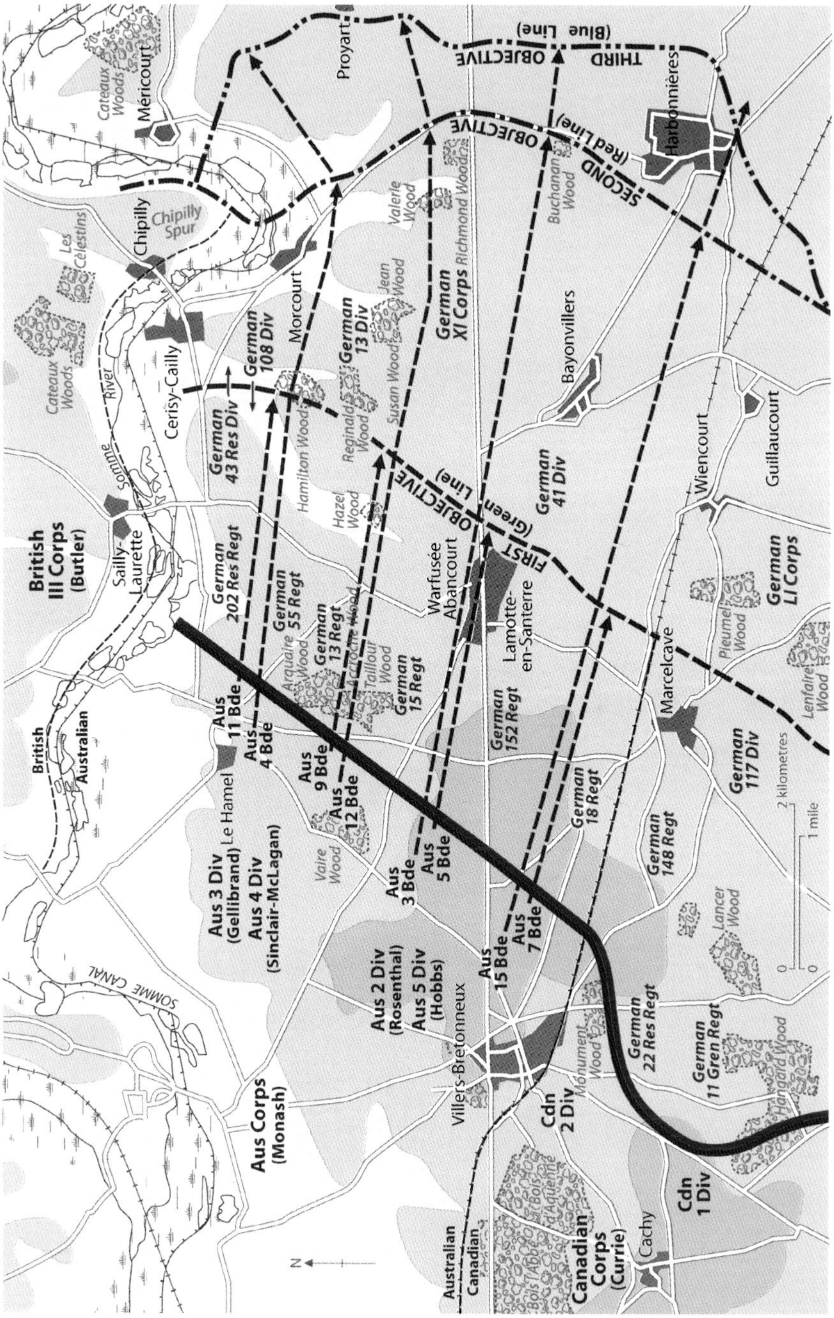

'The biggest day', Battle of Greater Amiens, Western Front, 8 August 1918.

Courtesy of Keith Mitchell of Canberra.

General Sir John Monash stepping out in full uniform, c.1918.
The Imperial War Museum London, after a recent upgrade to its portrayal of World War One, still has no mention of Monash.
Courtesy of the Australian War Memorial, A02697.

Clery on the Western Front, 1918, where John Winston Howard's grandfather met up with his father. Note the use of Decauville narrow-gauge track laid quickly on standard-gauge sleepers.

Courtesy of the Australian War Memorial, E03179.

King George V knighting Monash, 12 August 1918, at HQ Château Bertangles near Amiens.

Courtesy of the Australian War Memorial, E02839.

AIF diggers had to be asked twice to give King George V three cheers in front of the HQ Château Bertangles.

Courtesy of the Australian War Memorial, E03895.

AIF and Allied troops in the Victory Parade, Paris, 1919.
Courtesy of the the Alexander Turnbull Library, Wellington, New Zealand, 1/2-014352-G.

Left: General (Four star) rank insignia.
Right: Field Marshal (Five star) rank insignia.
Courtesy of the Australian Army History Unit.

Monash Memorial Hall is located in the Riverland of South Australia, the soldier settler irrigation settlement and township which was created in 1920 and named in honour of General Sir John Monash.

Courtesy of Dave Degrancy.

Princes Bridge, Swanston Street, Melbourne: the first job Monash had in the role of assistant engineer.

State Library of Victoria, Charles Weetman collection, H92.342/356.

Monash's pistol, proudly held under lock and key at Scotch College, Melbourne.

Courtesy of Nick Anchen of Sierra Publishing.

Foundation stone at Scotch College, Melbourne.

Courtesy of Nick Anchen of Sierra Publishing.

Morell Bridge across the Yarra, built in 1899, aguably the best bridge created by Monash from go to whoa.

Courtesy of Nick Anchen of Sierra Publishing.

Pathway of the magnificent Monash Outer Circle Railway, where it passes under Canterbury Road, between Camberwell and Fairfield.

Courtesy of Nick Anchen of Sierra Publishing.

The uplifting State Library of Victoria dome, which engineer Monash assisted with. A small plaque in a corner of the room below testifies to this.
Courtesy of Nick Anchen of Sierra Publishing.

Family residence of Louis Monasch, later Monash, at 30 Jerilderie Street, Jerilderie. Extensive stables were built behind to assist the Monash horse-trading business.
Courtesy of the Faith Bryce family, Jerilderie.

Victoria Barracks, Melbourne, Defence Headquarters in Australia throughout World War One.

Courtesy of Nick Anchen of Sierra Publishing.

The historic Jerilderie Cenotaph.

Courtesy of Laurie Henery, Jerilderie.

The superb Melbourne Shrine of Remembrance, which Monash greatly helped create, defeating an alternative proposal for a large cenotaph in Spring Street.
Courtesy of Nick Anchen of Sierra Publishing.

A monument to Monash, tucked away in the gardens in front of the Shrine of Remembrance. On Anzac Day 1931, on a horse, he led the parade in Melbourne for the last time.

Courtesy of Nick Anchen of Sierra Publishing.

when one day renewed German shelling totally interrupted classes. It was a direct baptism in German artillery shelling that Foch would never forget.

The military career of Foch steamed ahead, and literally so as twice he caught a train to Paris to see the then French prime minister and argue his case for promotion or a posting, notably to be commandant of the Ecole Militaire, the national military academy of France. It was the kind of direct action or intervention that Foch greatly favoured. It is said that Foch, who was from the streets rather than the elites, had a better understanding of what went astray for France in the Napoleonic wars and Franco-Prussian war than anybody else.

In turn this helped him, like Monash, develop his own distinctive strategic approach, distinct from what was the decreed dominant thinking of the day. It was a particular approach or template that had a strong offensive or attack-mode element, involving all components on a holistic basis. Foch wrote much about best strategies for battle and war. He was steeped in officer training and he had a personal axe to grind against Germany.

In the first few months of World War One Foch lost his son and his son-in-law in the intense fighting surrounding the big drive by the German Army through Belgium and on into France. He did not have time to shed tears as he was successfully conducting the first battle of the Marne. Suddenly he had to fill a big gap in the Western Front line. This he did and he successfully halted the German advance for a vital period. He was commanding the Ninth Army and reputedly said on one occasion, in late 1914: 'Hard pressed on my right, centre is yielding, impossible to manoeuvre. Situation excellent, I shall attack!'

Foch had a certain flair and determination. At one stage British general and later field marshal Sir John French stated that Foch was the greatest general in the world. He had his critics but he tended to get the job done, keeping a cool and calm countenance in the most trying of circumstances.

Now in early August 1918, after the Allies by the narrowest of margins had turned back the Ludendorff lunge, the Allies and their key military leaders were shifting to the offensive again. The Battle of Hamel had been a useful template and boost to the tired Allied forces in early July 1918.

The small, Monash led victory had resonated up the chain to Rawlinson, then Haig and now to Supreme Commander Foch.

The very first week of August 1918, with summer in France at its zenith, was the last week of World War One when most historians concede either side could have still won. The German military machine could still burst through, capture both Paris and the key channel ports, cut off the BEF forces and so in turn dictate terms for any Armistice. But the tide was turning.

This was all about to change and massively so on 8 August with the Monash-led Battle of Amiens. The Australians and Canadians produced their own brilliant lunge forward and created the 'black day' for the German Army.

There were seven factors in play during that pivotal week that was to be the end of the trench war stalemate, give or take a push here and a shove there.

Firstly there was the near exhausted British Expeditionary Force still holding a large northern portion of the Western Front, and the Allenby-led forces still steadily marching towards Damascus and conquering large parts of the Middle East. With thousands killed and wounded, there had been a total turnover in many units and raw, under-trained and too young conscripts were now stepping up into the big holes in unit manpower.

Secondly and thirdly there were the Australian and Canadian units, now under the operational leadership of Monash and Currie respectively. Bruised and also with many raw recruits in their ranks, they had become above-average machines of military capability with the capacity to add greatly to a knockout offensive on the Western Front.

Likewise the long-serving French forces, as the fourth factor, were still in the trenches, despite some mutinies in 1917 that had had to be carefully handled to avoid a total collapse of French resolve after four long hard years of fighting. In the disastrous 1916 Battle of the Somme the French had made some real progress and advances against the Germans, though the concerted lunge by Ludendorff in March 1918 had reversed much of these.

Foch and the dynamic of an overall Allied command had arrived as the fifth factor, though Foch still had to cajole the likes of Haig, Pétain and Pershing, all now technically under him, to follow his directives. Haig could and did appeal to British prime minister Lloyd George on any Foch decision that he strongly disagreed with. Foch was also beholden to Clemenceau.

Still Foch made his approach clear, especially around Amiens during the middle months of 1918, after the giant German attack of 21 March 1918. He told Clemenceau: 'I would fight in front of Amiens, I would fight in Amiens. I would fight behind Amiens. I would fight all the time and, by force of hitting, I would finish by shaking up the Bosch, he's neither cleverer or stronger than we are'.

The situation was eased by the now British general officer commanding (GOC) Sir Henry Wilson and the fact that these two longstanding friends, Foch and Wilson, remained very close throughout most of the war. Whatever actual positions Wilson held, including briefly but not successfully upfront in 1917, he might be accurately dubbed the supreme defence attaché of World War One.

Foch and Wilson saw to it that many liaison hiccoughs and Anglo-French tensions were overcome, and there is evidence they also protected Haig and Rawlinson from being sacked in relation to the opening dreadful day of the 1916 Battle of the Somme.

One extra available resource was the arrival of new generation tanks on the Allied side, with Monash and others showing how best they might be webbed into planned offensive battles, to drive forward through heavy German wire protected trenches. The new tanks were the sixth factor and were gaining in status with infantry commanders in the field, especially after the Battle of Hamel.

The seventh factor was the arrival of the Americans upfront at last, more than fifteen months after a reluctant President Woodrow Wilson had addressed the US Congress urging a path of a formal Declaration of War against Germany in order to keep the world safe for democracy. On the Tuesday before Easter 1917 the president had laid out his case for war and the Congress had given him a standing ovation.

Both Houses of Congress quickly passed resolutions and on Easter Saturday President Woodrow Wilson formally signed the Declaration of War.

The capable Pershing had been selected to lead the US forces to France and into actual battle on the southern portion of the

Western Front. His career in battle against the Mexicans and in the Philippines and as a defence attaché covering the Balkans but based in Paris made him a good fit for the big job. His instructions were clear enough from the president. These were to create a US Army on the ground in France and smash through the German opposition, most likely, it was thought, in early 1919. This was to be as a united US standalone effort and so create the conditions for President Wilson to have maximum sway in dictating peace terms and drawing the boundaries of the postwar world.

It was in late July and August 1918 that the major military leaders on the Allied side began to reckon on a victory in late 1918 and to consider it a waste of time planning a huge spring offensive in 1919. Foch, Haig, Currie and Monash were as one on this as August unfolded. Foch by now also had the status and practical standing of having been made a marshal of France.

So on the penultimate day of August 1918 Foch descended on Pershing at the US general's headquarters and laid out the grand strategy for a September offensive. Initially the plan had the US playing a small supporting role, including with some of their units being rolled under the command of lieutenant generals of the Allied forces, such as Monash.

For three long summer days they haggled on and off, head to head, because Foch was really asking Pershing to break his overarching orders and play second-fiddle to a British-French grand finale with the Australians, Canadians and others fulfilling medium-sized roles broadly commensurate with the size of their fighting units.

Pershing was persuaded and broke orders, accepting one relatively easy task, to close off the Saint-Mihiel salient or narrow spear created by Germany years ago into France, and also then to attack outright towards the Hindenburg Line in the area of what became known as Meuse-Argonne.

If communications between the Situation Room of the White House and the Pershing HQ had been as good then as now, then the military flexibility on the ground exercised by Pershing might have been vetoed. It was a situation not unlike the breach of strategy and orders that President Harry Truman encountered, in part due to better communications and so less wriggle room, with General Douglas MacArthur, over the see-sawing Korean War.

The truth is that Pershing had signed on for an 'all-in' big push masterminded and approved by the Supreme or Allied War Council to end the war in 1918. It involved much closer integration of effort amongst all Allied forces. As an example, a US regiment was to be placed under the command of Monash only two months after 1000 US troops were removed from his command.

And this increased integration worked. Foch had the honour, and the luck, to be the overall commander when victory was obtained just a few weeks later.

The huge push was on but there was still much for Monash and the Australians to overcome. Like two old boxers bloodied and exhausted, each side had a capacity for one last knockout blow but the tide was about to turn, once and for all, as we will now see.

Chapter 8

FROM AMIENS TO ARMISTICE

'Some critics have declared that in the last grand advance Monash overworked and overdrove the Australians. But I have never heard the fighting men say so. They were pushed on with heavy wastage to the verge of prostration; but it was victory all the way. The result was the justification'.

(HS Gullet, Journalist, AIF member and later Australian federal minister, reflecting in 1923.)

It was the black day of the German Army, 8 August 1918. Brooding in its aftermath and starting to feel and see the first conclusive signs of defeat, and that a snap breakthrough and victory that had been possible for most of the year, was now out of the question, German general Erich Ludendorff put it definitively: 'August 8th was the black day of the war, it put the decline of our fighting power beyond doubt. The war would have to be ended'.

It was the darkest day for the Germans, the biggest day for the Allies and the commencement day of what is somewhat confusingly named the 'Battle of Amiens'. Amiens had been in Allied hands throughout 1918 and was now some distance behind the frontlines on the Allied side, still recovering from massive heavy shelling by long distance German guns.

Perhaps a more accurate name would have been the 'Battle of Greater Amiens' or even 'Battle of Bayonvillers', as Bayonvillers was the name of a village captured on the first day and in the centre of the recaptured zone. Alternatively, running through the area was the Somme River, but there was no way that name was going to be used a second time.

I reiterate on balance it might have been better to call it the 'Battle of Greater Amiens'. It is never too late for the Imperial War Museum (IWM) of London to meet with various other relevant museums in Auckland, Canberra, Paris, Ottawa and beyond and agree to adopt secondary battle names with regard to 1918, such as the 'Battle of Anzac Amiens' for that of 25 March to 25 April, or the 'Battle of Greater Amiens' for that of 8 August.

Basking in the afterglow of the Hamel victory, Monash now had huge influence and held sway at many gatherings of senior military personnel. Lieutenant general he may have been, the correct rank for commanding a corps, but he was acting as a de facto full general, at the behest of his seniors who were seeking his ideas and opinions.

Monash played a part in the planning to initiate a big offensive from 8 August.

Doing the heavy lifting, providing the hammerhead to smash through the German lines, were the Australians and, to a greater extent, the Canadians, who had a tougher sector to account for.

This allocation of tasks was due to a large part to the capabilities of the two key military leaders of Australia and Canada, Monash and Currie. Like Monash, Currie was also militia, an outsider as a colonial, and with a fierce determination to think holistically and apply some lateral thinking based on modern developments. Indeed there were many similarities between Currie and Monash.

Both had a slight adjustment to their surnames, from Curry to Currie in the Canadian's case. Both were in a business that almost went broke before World War One. Both were involved in different ways with libel litigation. Both were knighted by King George V in France just to the east of Amiens, Currie on 17 June 1917, and Monash on 12 August 1918. Above all, both challenged orders from on high, notably from British generals still locked into a defensive mentality belonging more to the Boer War. The practical Arthur Currie had made it from the lowest rank to the highest rank and, like Monash, entirely on merit.

So Monash and Currie started detailed planning for the huge Battle of Amiens, the last battle to be conducted from the now well-established headquarters at Château Bertangles (prior to Monash having to move his headquarters closer to the action, further east towards the Hindenburg Line).

Monash knew that the advent of widespread use of gas by the German armies, especially gas that acted as 'poison on delay', was a wildcard as the clocks ticked down to 4:20 A.M. on 8 August. Any inkling to the Germans of a forthcoming major battle and gas canisters would rain down. The Allies had also improved their use of gas and, happily, had also gradually developed more helpful gas masks.

All hell broke loose at 4:20 as hundreds of artillery guns blazed away at enemy positions and as the tanks crept forward; improved tanks with real grunt and fire power. Fog and smoke provided advantage and disadvantage as the Australians and Canadians swept eastward, overpowering the enemy. Soon enough lines of German prisoners formed and were being marched back to enclosures behind the Allied start line.

By noon it was clear the ascendency had been gained and much of the Red Line objective obtained. The Australian flag was flying in Harbonnières. By sunset even more ground and villages had been captured and by combined effort – British, Australian, Canadian and French – over 16,000 prisoners were also captured, along with a huge haul of weapons and munitions.

By now for many German soldiers becoming a POW was a fast way out of the frontline and a chance they might just survive World War One. A certain weariness had taken hold and many were not your professional battle-hardened soldier from the Eastern Front but raw recruits struggling with every aspect of being in the theatre of war and regularly under fire.

In the circumstances Allied casualties had been minimal and by now Monash, as part of the all-encompassing Monash strategic approach, was insisting on maintaining a commitment to the troops to provide prompt evacuation of the wounded to Field Hospitals, with priority for the ambulance vehicles running shuttles from the pick-up areas back to the rear zones.

It was absolutely clear by sunset on 9 August that the Battle of Amiens had been a massive victory and the word of the victory was to be telegraphed around the world. The German divisions had been pushed back and back, beyond their artillery lines and towards the Hindenburg Line itself. A huge tract of the Western Front had been gained by the Allies.

There was some messiness on the second and third days as different rates of progress by the various corps and divisions created confusion and gaps that Monash was slow to get on top of but, in fairness, was able to, in difficult conditions. Snap orders from Rawlinson given on 9 August did not help.

The diaries of young gunner Edgar Webb (AIF 27200) from Lockhart, New South Wales, point to the movement on the ground over those three extraordinary days from 8–10 August:

> 8 August worked all night carting ammunition. Fired 300 rounds a gun for the hop over.
>
> 9 August moved the whole battery forward 5 kilo to new position, action in the open, great movement of troops.
>
> 10 August pulled the battery up about 2 kilos and intended to move in the morning, guns near a lot of Fritz captured naval guns. Bombed us all night 11 horses killed, 1 man killed, 8 men wounded.

Where for months there had been no movement in the frontline and the first and second row of trenches, this '5 kilos plus 2 kilos', read about 7 kilometres forward, over heavily defended ground captured from the Germans, did constitute dramatic movement. The bonus was thousands of German prisoners and guns were captured and permanently taken out of the war.

As Monash summarised: 'We and the Canadians on our right effected a penetration greater than had ever been attempted in the war and with complete success'.

In turn the big victory brought forward a steady stream of VIP visitors to headquarters at Château Bertangles, including one ex-first lord of the admiralty and now minister for munitions, Winston Churchill.

Early on the morning of 11 August 1918 Churchill, who was born again as the minister for munitions after a long stint out of Government serving on the Western Front himself, hastened to salute the efforts of Monash in the typical vibrant Churchill way and on French soil, still in earshot of the guns blazing away to the east. Typically Churchill had flown himself over the English Channel the day before.

Nearly twenty years earlier at the relief of Ladysmith and related Battle of Spion Kop, Churchill had met with and observed Australian soldiers in fierce battle. In return they had closely watched the colourful Churchill, causing Arnold Brissender of Melbourne to observe: 'Winston Churchill … was with us on the hill. He is as game as a bantum and full of fun'.

Churchill was on that hill, or Spion Kop ridge, with two other people who went on to become giants, Louis Botha of South Africa and the Mahatma, Ghandi of India, though they were not all on the same side. They were fortunate, or some believe an omnipotent force ensured, that three more bullets did not kill them off there in their twenties. One bullet went close to doing so to Churchill, according to his biographer Roy Jenkins, creasing his hairline and parting the feathers on the Churchill headgear, but missing the huge skull.

Churchill befriended Louis Botha and Monash and these three sat together at a very momentous dinner at Buckingham Palace examined in the next chapter. Alas Churchill remained throughout his long life dismissive of Ghandi, once describing Ghandi years later in 1931 as a seditious Middle Temple lawyer now posing as a fakir.

Early on the morning of 11 August the minister for munitions Winston Churchill dashes to the Monash HQ at Château Bertangles to confer with and congratulate John Monash on the Battle of Amiens.

Churchill was at this time in full praise of Monash and the work of the Australian Army Corps and also keen to discuss tactics and munitions technology. There was not much time for any fun, even for having a good cigar with Monash or sharing a good bottle of red on that busy morning, as later in the day Monash would convene a huge conference involving his divisional commanders. The weather was fine so Monash selected an open air venue under a bunch of trees on the western or Amiens side of Villers-Brettoneux.

Part by good planning and part by sheer chance, what then unfolded on this afternoon of 11 August was the largest gathering of the Allied leaders anywhere and at any time, held on the Western Front, with Monash playing host. In addition to chief of staff Blamey and the five Australian divisional commanders, Haig and Rawlinson also descended, plus Currie, along with various other top brass including Sir Henry Wilson.

It was interesting that Rawlinson as always disguised his anti-Semitism. Later on in 1920 he wrote to his deputy Sir Archibald

Montgomery describing Edwin Montague as a 'clever slippery creepy crawly Jew – not unlike Monash'.

Four other significant figures present were Cavalry Corps Commander Lieutenant General Kavanagh, Acting Third Corps Commander Lieutenant General AJ Godley, Tank Corps Commander Major General Hugh Elles and RAF Fifth Brigade Commander Major General LEO Charlton. On top of this high powered group, along came Clemenceau and Foch plus the then French finance minister Louis-Lucien Klotz.

Rawlinson had to defer his detailed planning conference as the dynamic of all the key leaders being present in one spot kicked in. This made it something like a grand victory conference but, in Australian Rules football terms, being held after the preliminary final and not after the grand final. It was certainly a grand conference in the field with the impressive Premier Clemenceau and the various key Allied marshals and generals. Had a group photo been taken then the assembled, listed here by seniority but with the AIF portion in one group, would have been an extraordinary first eighteen: Blamey, Glasgow, Rosenthal, Gellibrand, Sinclair-MacLagan, Hobbs, Monash, Clemenceau, Klotz, Foch, Haig, Rawlinson, Wilson, Currie, Godley, Kavanagh, Elles and Charlton. Plus there was Rawlinson's deputy Archibald Montgomery (not to be confused with Montgomery of Alamein).

One long distance artillery shell from the damaged but still lethal German heavy artillery lurking to the east on top of Mont St Quentin could have wiped out one national leader and eighteen of the Allied top brass.

The best offensive strategy was now firmly under consideration at what had become an impromptu Allied leaders conference under trees near Villers-Brettoneaux, even if the details had to be deferred for the greetings and brief celebrations and speeches of salutation. Currie and Monash received the lion's share of commendation from those present, including Haig, who praised the enormity of what the Australian and Canadian forces had achieved.

Years later Monash said that day and the next were incredible days in his life, in so many ways. On the next day, King George V turned up at Château Bertangles and reviewed both a representative parade of the Australian Army Corps and a huge display of captured German guns and various military equipment captured just four days before. In front of the huge entrance portal of the Château, after a short delay while a sword was located, the king knighted Monash in the field.

The diggers of the AIF forming the guard of honour were apparently not too impressed on the occasion, even if it was a sunny day. They had to be asked twice to give a respectable round of three cheers, the first being barely audible. It was another reminder that the diggers were not greatly impressed by pomp and circumstance.

As push-and-shove minor battles and raids unfolded, the grandfather and father of John Winston Howard, Australia's second-longest serving prime minister, both foot soldiers under command of Monash, met near the Somme River. 'Met Dad at Clery', Lyall Falconer Howard, then 21, recorded in his diary. Walter Herbert Howard was then aged forty-five. It was a busy time and a brief encounter between two who survived the war but suffered indifferent health thereafter.

Already Monash was gathering thoughts and plans for another big attack that was to unfold on 1 and 2 September, the Battle of Mont St Quentin and the related Battle of Péronne, a nearby town to the south of Mont St Quentin.

Some controversy still exists about these days of the big push forward. Was it too far too fast? Was it properly reconnoitred beforehand? Were the freewheeling movements that became a critical part of the Monash design the decisive factor or merely part of events rapidly unfolding from developments on the given day, all helping to achieve victory?

This was the Monash justification for pushing hard: victory. Victory that was never going to be easily obtained.

Once again fast thinking by Monash and the true grit of the Australian diggers ensured victory and the Australian flag being placed on top of Mont St Quentin on the first day and Péronne being captured on the second day. Captain WJ Denny MC, later a South Australian attorney-general, served throughout World War One while being a South Australian State MP. Re-elected in absentia, he wrote about Mont St Quentin:

> The capture of Mont St. Quentin stands out in bold relief in a war that had hitherto largely consisted of monotonous trench warfare. Its story reads more like a military romance of the olden times; though in certain respects it was not unlike the famous Gallipoli landing. Sir Douglas Haig using strictly official language in his recent dispatch says it 'ranks as a most gallant achievement'. Other writers unfettered by the strict necessities of Army formality use language of a much more eulogistic character. The Germans, as we learnt after the attack, knew the formidable character of the forces operating in front of them. An order signed by the Commanding Officer of a German Battalion and subsequently captured contained the following warning to the enemy:-
>
> 'Forces confronting us consist of Australians who are very warlike, clever and daring. They understand the art of crawling through high crops in order to capture our advanced posts. The

> enemy is also adept in conceiving and putting into execution important patrolling operations. The enemy infantry has daily proved themselves to be audacious.'

Even with this tribute it was, however, never conceived possible by the Germans that this great natural fortress, supplemented by the aid of every clever device of skilful leaders, would in a few hours not only fall, but that the whole of its garrison would be killed or captured. On that eventful day of 31 August Australian troops, in addition to the large number killed, took 1500 prisoners of the Prussian Guards and, as Sir Douglas Haig states, left the way open for the subsequent capture by the Australians of Péronne.

At Mont St Quentin yet another VC was won by a Monash soldier, Sergeant Albert Lowerson of Myrtleford and Adelong, where he had been a gold digger. Lowerson took a small team forward and cleaned out a major enemy machinegun hub with a dozen machineguns spitting deadly fire, in the process capturing twelve guns and fifty prisoners. He continued the fight even though wounded and after surviving World War One backed up to serve throughout World War Two, taking his discharge in August 1945 but dying a few months later. Not many VCs made it through both World War One and World War Two on active service.

Again the German Army was in retreat. Since the 8 August black day, things were getting still blacker. Though there was still no large-scale collapse or mutiny throughout the German forces, Ludendorff at one stage ordered a fall-back to the Hindenburg Line to regroup.

Since his last visit to Monash back in July, Prime Minister Billy Hughes had been basking in the reflected glory of the victories by the Australian units, and said publicly of the Battle of Hamel that 'Monash had conceived the whole thing and carried it out in a masterful fashion.' After the hectic and victorious first week of September, Hughes turned up with journalists in tow, including that pair of trouble-makers for Monash, Bean and Murdoch.

Hughes demanded that the AIF be rested by early October and that the original Anzacs be granted two months leave back in Australia. Otherwise, he said, he would take direct action on the matter. In other words he would sack Monash and find a senior officer who would comply.

There is no doubt Monash thought that both his men and for that matter his HQ staff and he himself should have some leave, a decent spell well away from the frontline. However there was one more big operation to pursue – to smash through the Hindenburg – before, he thought, the rotations and leave should apply.

Had this leave gone ahead in the timeframe set out by Hughes, one suspects that not all those who took the leave would have turned up to re-embark for Europe if required, after a taste of 'home sweet home'.

Monash massaged the issue of the demands from Hughes and coped with disturbing issues involving disobedience and minor mutiny in the ranks, especially over breaking up and disbanding some units. He did this with his flexible and diplomatic best endeavours. He secured a resolution to allow one more big attack that would effectively end any German military action on French soil and help bring the war to an end as soon as was possible.

Indeed Monash was continuing in a masterful fashion throughout the 100 day effort through to Armistice and victory.

This last lunge was not to be by a dissipated ragtime band, cobbled together from some raw recruits and unit mergers, but rather by the Australian Army units at their zenith. Monash could rightly have faith in their capacities. During this period he was at times commanding eight divisions and over 200,000 troops, including American units, a number normally commanded by a four star full general.

In late September the battle to smash through the Hindenburg Line was launched and there were intense pockets of resistance and heavy fighting, often bringing about very brave individual action by Australian NCO ranks, with individuals charging forward and heroically taking out German machinegun nests and pockets of fortified trenches.

The last Australian VC of the war was deservedly won by Lieutenant George Ingram of the Sixth Brigade when he singlehandedly snuck into Montbrehain and located a sniper in a ventilator shaft close to ground level. He fired his revolver at close range and took out the sniper and then raced around the back of the house to capture the team in support of this sniper's nest, all thirty of them.

It was a case of seven final days that broke the backbone of the German forces on the Western Front, from 29 September to 5 October 1918. The Bellicourt tunnel was a key capture and the German units did not give it up lightly. By the final day for the brave Australian diggers, before their rotation, towns like Joncourt, Ramicourt and Wancourt, well east of the Hindenburg Line, had fallen and were free at last.

Soon the Allies were so far through the Hindenburg main line of defence as to allow thoughts of pushing on into Germany itself.

Foch said to Haig, in his ever frenetic negotiations to plug holes here and advance there, that he needed forty divisions, to which Haig said he had none available. Foch then reportedly replied: 'That is alright, just send me two divisions of the Australians instead'.

But for the exhausted AIF, there now had to be time out and so the rotations began, including for Monash himself, who very quickly repaired to London.

Once word was out that Monash was in town invitations flowed and Monash spoke at the Dominion Club, preceded on the occasion by British foreign secretary Arthur Balfour. Balfour had signed the famous letter known as the 1917 Balfour Declaration, laying out the British Cabinet declaration in favour of creating a Jewish home state in the Palestinian mandate. It was, in the account of those present, another triumph for Monash. He upstaged a dreary Balfour with a bright account of prospects, stating that the long war was almost over.

Monash correctly believed that victory was just around the corner and he carried these thoughts back to France, after his short break. The Armistice, to take effect at 11:00 A.M. on 11 November, was announced soon afterwards. As mentioned earlier, on the day of the announcement Monash was for most of the time in a car, starting to shift his headquarters forward across eastern France to Le Cateau. And no doubt he shared in the general relief expressed by people in extraordinary and what would become iconic scenes, in cities and towns from London and Paris to Sydney and Narrandera in Australia.

Chapter 9

A BITTER-SWEET END

The Last Day of the Great War

'In sight of Big Ben, London:

And suddenly the first stroke of the chime … then from all sides men and women came scurrying into the street. The bells of London began to clash … people in hundreds, nay thousands running hither and thither in a frantic manner, shouting and screaming with joy. All bounds were broken. The tumult grew. It grew like a gale but from all sides simultaneously. Flags appeared as if by magic. Almost before the last stroke of the clock had died away, the strict, war straitened, regulated streets of London had become a triumphant pandemonium.

Now the war was over. Victory had come after all the hazards and heartbreaks in an absolute and unlimited form. Safety, freedom, peace – all after fifty-two months of gaunt distortion.'

(Winston Churchill, 11:00 A.M. on the eleventh day of the eleventh month 1918, Whitehall, London.)

In the first year of the war, back in 1914, Churchill had been somewhat cavalier, telling Lady Margot Asquith (wife of the then UK prime minister) that 'I would not be out of this glorious, delicious war for anything this world could give me'. Quickly Churchill asked Lady Asquith not to repeat the word 'delicious', as well he might, but by the end of the war it was a much wiser and wearier Churchill, back at Whitehall after a stint in the trenches.

Likewise so many learnt so much during the years of war, with many extraordinary tales to tell. Arguably Kiwi-raised Bernard Freyberg was first ashore at Gallipoli and on the last day he was in action again, saving a bridge at Lessines at 10:59 A.M. on 11 November 1918, so earning his third DSO, already having won a VC on the Western Front. Churchill described his friend Freyberg as a 'Salamander', due to his ability to withstand enemy fire and survive – right through to 11:00 on the eleventh day of the eleventh month and in action again to the last moment.

Amazingly, the ceasefire held tightly across the Western Front, both sides having clearly had enough. Both Austria and Turkey had sought armistice and effective surrender in the course of the previous fortnight and this had been agreed to, so the Great War fighting was really over, save for some conflict involving small Allied units (including one led by Australian general Savige) around Baku, relating to the melee and mess of Greater Russia.

On the top of Anzac Hill at Alice Springs the World War One memorial has in large letters on the side facing the township: '1914 to 1919'. This is the case with many memorials around the world and reflects the fact that many soldiers did not get home until well into 1919.

Sydney had started celebrating prematurely, three days before the official announcement, due to a mixup and incorrect advice being passed on that the Armistice had already been signed. In the small Riverina town of Narrandera, that Monash had visited twice on holidays to see his uncle Max Monash, the general storekeeper, the young journalist Bill Gammage was anticipating the big news. He worked for the Narrandera *Argus* and had a close liaison with the local telegraph office across the street. He arranged to be tipped off and given the first word when the telegrams began pouring through with the news of the actual Armistice from London.

It was well after sunset on the spring evening of 11 November when the word arrived and Gammage sprang into action. He soon had the Church bells of Narrandera peeling and the people out on the streets on that very night, simultaneously with the crowd surges on the streets of London that Winston Churchill so evocatively described. The mayor of the day was less impressed, saying it was a bit late in the day, but the party of all parties had commenced and was to run for two days and two nights. The district, like all country districts and cities of Australia, had sent so many of their best sons to the Great War, never to return.

Post office after post office right across Australia became the clearing house for bad news from the Great War. The deluge of official telegrams and letters advising casualties continued from August 1914 to and beyond November 1918.

Springdale near Temora and Tumbarumba, both in the Riverina, had lost a huge chunk out of the rising generation, in the case of Tumbarumba forty-eight killed in action or dying of wounds and other causes during the war, out of some 255 AIF enlistees from that district.

These huge death ratios were indicative of those in towns and hamlets large and small right around the Empire. In Scotland the tiny location of Raasay near Skye lost eighteen out of twenty-six in service in the Great War.

There are debates about the various casualty counts. Prime Minister of Australia Tony Abbott said on Anzac Day 2014 that Australia, with a then population of just under five million people, sent 332,000 overseas in World War One from a total of 417,000 enlistees, and that some 61,000 were killed and 152,000 wounded. Historian David Noonan has argued the 61,000 figure of killed was understated and it should be at least 62,300. He called in 2014 for a new official review of all World War One statistics.

For the Australian soldiers in France and Great Britain the news quickly spread by word of mouth. Chaplain Sidney Beveridge rushed through the wards of the Third Australian General Hospital conveying the welcome news that the Great War was over. The diggers demanded an immediate Thanksgiving service and this took place not long after the eleventh hour on the eleventh day of November 1918.

Gladstone Robert McGowan had survived the Western Front despite having the job of laying the marker tapes way out in front of the lines in the dark ahead of the next stunt, or battle, to guide the AIF troops as they surged forward under fire, often enveloped by fog and smoke. He wrote in his diary that he was at the local cinema not far from the action when the news came through.

'J'ai beaucoup de plaisir de announce que l'armistice sur Austrich a ete signe aujourdui' was the announcement and the audience immediately sang the Marseillaise. Within hours all the houses had flags flying and crackers were going off. McGowan was on orderly duty and wrote he had trouble maintaining the peace on the first night of peace as much cognac and liqueur had surfaced from various French cellars.

For many other AIF members, it was the local newspapers that delivered the news of the 11:00 A.M. armistice, on the very morning of Armistice Day. As their trains loaded to move further east around Le Cateau, the newspaper headlines created a huge stir and there was much rowdiness and cheering. When operational circumstances permitted, the London newspapers became available in large quantities along the Western Front around 11:00 A.M. each day, after being rushed to Dover, ferried across the English Channel and distributed. Monash recalled seeing a young French girl selling London newspapers to the troops as shells, which in their regularity had taken on a degree of normalcy, landed around them. The availability of these London papers was one factor that drove Monash to press for portrayal of Australian breakthroughs being correctly credited and not just absorbed under a banner headline heralding a British victory.

In the Middle East the capture of Damascus had not been properly accredited to the Australian Light Horse under General Chauvel. These soldiers would have to face putting down their brave horses, who had carried them loyally from Cairo through Romani, on the charge at Beersheba, onto Jerusalem and Damascus and then onto Aleppo.

For soldiers on a rest break way behind the lines, the day of the Armistice announcement actually passed quietly.

After a resolution of Hughes' demands that the Australian divisions be properly rested, involving a compromise of just one fortnight break, the Australian units were coming back onto line and as noted on the 'last day' Monash was being driven through pleasant captured countryside to a new Château headquarters at Le Cateau.

This was to be the last headquarters of Monash in the field. However there was a swirl of adjustments and various appointments for him to attend to, including monitoring the remnant German

Army that had two weeks, until 25 November, to withdraw from all of Belgium and France.

Two days later he was recalled to London by Hughes, with the request that Monash take on the role of director-general of Repatriation and Demobilisation, based in London. Monash readily accepted and took the opportunity to celebrate in London and soak up the hard-won victory.

Prime Minister Hughes was in London for the 'last day' and starting to plan ahead in a rapid and decisive way for the huge repatriation and demobilisation tasks, before taking up the cudgels to win for himself and Australia a place of influence at the Versailles Peace Conference. The large and imposing Australia House, opened on the Strand during the war, was the focus of much activity.

Long-serving Canadian prime minister Sir Robert Borden, New Zealand prime minister William Massey and South African prime minister Louis Botha were like Hughes beavering away to ensure direct representation for each Allied country at Versailles. Borden spearheaded these efforts and eventually US president Woodrow Wilson backed off and agreed to direct representation of the smaller countries, who had given more in blood than the USA per capita and given it for the full duration of the war. Back in 1914, Prime Minister Massey of New Zealand had sent a telegram that read: 'All we are and all we have are at the disposal of the British Government'. Now in the aftermath some recompense was expected.

For Botha the last day was one perhaps of some bemusement, as less than two decades before, as a Boer commander, he had captured a young Winston Churchill and placed him in prison in Pretoria, from which Winston had later famously escaped. Now he had just spent four long years and more arm in arm with Churchill to beat the German Army.

It had started back in Sarajevo over four years previously with the firing of a pistol and the assassination of Archduke Ferdinand and his wife on a pleasant Sunday near a park and the Latin Bridge. It had ended after rivers of blood all over the European continent and beyond. There were 61,000 men lost from Australia alone, with a then population of just over four and a half million people.

Per capita Australia, New Zealand and the UK had been hit hard. A whole generation had been decimated, with in each case more than ten times the per capita rate of military deaths than that endured by the USA, though the USA lost close to double the number of troops lost by Australia.

In total the loss of life on all sides was over ten million, in military terms, but around thirty-seven million people overall, the majority of whom were civilians.

By mid-November 1918 not only was the fighting over but the diplomats were on the move, negotiating manoeuvres had commenced around the various foreign offices in the capital cities of the Allies, and preparations were being finalised for the disastrous Versailles Peace Conference, to be held throughout the first half of 1919. This was the treaty that is correctly judged to have set the stage for not only World War Two but wars in the Middle East and elsewhere.

Still, as we shall see, the same said Treaty gave Australia some advantages that enhanced its strategic situation leading into World War Two in decisive and important ways. Australia and New Zealand, more than other Allied countries, were nations that emerged emboldened for all that lay ahead.

Monash rolls east on Armistice Day 1918 to new HQs at Le Cateau

Had this great war been the war to end all wars then just maybe the huge loss of life, destruction and suffering might have been worthwhile, but sadly within twenty-one years it was on again. The treaty that came from this first world war was to sew the seeds of a second.

The final negotiations for the Armistice had been conducted in a forest at Compiegne, in carriage No 2419 of the private train of Ferdinand Foch, and this is where the Armistice was actually signed around 5:00 A.M. on 11 November, with Foch present and overseeing. The carriage was to be captured by the Germans in World War Two and used by them for the formalisation of the French surrender, before being taken to Berlin. Towards the end of the Second World War it was destroyed by the SS for fear it would be used for a surrender ceremony again.

By this time the sons of the survivors of the World War One Allies were well and truly back in harness against the German Third Reich and ex-Western Front corporal Adolf Hitler.

SECTION THREE
MONASH POSTWAR

Chapter 10

THE BUCKINGHAM PALACE BANQUET OF BANQUETS

'This is an historic occasion and your visit marks an historic epoch. Nearly 150 years have passed since your Republic began its independent life; and now for the first time a President of the United States of America is our guest in England'.

(King George V, Buckingham Palace 27 December 1918.)

'There is a great tide running in the hearts of men ... and it will be our high privilege, I believe, sir, not only to apply the moral judgments of the world to the particular settlements which we shall attempt, but also ... to make the right and the justice to which great nations like our own have devoted themselves the predominant and controlling force of the world.'

(President Woodrow Wilson in reply to the toast of King George V at Buckingham Palace near midnight, 27 December 1918.)

How the mighty gathered, the king and queen of the Empire, the president of the USA, five prime ministers – from Australia, Canada, Great Britain, Newfoundland and South Africa – admirals and generals at a banquet of all banquets, never matched before nor since.

There were 115 guests in all, hosted by King George V and Queen Mary.

One month on from the end of the war, during that halcyon period of sheer relief that the war was over, the plans were drawn up for this banquet, to be held on 27 December in the grand ballroom at Buckingham Palace. This was to honour the state visit by US president Woodrow Wilson to London and Manchester in salute of victory and the fallen. It was also to start the planning of the Versailles Peace Conference.

Woodrow Wilson and his wife were received by rapturous crowds at Victoria Station, having arrived from France by Channel ferry and the connecting boat train. They travelled slowly along the mall to the palace with the crowds continuing a warm welcome and waving flags. They arrived at their destination in time to rest and get ready for the big banquet the night after Boxing Day.

'The King and Queen gave a banquet at Buckingham Palace this evening in honour of the President of the United States of America and the following had the honour of being invited.' The guest list of 115, recorded in the Court Circular section of the *London Times*, reads like an ultimate 'A list'. This included the future King George VI as well as the Duke of Connaught, who was the third son and seventh child of Prince Albert and Queen Victoria: Arthur William Patrick Albert. The Duke had been appointed a field marshal of the British Army as well as a field marshal in the Prussian Army by his cousin Emperor Wilhelm II. No doubt no insignia relating to the latter position was worn by the Duke that night.

The archbishop of Canterbury and the archbishop of York headed the religious leaders invited. There were no rabbis or Roman Catholic bishops invited. On the diplomatic front, the French, Italian, Spanish,

Japanese and US ambassadors were in attendance plus a party of seven from the US Embassy, not unreasonably, including Admiral William Sims heading the defence attaché group.

The particular grouping of five prime ministers can never be repeated as it included WF Lloyd, the prime minister of Newfoundland, which merged or more accurately confederated with Canada in 1949.

Lloyd George as prime minister of Great Britain, a country possibly at its very zenith that Christmas in 1918, led a huge Cabinet contingent including Foreign Secretary Arthur Balfour, HH Asquith, Austen Chamberlain and the then chancellor of the exchequer, Bonar Law. Churchill was there as minister for munitions. Having completed a stint of service on the Western Front as a colonel he was now very much back on deck as a minister and MP.

WM Hughes was the fifth prime minister present and, short of height and with no medals or sash or ribbons to wear, he may have felt out of it a little and not have clicked into the proceedings all that well.

The speaker of the House of Commons, JW Lother, and the lord mayor of London, Sir Eric Drummond, were present and also Sir Robert Cecil. It was a case of anybody who was somebody being there for this victory and alliance salutation.

From those who did or supervised the fighting there was a huge line up of admirals, including Viscount Jellicoe, Sir David Beatty, and Sir Rosslyn Wemyss and others. However the Allied armies dominated with field marshals including Viscount Sir John French and Sir Douglas Haig, Generals Sir Henry Wilson and Sir William Robertson, plus lieutenant generals: Canadian Sir Richard Turner VC and Sir John Monash, listed as director of Demobilisation, Australian Imperial Forces.

Even the fledging Royal Air Force had a Guernsey, plus significant people like Sir Joseph Thomson, president of the Royal Society, Sir George Makins, president of the Royal College of Surgeons, and Dr Norman Moore, president of the Royal College of Physicians. It was a rich cross section of triumphal British and Commonwealth society matched up with their helpful cousins from the USA.

The diary notes of John Monash detailed the seating in his area. He sat in the vicinity of Churchill, Botha and the portrait painter John Singer Sargent. Directly beside Monash on one side sat Rudyard Kipling then next to Kipling was the Nobel Prize winning physicist Sir Joseph Thomson. On the other side was Lord Burnham, the owner of the UK *Daily Telegraph*, and beyond him General Wilson. The conversation at that end of the table was set to sparkle.

The menu for the occasion had been especially created with an eye to the celebration of victory:

BUCKINGHAM PALACE

Consommé des Alliés

———————

Filets de Sole à la Victoire

———————

Noisettes de Mouton Châtelaine

———————

Poulardes à la Danoise

———————

Asperges Sauce Mousseline

———————

Mousse glacée à l'Américaine

———————

27 Decembre 1918

In early 2014, at my request, the official menu and the carefully crafted seating plan for this occasion was provided to me by Buckingham Palace.[1]

President Wilson had arrived after spending Christmas with his wife in Paris, where he had been welcomed by thousands. Likewise when he arrived in London and travelled from Victoria station up the mall to Buckingham Palace, thousands were on hand to wave flags and extend warm greetings.

Monash wrote in his own diaries that on the night the guests arrived through the arch and into the courtyard and main entrance. Upon being greeted by footmen and ushers, the attendees turned left to climb the sweeping grand staircase from the inner foyer to be presented to King George V, Queen Mary and the Wilsons in the White Drawing Room. They then mingled before being ushered along the superb Picture Gallery and the East Gallery into the Grand Ballroom, which is complete with a large grand organ. The beautiful State Dining Room was judged too small for this special occasion.

The seating plan provided by the palace reveals a huge open U table layout with the open end of the U at the organ end or southern end of the Grand Ballroom. Across the joining section of the U at the top of the Banquet table, in the centre, sat the king and queen as hosts.

The protocols of seating and dealing with the proximity to host and hostess when you have over 100 guests today require a computer

---

1 I lodged the request through the then high commissioner in London, Mike Rann. To his credit, he knew exactly who to contact in the large palace official household. Within two weeks the unique material was found and sent across to Australia House. Her Majesty Queen Elizabeth II then gave permission to allow the material to be published, much of it for the first time ever. So it is that the content of the menu can be detailed.

with algorithm capacity, to sort. The overall deciding factor is seniority but that criterion is often applied with a twist or two. In the case of a large U layout, other subtleties come into play. The more senior sitting is not necessarily the best. On this night all ambassadors present were to rate more highly than prime ministers, so the top table section read as follows:

United State Ambassador

Princess Patricia of Connaught

The Spanish Ambassador

Princess Christian

The French Ambassador

THE QUEEN

The President of the United States of America

THE KING

Mrs Wilson

F.M. Duke of Connaught

Princess Mary

The Italian Ambassador

Princess Beatrice

The Japanese Ambassador

Marchioness Imperiala

There are subsets within nominal and actual seniority. This explains why the US ambassador was not closer to the host as he was junior, in years at the Court of St James, to the three European ambassadors present. All diplomatic seniority is based on a countback to the actual day the ambassador presents credentials, and in this context any inexplicable variations to this can cause huge animosity and tension.

The crucial point in the seating, in relation to Monash, was that although Monash had technically a lower-order seat to Hughes, his was a place that commanded attention from the whole banquet, from the king on his far left to the most junior guest, notionally, the master of the household, on his far right. Hughes had his back to half the guests at the banquet and would have to stand up to see the top end of the table containing the king and president.

What then cuts in is the personalities of those present along particular parts of the one long U-shaped banquet table. Here Hughes has much to lament. He was sitting opposite the hapless Austen Chamberlain, minister without portfolio and older step-brother to Neville Chamberlain. On Chamberlain's left and right were two admirals, Sir David Beatty and Sir Rosslyn Wemyss. On Hughes' immediate left was a Nobel Science Prize winner and seventy-six-year-old renowned physicist Lord Rayleigh and on his right an-up-and-coming thirty-one-year-old US general staff officer, GM Barnes. On paper Hughes had little in common with his immediate company. Almost nothing at all.

Contrast this with Monash who had on his right Kipling, who he had met before the war in Melbourne and had greatly enjoyed his company. On his left was Lord Burnham of media fame, General Sir Henry Wilson of defence liaison fame, at the highest levels between France and Britain, and then there was Churchill. Directly opposite Monash was the renowned portrait painter

JS Sargent. Monash had been sitting for a portrait in London and would likely have been interested in raising queries with Sargent.

The portents for the visiting Australian prime minister delivered up by providence and the protocol and seniority calculations were not splendid. For the dashing lieutenant general Sir John Monash, however, they were excellent, and he made the most of it.

Monash wrote that it was a splendid setting and a superb evening of fast moving conversation with Monash at one stage being able to volunteer that he had met bushranger Ned Kelly in Jerilderie some forty-one years before. It was a stellar night as adversity had driven so many nations and so many high-achievers together. This at last was the night of celebration for 'the best of the best'.

For Billy Hughes could this have been a night that made him resentful towards Monash, as this Australian Jewish militia lieutenant general had more allure and realpolitik standing than he did as the actual prime minister of Australia? Yes he had praised Monash after the Battle of Hamel but Hughes had been increasingly disturbed by the ascent of the Monash star.

Throughout that December 1918 Monash and Hughes had clashed about aspects of the repatriation, most notably the speed at which the troops were to be sent home. Monash favoured getting them home as quickly as possible but providing education and vocational training while they waited for scarce shipping. Hughes was concerned about voting blocs and also employment prospects for the troops returning, and perhaps more so for his own onward employment prospects as prime minister.

At a luncheon of the Australian and New Zealand Club that month, Churchill and Sir Ian Hamilton, the sacked general from the Boer War and the Dardanelles campaign, both went out of their way to praise Monash. This attracted applause and much support from the audience. When Hughes spoke at the same luncheon, he gave scant reference to Monash. Their various meetings and encounters lacked goodwill.

Was it the last straw for Hughes that at this banquet of banquets with the Allies all represented at the highest level, King George V was more friendly and unashamedly happy to converse with Monash than with the Australian prime minister? Was it the very aura and presence of this lieutenant general, dressed in splendid Military Mess Kit, with medals gleaming, that got under the skin of the diminutive Welsh prime minister?

Many believed that it was about this time that Hughes began to strongly dislike Monash.

The speeches, in the form of toasts, delivered by the king and then the president were short but brilliantly pitched for the occasion and built on the links of history between Great Britain and the USA, with an emphasis on freedom and liberty and above all, justice.

The string band of the Royal Artillery played throughout the night and the conversations and wine flowed among these great achievers and, just for one evening, for those present it was a chance to celebrate a hard-won victory together and ease back from the massive burdens of the war.

After the formal dinner, served on special golden plates from Windsor Castle as every effort was made to enhance the night, the hosts led the guests to the State Drawing Room for coffee and intermingling, a chance for informal commending, for greeting and networking aplenty, and no doubt to sample some good port.

At midnight the king and queen with the president and Mrs Wilson retired for the evening. The palace staff ensured the guests were moved along to their carriages and cars and this glorious night of celebration came to an end. As the crowd of super-VIPs dispersed, again it was Monash who was the subject of attention and greeting, while Hughes was farewelled by the protocol staff, properly but perfunctorily.

There is one extra tale from the banquet, passed down amongst historians over the decades and while not verified it would have been a distinct possibility. During the night of nights it is said that at one stage in the Buckingham Palace White Drawing Room, King George V came across to a group and in the process initially overlooked the Australian prime minister WM Hughes to greet warmly his good friend Lieutenant General Sir John Monash, standing alongside.

It may have happened. Certainly Monash was there in full regalia and riding high, Hughes was playing second fiddle to other prime ministers including the other prime minister of Welsh heritage, Lloyd George. Monash was not playing second fiddle to anybody as the only other Australian in the room.

It seems this grated on Hughes during the dull winter days in London between Christmas and New Year, and just as the happiest New Year in recent years arrived a bombshell arrived out of left field. Monash was given the title of 'Knight Grand Cross of the Order of St Michael and St George' (GCMG) in the New Year's Honours list. Monash was now a kind of double 'Sir', promoted at the behest of King George V but robbed of actual rank at the behest of WM Hughes.

Again the king had acted and Hughes had to put up with the situation. Clearly Monash had momentum and standing and, it seems, Hughes was determined to clip his wings in the only way possible, by declining to promote him to general.

Where Haig and all other key leaders received extra awards and in some cases promotion to the House of Lords. The only awards Monash received were foreign. Incredibly, there were none from the Australian Government.

The last week of 1918 had been momentous for Monash, along with the first day of 1919, as a new era unfolded with a new big task for Monash to be conducted still a long way from home.

Monash returned from London across the English Channel to a now peaceful but threadbare France, to pack up and then formally take his leave of the Australian Army Corps with a banquet at Le Cateau. He then returned to London and settled into his new task of arranging the return to Australia of over 180,000 restless, magnificent diggers.

Hughes it seems had carefully planned a form of retribution: tie Monash up with the complexities of sending home thousands of Australians from a base in London while keeping him one step in rank below the military rank he should have been afforded. Thus he could and did block the promotion of Monash from lieutenant general three star to general four star, even though this promotion would have helped Monash to deliver in the endless negotiations over shipping and training of the many soldiers returning from France through Britain to Australia. Shipping was in short supply and Canada, India, South Africa and the USA all had large numbers to shift.

Eventually Hughes was to return to Australia but in all his utterances and in his much anticipated first speech to Parliament in the wake of World War One and the Paris Peace Conference, delivered in Melbourne, there was not one mention of Monash.

It was Hughes and his bloody mindedness, perhaps locked in on the night of the banquet of all banquets at Buckingham Palace, that blocked the promotion of Monash, a deserved promotion and one that could have come earlier. While it is readily conceded that until 11 November 1918 technically Monash held the correct rank, after 1 January 1919 Monash was clearly one step in rank below where he could and should have been.

For those who were wary of Jews, including the governor-general of Australia at the time, Sir Munro Ferguson, the Monash rank saga was a kind of get-even, indeed a dimension of the fabled tall poppy syndrome. Ferguson was not happy that Monash was held in such high regard by the palace and even less happy that the king had given Monash the same senior knighthood (GCMG) as he himself held.

Monash had survived the Great War and as he celebrated his GCMG and the start of the new year of 1919 he was too busy to dwell much on his actual rank or to lose much sleep wishing for promotion. But this was a massive wrong call by Hughes and it had ramifications.

If Monash had not been invited to Buckingham Palace for that banquet of banquets then perhaps Hughes would have relented and allowed or even initiated the promotion, realising that around London rank does matter and always has. However Hughes knew exactly what he was up to. It was not something he had overlooked. Rather it was a deliberate ploy to put personal issues and perhaps domestic politics ahead of what was right and what might have even helped expedite the repatriation of thousands.

Today during summer months it is possible to visit Buckingham Palace and see first-hand where this banquet of banquets took place, to walk up the famous palace staircase and to pass through the Portrait Gallery. The organ, referred to by Monash in his diary writings about the night, anchors exactly the giant ballroom.

Hopefully on the centenary of this unusual banquet, on 27 December 2018, a commemoration might be held at Buckingham Palace. It would provide for the opportunity of bringing together an interesting line up of modern day Monarchs, presidents, prime ministers, ambassadors, admirals and generals.

Monash and Sir Rudyard Kipling at Buckingham Palace on 27 December 1918 for arguably the greatest banquet ever held at the palace.

Chapter 11

REPATRIATION AND DEMOBILISATION

A Year of Reflection in London

> 'Never can there be any questions about Monash's brain. It is there, a living, searching, strong intelligence, breeding ideas, and judging them shrewdly. His motto is action, and his energy already pulsates through the demobilisation scheme.'
>
> (Sir Keith Murdoch, 28 February, 1919.)

The year 1919 started with Monash having his head down, buried in planning and making key appointments to his new team for Demobilisation and Repatriation. He wanted men he knew and men that would perform the many exacting tasks in support of getting the Anzacs home safely and as quickly as possible.

As the cold days of January 1919 further unfolded, Monash drove forward with ideas and concrete plans on how best to galvanise the complex administrative apparatus for demobbing thousands who had to be well fed and housed while awaiting return to Australia. It was not an easy task and required close liaison with senior federal ministers, one or two of whom had eventually come up to London to ensure they looked like they were doing everything possible to expedite the task and at the same time to second-guess Monash.

Defence minister George Pearce, who served in that role for over a decade and right throughout World War One, arrived in March 1919 in London with his young family, and he was smart enough to agree with most arrangements that Monash had put in place and which were already despatching thousands for home.

Pearce was a capable defence minister from November 1908 to December 1921 and again later in the 1930s. He grew up in Western Australia and was elected as a senator from that state but due to the location of Parliament in Melbourne for the first twenty-five years of its existence, Pearce and his family ended up living mostly in Melbourne.

Later in his career, in 1923, he changed from the WM Hughes to the SM Bruce regime, almost seamlessly but holding a range of different portfolios, including minister for territories. His negotiating skills built up over many decades of rough and tumble, especially in Western Australian trade union circles, were very well regarded. In the 1930s he became a minister under Prime Minister Joseph Lyons, including minister for external affairs where he again won praise for his negotiating skills.

In London in 1919 Pearce worked comfortably with Monash. However at all times he chose not to trumpet the cause of Monash for Australian recognition and promotion. By this time Pearce and Hughes had worked well together for years, switching from the ALP to the Nationalist Party. Pearce complied with Hughes' apparently 'locked in' decision of no promotion and no Australian recognition of Monash, for each year he was defence minister after 1918.

The basic shape of the Monash demobbing plan soon emerged. It was to divide all into groups of about 1000, a neat ship load and set of train loads, and to give priority to those who had the longest war service. While all waited uplift, the troops were provided with extra education and career training around England. This was to include, for some, vital university preparation courses right through to practical bricklaying trade courses.

In the processing, medicals had to be conducted of all members of the AIF and various mustering into categories took place, the main category being unaccompanied AIF members judged fit for travel, be they single or married. Other ship loads were reserved for AIF members who had married British wives and in some cases already had children, young families who wanted to stay together and travel together back to Australia.

The hundreds of wounded adjudged fit for travel were clustered onto designated hospital ships, with extra doctors and nursing staff.

All of this had to be carefully managed and the right AIF grouping married with the right ship at the correct departure port and with adequate supplies for the – on average – six week voyage on mostly coal-fired HMAT transport ships.

There were two parallel repatriation and demobilisation hubs operating for the AIF; one based in Great Britain under Monash and one in the Middle East under Chauvel. Both had to cope with incorrect diagnoses of the health of AIF members, including from the then lack of knowledge about 'shell shock' and mental health. Today many of these conditions are labelled quickly and outright as Post Traumatic Stress Disorder.

Hector Thomson from Gippsland was diagnosed with malaria in March 1917, after having served in the Light Horse in the Middle East and been awarded the Military Medal (in August 1916). His grandson Alistair Thomson, Professor of History at Monash University, Melbourne, dived into all the records relating to Hector to discover it was really mental illness he was primarily suffering from, with severe bouts at times.

Mental illness, however, was not spoken about but, rather, hushed up. In his excellent book *Anzac Memories*, Thomson details the family agony created by the terrible postwar condition of Hector, which was to have an impact on his family that was to go on well beyond World War One and even after World War Two.

For against all odds, Hector managed to falsify his age to serve in World War Two, notwithstanding ongoing bouts of illness and the demands he faced as a widower bringing up his two sons, at least when he was on deck. His two sons, Colin and David, also against considerable odds, achieved a great deal including service in the occupying force in Japan at the end of World War Two. In the case of David, he gained much from a short stint at Scotch College, where Monash had been equal dux, and he had an add-on career after his military career as House of Representatives member for Leichhardt and federal minister for science and yechnology.

The amazing thing is that a soldier of ill health, indeed considerable ill health in the case of Hector Thomson, could soldier on into another world war.

Clearly there were thousands of PTSD and other mental health cases for both Monash and Chauvel to wrestle with, as a dimension of the whole repatriation system. In terms of the success of the system in dealing with these challenges, as the Hector Thomson case shows, this was hit and miss. Mental health, in any case, was yet another set of challenges for exhausted leaders who had given so much since 1914 and now had to handle a different set of problems.

The war might well have been over but very sadly some shooting was to continue as Australia, along with Canada, India, South Africa and the USA, wrestled with huge numbers of restless troops. In March 1919 deadly riots broke out among Canadian troops awaiting return to home, fuelled by rumours that grain ships were returning from Liverpool to Canada, empty. Military Police stepped up and so Canadians were killing Canadians as spring 1919 was just starting to unfold in the UK.

Meanwhile, overall, London in the first half of 1919 was a bustling confident capital city, a hub picking up the pieces after the war and getting ready to swing into the roaring twenties. As is often the case expat Australians kept bumping into each other, attending the same functions and circulating around the two square miles around Westminster, the West End and all the military clubs and other clubs, through to the palace area. Further to the west was the Royal Albert Hall and central museum precinct, to the east Fleet Street and Threadneedle Street as well as Christopher Wren's giant creation, St Paul's.

AIF diggers on leave took the opportunity to soak up everything London had to offer, including a great deal of live theatre. The diaries of diggers often referred to theatre outings, complete with a pithy review of the play or musical attended. For many it was their first and last visit to this big powerful city and memories of it were preferable to memories of the Somme.

Australia House was the epicentre: a substantial building right on the Strand. And it was where dignitaries took the salute as the Anzacs marched by, led by Monash on the first Anzac Day after the cessation of hostilities, 25 April 1919. Hughes had his main office there and Monash even kept a small office there to facilitate liaison. Despite this, by now Hughes was no longer prevaricating. He had locked in his decision not to promote Monash as he prepared to move to the next phase postwar, the Peace Treaty preparatory negotiations and midyear formal sessions and signings in Paris or just west of Paris at the actual historic Palace of Versailles, where the Peace Conference was held.

It was at this conference that Hughes was at his best. When challenged by President Woodrow Wilson as to how many he actually represented, Hughes snapped back that he represented 60,000 dead. Eventually Hughes signed the fateful Peace Treaty that set the stage for World War Two. He then returned to London by the boat train for a round of farewells and sailed for Perth.

Meanwhile function after function in early 1919 around inner London saw Hughes and Monash in the same room but not happy with each other and seething tensions continued. Monash had reached a stage in life where he was not in awe of anybody, from the king and prime ministers downwards. He could see petty political games being played, a mile off. He observed polite protocols but both he and Hughes were keeping their relationship to a minimum.

The curious thing is that Hughes himself might have been enhanced by swiftly and deservedly promoting both Chauvel and Monash to general in the first quarter of 1919; he could have had a kind of reflected glory, but this was not to be.

Vic, with daughter Bertha, arrived in London from Australia by ship on 29 April 1919. It was a great family reunion but by degrees tempered by the ongoing relationship Monash had with Lizette Bentwitch. Monash maintained communications with Lizette even when escorting his wife and daughter to various functions around London.

Vic Monash knew Mrs Hughes well. She had also long awaited joining her husband in London and the Monash couple took Mrs Hughes out to dinner and a show but, as Roland Perry has detailed, Billy Hughes did not choose to make up the foursome. The tensions continued.

Even on the Australian prime minister's final departure from London there was barely a polite farewell between Hughes and Monash. Basic civility was maintained but no more than that.

Back on home ground, Hughes soaked up huge applause as he made his way across Australia by transcontinental train, from Perth to Kalgoorlie, across the Nullarbor to Port Augusta, as the returning PM who had tackled Woodrow Wilson and much more.

At the big platforms that form Port Augusta railway station, Hughes had to change trains from the Stephenson standard gauge to the Anglo Cape narrow gauge and proceed up the beautiful Pichi Richi Pass to Quorn. This section still operates today as a tourist train. Hughes was the first of many prime ministers after the Transcontinental was completed in 1917, who rode the steam train through the Pichi Richi pass to make the east-west connection across the continent. Then the rail journey turned south to Terowie where there was another change of trains, from the narrow gauge to the Irish Broad gauge for the run into Adelaide and a huge welcome. Then it was onto Melbourne by the overnight train. Hughes the returning hero was riding high; so high that he had perhaps over-concerned himself about the status and location of Monash.

For Monash, as 1919 gathered momentum, the work pressures never abated . Any hiccough or delay in returning the heroes of the AIF to their families in Australia was widely reported, so the weights were on. In any event Monash wanted to do the right thing because he had the utmost respect for all those who bore the brunt of the fighting.

Ship after ship departed Southampton and Tilbury for down under and on arrival in ports around Australia, huge crowds turned out to give a big welcome. Later, on arrival in large and small country towns, there were impromptu and more formal welcomes. In some towns local mayors pleaded for early information on AIF heroes coming on the local mail train or its connections, to ensure that a full and proper civic and town welcome was extended to the returning diggers and nobody was overlooked.

One suspects some of the diggers would have been happy to mingle in the crowd and quietly vanish back into family circles as they wrestled with Post Traumatic Stress Disorder. For some such as Senator Pompey Elliott this was to lead to suicide, even though the great Pompey had much to live for. Acts of valour were no protection. Hugo Throssell VC became an activist against all war but committed suicide at Northam, Western Australia. While Monash would not have had a modern medical understanding of PTSD at the time, he knew the men now needed a letdown period, a period of recovery helped along where possible by a flexible command approach.

For Monash personally it was a case of balancing his workload with writing a book on World War One: *The Australian Victories in*

France in 1918. More than 100,000 words were required and to meet deadlines this had to be pumped out in about two months in the late London summer of 1919. This meant some cutback in the evening social swirl, as Monash tackled writing in earnest.

This book project led Monash to reflect on the war but in particular to address the crucial period of the last six months of fighting. Monash thought victory had been honourably obtained and that Australia had done its fair share of heavy lifting. Now he sought to nail down this contention in a book that never really took off, although he as author made a small profit.

In May Monash fronted at Buckingham Palace to receive his GCMG and was back there on 12 August for a lunch with the king and queen, in salute of the knighthood Monash received in the field exactly one year earlier near Amiens.

Think about this: there were many new knights around London in 1919 and many colonels, generals and field marshals floating around but King George V made a point of bringing about, creating and hosting this timely lunch with Monash.

Vic Monash was trying hard to keep up but was starting to endure severe ill health and weakness, so she cut back on some functions but with daughter Bertha the family made it to Cambridge and Oxford Universities to watch Monash pick up honorary degrees. Monash or in fact his family would be annoyed to learn that decades later Cambridge University had completely overlooked their honorary-degree graduate in their three volume history of World War One.

This custom of awarding honorary degrees continues to this day; indeed Churchill took Menzies to Bristol University in the darkest days of World War Two to award him an honorary degree, in the hope

Menzies might then decide to go home to Australia (Churchill never visited Australia). Many more recent Australian prime ministers have received honorary degrees in the northern hemisphere.

In what must have been an extraordinary five hectic days in May 1919, Monash took his daughter across to France to tour the battlefields from Amiens through to Flanders, visiting many war graves and places where battle raged less than nine months before. The visit allowed Monash to explain to his daughter the strategic linkages with the devastated landscape and where key HQs were and battles took place. She wrote: 'Dad explained the importance of the high ground at Villers-Brettoneaux which overlooked Amiens ... [R]eached the summit of Mont St Quentin ... [A] few people back in Perrone [sic], a few wooden huts being erected, a little restaurant open'.

The slow recovery of the cities, towns and villages comprising the Western Front had begun, reflecting the resilience of the French and Flemish people and of humankind more generally after great adversity and large-scale death and destruction.

As the northern autumn arrived in 1919 the largest part of the repatriation task had been completed. Monash and his family prepared to pack up and say farewell. At long last they boarded the *Ormonde* and set sail for Melbourne. Australia beckoned and by now Monash had been in a sense one year in the sin bin at the behest of Hughes, while Hughes won a federal election easily and without having to contend directly for attention on home soil with a distinguished war hero.

It had been a huge five year effort by Monash, one that had aged him, slimmed him down and also in moments of big stress towards the end resulted in him getting a nasty nervous twitch in his hands.

At times he encountered periods of exhaustion, not unreasonably, but he soldiered on.

He had carried his burdens very well, despite some internal opposition and a raft of near misses with incoming bullets and shrapnel from the enemy, particularly at Gallipoli. He was lucky in as much as he was alive and ready to resume life in Australia while 61,000 AIF members lay dead and buried on the soil of Greater Europe and the Middle East and of course at Anzac Cove in modern Turkey. Further his reputation as a senior military commander was intact, although he was to face various accusations, including one of cowardice that will be examined later.

All in all Monash with his family could depart London and Europe with his head held high after a job well done, indeed an incredible set of tasks allocated to him over five years completed effectively and efficiently. Monash was keen to return to Australia. He could walk tall and be proud and begin to think about the next phase of his life postwar and post the extra year working on repatriation.

Chapter 12

POSTWAR DISCRIMINATION FROM BEAN AND HUGHES

'A man like John Monash is not the man to handle the AIF at a critical moment like this.'

(CEW Bean writing in September 1918 from France, just after the Monash led victories at Mont St Quentin and Péronne and just ahead of further Monash led victories through the Hindenburg Line.)

'Monash was a leader of whom it could be said that he would command a division better than a brigade and a corps better than a division.'

(CEW Bean, *Official History* Volume II, 1924.)

It was a superb summer's day on 26 December 1919, Boxing Day, when John, Vic and Bertha Monash sailed up Port Phillip Bay and arrived at Station Pier, having left London on the *Ormonde* in mid-November 1919. It had been a long leisurely voyage but with hectic ports of call at both Perth and Adelaide.

On board the *Ormonde* for the duration of the voyage was General Sir William Birdwood, the ultimate general officer commanding the

AIF but an India-born English officer with Sandhurst training who, after World War One, would return to reside in India.

Here was a regular Sandhurst officer of true-blue British military output turning up in Australia for a grand tour at the invitation of Prime Minister Billy Hughes, even though Birdwood had been surpassed and had played no role in the critical Australian Western Front battles of the second half of 1918 in France, from Hamel through Mont St Quentin to and beyond the Hindenburg Line. Birdwood was quite popular with the AIF but he was not truly one of them.

Birdwood and Monash had to endure each other, for some two months, no doubt on the captain's table but also around the upper echelons and saloons of the *Ormonde*, with brief stops at transit ports. At Perth the VIPs on the *Ormonde* disembarked for official welcomes with General Birdwood leading on the occasion, receiving a huge welcome from the large crowds.

It was a case of the regular officer, the professional soldier officer, versus the irregular militia officer who was still part-time in service as late as July 1914. In a perhaps accidental but nonetheless ultimately insulting promotion, for Australia, Birdwood was made a field marshal on 25 March 1925, even before he became commander in chief of the Indian Army.

So for the record Birdwood ended World War One a general, having been promoted to general on 23 October 1917, initially with a view to commanding the Australian Army Corps in France but after May 1918 commanding the Fifth Army. Monash ended the war as a lieutenant general, just one step behind Birdwood and in command of the Australian Army Corps, confirmed after a wobble engendered by Bean and Murdoch. This was the gap in rank situation until 1925, when Monash quietly endured the further promotion of Birdwood one final extra step up, to the rank of field marshal.

On arrival and despite the fact it was Boxing Day, a large crowd of former AIF soldiers, some officials, and members of the grateful public, were all on hand to extend a big warm welcome to the capable, popular, proven but exhausted Monash. Hughes was in Melbourne that Christmas but chose not to show up for the welcome.

What was more significant than Hughes' flippancy here was the failure of the Army to push for the promotion of Monash from their headquarters at Victoria Barracks along St Kilda Road, in effect at any time after 11 November 1918; or even push for promotion of the other lieutenant general of particular renown at the end of the war, namely Sir Harry Chauvel.

Chauvel had brilliantly commanded the Australian Light Horse in a superb contribution to the campaign from the Suez Canal through a charge at Beersheeba, onto Jerusalem and into Damascus, three days before General Allenby and Lawrence of Arabia arrived. Chauvel had a prickly meeting with Lawrence in Damascus before Chauvel led his troops on to Aleppo.

Chauvel like Bean was somewhat wary of Jews, of whatever rank. Today, buried away in a folder in a restricted archive of the Australian War Memorial in Canberra, there are some interesting writings of Chauvel reflecting on Monash, critical stuff that in part will be detailed in a later chapter.

Both had to wait for nigh on another decade before being finally promoted to full general, or four star general in today's parlance. It was a form of collective bastardry at the highest levels, with the Army HQ apparently knowing that a push for promotion of Monash and to some extent Chauvel would be unwelcome around the office of the prime minister. Remember the prime minister's office and Victoria Barracks headquarters in Melbourne were close together, just a short walk across the Fitzroy gardens and over the Yarra River and along St Kilda Road.

Further it seems the defence minister Senator George Pearce, a self-made man of considerable standing with Hughes, chose not to stand up to Hughes and try to insist on overdue promotion for Monash. Despite the Hughes snub, Monash was feted for some twenty-five days all over Melbourne with a huge bundle of invitations arriving in the mail at the Menzies Hotel in Collins Street each morning. It was publicly known that Monash was staying there initially, before returning to 'Iona' in Toorak.

Typically Monash stopped accepting the stream of invitations in order to gain some control and balance in his life now that he was back home. He attended two functions in Melbourne for the visiting Birdwoods, on 18 and 20 January, and then retired for a period from the social milieu. He maintained a huge effort in these busy days in replying to a heavy load of correspondence, for example writing a letter dated 28 January 1920 in reply to a letter he had received just six days before, relating to the death of Major Terence Garling, who died of wounds on 5 April 1918 in France. Mrs W Elliott of Jerilderie was the aunt of the late major and his letter in reply was especially generous and consoling.

However his hands were full on another front, with the rapidly deteriorating health of his wife Vic. He chased down the best specialists in Melbourne but the diagnosis was cancer and Vic Monash died in late February 1920, less than two months after returning to Melbourne from London. It had been a troubled marriage but one in which Vic had maintained total fidelity and been very proud of her husband and his military exploits. Equally Monash had enjoyed many high moments of marriage but also carried out an affair, in the height of the darkest days of World War One, while on leave from the dreadful front line action.

It could be contended that unless one has firsthand experience in trench warfare and trench warfare command, it is difficult to be judgemental about all that happens throughout the war, as Monash wrestled with his own personal demons while maintaining at all times a confident and positive demeanour and careful correspondence with his family.

Hundreds of letters and telegrams of condolence arrived at 'Iona', addressed to Lieutenant General John Monash. Lengthy hand-written letters came from state premiers, the federal minister for defence George Pearce and from members of the High Court, including Sir Isaac Isaacs. However from Prime Minister WM Hughes there was a telegram of only six curt words and I quote: 'Deepest sympathy in your sad bereavement'. Again it is apparent that Hughes was observing minimal protocol in respect of Monash.

Is this an unfair judgement? I do not think so and I am fortified in the judgement when I see and read all the other letters written by busy people to Monash.

After a period of mourning, there was a perhaps inevitable journey from London to Melbourne by Lizette Bentwitch and not long after Monash and Bentwitch were an item around Melbourne. However daughter Bertha made it clear to her father that she would cut off relations if Monash married Liz and certainly would not allow Liz to come to live in 'Iona'. Bertha and her husband Gershon Bennett lived at 'Iona' with Monash after they had married in 1921 and later three grandchildren arrived.

At no stage during the two major affairs – with Annie Gabriel or Lizette Bentwitch – did Monash have to pick up a newspaper in London or Melbourne and see his love trysts bandied about on the front cover. In April 1919 he even announced publicly in the *London Times* that his wife and daughter were about to arrive in England. It was another era alright, as there were no headlines 'general faces decision time: wife from Melbourne or London lover?'

Despite the adoring and at times madding crowds, Monash did not find himself a lonely, ageing man, without a partner in Melbourne. Indeed he happily stepped out with Lizette to functions and theatre opening nights but as a couple they were never invited to Government House or national parliamentary functions, remembering both were located in Melbourne at the time. The lack of invitations to Monash when Allenby and others were visiting Melbourne became an issue raised in Federal Parliament, sitting in Spring Street.

As Dame Elizabeth Murdoch said so stridently to me at Government House in Melbourne in 2009, Monash had a mistress and this was certainly known in the roaring 1920s up and down Collins Street and Spring Street. Hypocrisy abounded as King Edward VII had a well-known mistress who was a hotel keeper in London and Queen Victoria found solace as a widow with a certain Mr Brown of Scotland.

Monash was no shrinking violet on the matter and took Liz to some big activities such as the Melbourne Cup but again this was not into the Victorian Racing Club (VRC) Committee rooms. No Victorian Racing Club chairman of that time would extend an invitation to the couple.

So a pattern of discrimination against Monash on this score continued until the last year of his life. It was subtle but ensured that both Prime Minister Billy Hughes and his successor Prime Minister Stanley Melbourne Bruce were never going to promote Monash or invite him to be governor-general, although there was some discussion about Monash for such an appointment. In respect of Bruce this was curious as both Bruce and Monash had been on very active service at Gallipoli.

An additional challenge for Monash was the continuing vital matter of club membership around Melbourne. It was then part of the mantra of the Melbourne Club in the Paris end of Collins Street that Jews, even famous ones that had done so much for king and country, could not be allowed membership of the club.

This contributed to the formation of an informal club with the curious nickname 'the KK Club', standing for the 'King of Clubs'. It was a monthly luncheon and dinner club formed mainly by Melbourne Club members for the express purpose of eating with the great Lieutenant General Monash. It was no doubt a sense of guilt at the time that drove the KK Club members along. Monash himself did not devote any energy into obtaining Melbourne Club membership.

The KK Club continues to this day, over eighty years after the death of Monash, and at a meeting in 2008 even discussed the question of his rank.

This matter of discrimination against Monash by the Melbourne Club should be kept in perspective. He was held in enormous regard by the public at large and was quickly offered and accepted membership of the Melbourne Rotary Club and of a range of other organisations. He was invited to turn the sod for various new buildings, some associated with the RSL. In other cases he laid the ceremonial foundation stone.

On the work front Monash was head-hunted to lead the embryonic Victorian State Electricity Commission, which was given sweeping powers to develop the Latrobe Valley brown coal deposits for electricity generation. Victoria was moving on from an economic base in agriculture, gold mining and national administration (the flow-on effects of possessing the nation's capital) to a new role as a major manufacturing base. This required a big supply of reliable and not too expensive power.

In 1919, back in London, Monash had organised a kind of postwar raiding party to proceed to occupied Germany and extract all relevant information on how Germany generated power, especially from brown coal, which has a weaker heat generation quotient than black coal and is often found to be with an unhelpfully high moisture content. Now this initiative was to reap benefits as detailed planning and a trial extraction of brown coal proceeded near Morwell.

About half-way through the construction phase the Victorian state cabinet took stock, and so did Monash. He realised the need to greatly expand extraction capacity and power generation capability. The adjustments were made accordingly and electric power soon flowed to Melbourne and right across Victoria. Even some southern parts of New South Wales were supplied by the SEC: Monash went to Albury on 20 March 1926 to switch on the connection there in southern New South Wales to the Victorian SEC grid. On the occasion he was greeted and saluted by the Albury sub-branch of the RSL.

As Roland Perry has researched and observed, Monash had standing and gravitas on the subjects he knew much about, and key people, including the then young Victorian state minister Robert Gordon Menzies, said that when Monash entered the Victorian state cabinet meeting all stood, all listened intently, and all were persuaded to the propositions that Monash laid out so succinctly.

It was the Monash ability to get the job done that really earned him respect in this context. There was seemingly no discrimination against Monash in the workplace. Indeed there was great respect, which caused Monash to attract attention as a possible 'Il Duce' or fascist type of national leader to respond to the rapidly unfolding Great Depression, at the end of the roaring 1920s.

Monash was loyal to the constitution, king and country. At no stage did he show the slightest interest in aspiring to some all-embracing role as a national leader, still less one with the constitution somehow suspended. Approach after approach was made, unsuccessfully, from a range of people and organisations.

Major General HW Grimwade from the powerful Grimwade family and later chairman of the very influential Australian Club in William Street, Melbourne, was one such person. He had served under Monash happily on the Western Front and was also from a family with extensive commercial interests in both Melbourne and Sydney.

There had been a New Guard organisation formed as the Great Depression gathered momentum, splitting from an Old Guard organisation. Both were dominated by ex-World War One returned servicemen unhappy to see the economy collapse and job opportunities dry up.

In the largest state, New South Wales, the Lang Labor Government was in a fierce clash with bankers and the Scullin Federal Government, there was massive unemployment in that state and all others, and the nation was experiencing a devastating drought. The restlessness and turmoil was destabilising the nation. Lang became the first and only state Premier to be sacked by a state Governor, in May 1932.

Meanwhile as the added problem of nationwide drought unfolded around 1930, there was more and more clamour against the inexperienced federal Scullin Labor government and there were more and more calls for dictatorial leadership of the kind provided by Mussolini in Italy and Franco in Spain.

As approach after approach was being made to Monash, he came under pressure to turn down an invitation he had accepted to represent Australia for the New Delhi Grand Durbar in 1931, so as to be on hand for whatever eventuality.

Eventually, for Monash, the deluge was too much to ignore. He replied to this correspondence with a direct rejection of any idea of him stepping up to be a kind of downunder Mussolini or Franco. In a formal letter of reply to those raising this possibility, Monash said it all when he said 'No', he would not lead a coup, and then added some words that have inspired many in politics in Australia over the years, and I quote exactly: 'Depend upon it, the only hope for Australia is the ballot box, and an educated electorate'.

Over the years I have to confess I have tended to fudge this quote into the statement that the best hope for Australia is the ballot box and good education for all electors. It certainly kept me going through some very tough times at the federal political level when under massive attack. For Monash it was part of his political mantra, his Australian citizenship mantra, and nobody and nothing would persuade him otherwise.

Now throughout the whole of the decade after his return to Australia Monash had maintained a good deal of positive notoriety pursuant to one cause after another, particularly relating to building the observance of Anzac Day and the Shrine of Remembrance, due south in total alignment with Swanston Street in Melbourne.

Clearly Monash had enormous sway not only with the returned diggers but with their families and the public at large. Had he decided to lead Australia via a coup, there is no doubt he could have done it and that there would have been enormous instant support for Monash.

Once again those who disparage him argue that, by now aged over sixty-five, Monash could not have organised a coup and it would have fizzled out within a week. Yet had he invited all available members of the AIF to fall in in front of the local post office at noon on a given Saturday, by the Monday the machinery of government would have been in his hands and without bloodshed.

The ex-AIF members would have walked across hot coals for Monash. From time to time Monash inadvertently demonstrated how true this was when he led huge Anzac parades and was hailed by the large crowds. The Anzac Day RSL banquet of 1924 further demonstrated his total hold on a large crowd of diggers and civic leaders as he gently lectured all, but also saluted all ex-AIF members, dedicating his various awards to the members of the AIF. This extraordinary night, in some ways overdue by the time it took place, is examined in a later chapter.

In his last year of life Monash was still in the ascendancy, in a professional sense, despite all the discrimination and spiteful statements that had been made against him over the decades. Today if you walk along Swanston Street over Princes Bridge and then have a good search in the parks leading up to the shrine, eventually you will find, somewhat tucked away, a statue of General Sir John

Monash of Jerilderie and Melbourne, Gallipoli and Hamel. He is nicely portrayed sitting on a horse.

After the banquet of all banquets at Buckingham Palace on 27 December 1918, Prime Minster Hughes turned his back on Monash to ensure he was never promoted to the rank of four star general.

In the Australian spring of 1919, Hughes returned from the Versailles Peace Conference as a kind of hero and was well received by large crowds. He had ample opportunity to speak in Parliament and salute the diggers and their leaders. The closest he came to this was on 10 of September 1919 in the Lower House chamber of Parliament on Spring Street Melbourne, when he delivered a full report on the war and formally moved the adoption and approval of the Versailles Treaty which had been signed in France on 28 June 1919.

That afternoon Hansard records Hughes rose at the Despatch Box at 3:04 P.M. and spoke with special extensions of time until 5:30 P.M., a total of 146 minutes. The first part of the speech addressed the huge contribution of the Australian forces in World War One with central reference to Villers-Brettoneaux and turning the tide in late March and April 1918 on the Western Front, and secondly to the victory in Palestine, in which he twice made specific mention of General Allenby of Middle East fame. To quote from Hansard for the House of Representatives, 10 September 1919:

> The whole of the Australian Army was brought down and placed in position in front of Amiens, and for a time the two lines swayed backwards and forwards, neither side seeming to gain the advantage; but in the end, little by little, that indomitable will to conquer, that resource and initiative, and that invincible valour, which marks the Australians, overcame all resistance, and backwards, faster and faster, the army of the Huns was forced,

> until, at the culminating point of the war, the offensive of the 8th August was launched, resulting in the final destruction of the last hopes of victory for the Germans.

Note carefully this description relates to but omits the period of the Battle of Hamel, in relation to which Hughes had sent Monash congratulations. Also in relation to 8 August 1918 and the big breakthrough, Hughes had previously specifically praised the creativity and leadership of Monash.

Hughes then went on in his two-and-a-half-hour address to speak about nothing but a miracle saving the day.

Clearly Hughes made a tactical decision to mention no Australian names in his tour de force first speech to Parliament after the Great War.

Fair enough, it could be observed. He did return briefly to salute those who served and those who lost their lives, stating that Australia, of five million people, 'has the right to be proud of the heroism of her soldiers and sailors in the Great War'. And it should be acknowledged that back in November 1918 when the news had come through of the Armistice, both Houses of Parliament passed worthy motions the very next day and sang the national anthem of the time, 'God Save the King'. Both Houses then had spontaneous bursts of three cheers, all recorded in Hansard, with one in the Senate for Ferdinand Foch by name and one in the Representatives for the king, some for the men who served as well but with no specific Australian names called out.

But I would say 'Wait a moment'. After all he had plenty of time on the long journey from London to map out a thoughtful and powerful address.

Think about the magnitude of this snub: direct references to the battle of Amiens, where Monash was Australian Corps leader and, with the help of many, created the black day for the German Army, the biggest day for the Allies, but no reference to Monash, the man who so successfully led the AIF in the field for the last six months of the war on the Western Front.

While this does not add up to the wrongdoing of say the French Dreyfus Affair, where a French officer of Jewish background was found guilty of trumped up charges, a decision eventually reversed but at great cost to the unity of France, I do accuse Hughes (J'accuse) of deliberately deciding not to mention Monash in this speech.

To achieve this and play safe, he decided not to mention one Australian by name. Not one. Not Chauvel or Monash, let alone any of the fallen, such as General Bridges, or even Private Simpson and his donkey, both killed at Gallipoli. Just the British general who was by then a field marshal, namely Allenby. With a wry smile I hereby state Hughes could be forgiven for not mentioning Haig or Rawlinson and their disastrous blood-filled track record.

The debate then carried on over several days and was quite feisty, especially over certain islands conceded to Japan at Versailles and also over aspects of the 'White Australia Policy'.

As usual, at the end of the debate, the prime minister and mover of the motion had a right of reply and this Hughes did on 19 September 1919, for over an hour. Again there was no mention by name of any Australians who served but a spirited swipe or two at some backbenchers opposite, especially over the issue of who started the war. This was in response to some comments earlier by the MP for West Sydney, a certain Mr Wallace.

Hughes nailed down this issue of who started the war in a masterfully fiery and freewheeling way. He even mentioned 8 August

1918 again but still with no mention of Monash or for that matter any mention by name of any AIF member of any rank.

So after the Great War, the Australian Parliament thanked many and all in a general way but at critical junctures not Chauvel by name and not Monash by name. Even the US Congress in 1919 swiftly created the new rank of general of the Armies and awarded this in the first instance to Pershing.

Hughes kept Monash out of the country for a whole thirteen months after Armistice Day and the end of World War One and when he returned, Hughes as prime minister ensured Monash was not offered any federal position of note or even the seemingly logical promotion from lieutenant general to general that the Canadians gave for Arthur Currie upon his return.

Later, on 4 May 1920, Hughes moved a comprehensive motion of salute to the AIF and all who served and this was agreed to after a relatively short debate, in order that it might be formally presented to representatives of those who served, in Queen's Hall the next night. Hansard records that Hughes did not speak when he moved the motion. Apparently this was for health reasons.

Eventually Hughes was to find some 'nice words' and indeed generous words to say about Monash on the floor of the House of Representatives, but it was not until 1931, during the condolence motion in salute of Monash's passing:

> The news of the death of General Sir John Monash will be received with great and sincere regret by the people of Australia, to whom he stood as the leader and living embodiment of the AIF, and all its glorious and imperishable achievements. One by one the great outstanding figures of the world war are passing away. Yesterday, Haig and Foch; today, Monash.

> Sir John Monash has gone from us ... of all who held high command in the Allied forces, his claim to military genius is least likely to be questioned. To him more than any other, is due the plan which inspired the great offensive of the 8th August, 1918, which plucked victory out of the jaws of defeat, and drove back headlong the exulting German legions along the Hindenburg line; sweeping irresistibly through the vaunted barrier, to victory, and to peace.
>
> This great soldier, this great citizen, has left us; but across the abyss that now divides us we waft to him our tributes of homage and admiration, of gratitude and esteem. We extend to his daughter and sister our deepest sympathy.

Monash was laid in state in Queen's Hall and it was to be a huge funeral. However this contribution from the by then ex-prime minister, 'The Little Digger' as he was known with whatever degree of irony, was in any fair judgement rather too little, too late.

As Hughes spoke in the Chamber in Canberra (the federal Parliament by then having moved from Melbourne) he might have paused to reflect on his having done wrong by Monash. However I doubt it. He had obviously decided long before to hold back the due recognition of this rival leader.

As the journalist and historian Les Carlyon was to conclude, in the wake of World War One 'The Australian Government did nothing to honour him. He was still the outsider, somehow not quite right for the establishment'.

In 1920 South Australia created the vital town and irrigation soldier settlement of Monash in the Riverland and to this day it has proudly a local hall called the Monash Memorial Hall. Decades later Victoria created the huge Monash University and later again the busy Monash freeway. Nationally there was nothing but a belated promotion one step in rank in 1929 for Monash himself.

After 1923, when the Country Party succeeded in bundling Hughes out of the prime ministership in favour of Stanley Melbourne Bruce, Hughes would live on to be the holder of the record for longest serving member of the House of Representatives and the longest serving 'Father of the House', a position without formal powers but not without responsibilities for helping to set the tone and example to younger members.

After an initial warmth, relations between Monash and WM Hughes became very strained, especially in 1919.

Meanwhile on the other side of Canberra, step by step the Australian War Memorial (AWM) and attendant huge museum were being created. The actual tomb of the unknown soldier came as a late addition to the complex but interestingly enough, the soldier's body placed in the tomb was from the Western Front.

The co-founding chairman of the AWM was CEW Bean. He was a good choice given his monumental writings on the war. He had completed writing the first six giant volumes of the *Official*

History of Australia in the War of 1914–1918, a magnificent effort. He then led the team that completed the full twelve volume set and in the process of review and reflection following on from the five years of brutal war conceded that he had been wrong about Monash and wrong about opposing Monash taking command of the Australian Army Corps.

However this did not bring about a full-scale rebalancing in relation to Monash. Indeed Bean had his favourites and he stuck with them during and after the war. Bean went out of his way to heap praise on and boost the image of Brudenell White and others. As a consequence Monash and his huge contribution was again portrayed in a less than adequate way.

As part of this Bean persistently portrayed Monash as 'eager for military glory'. To be fair, Bean did allow that Monash was probably 'the ablest and most successful British (sic) corps commander in France'. But he had clashed with Monash on day one, at their first meeting at Gallipoli, and a decade after the death of Monash still put in the odd jab against him in the *Official History*.

Did this lead to any kind of 'mea culpa' evident in the construction and layout of the AWM? Alas not and in fact the opposite. For decades Bean ensured or at the very least took no steps to alter an imbalance. The result for decades was that in the World War One section there was a whole table and display of iconography of Chauvel, with narrative, but for Monash one lonely misplaced portrait painting and, scattered elsewhere, just two other items from his uniform.

Of course tucked away in the vital research section of the AWM there is much material pertaining to both Chauvel and Monash, including some interesting writings by Chauvel pertaining to

Monash examined in the chapter on 'dinkum' Monash. At the time of writing, in 2014, the Word War One exhibits and gallery are under reconstruction. The magnificent heritage dioramas are all being kept and this is a good thing but it is not clear if or to what extent either Monash or, for that matter, Chauvel, Bridges or Brudenell White, might feature.

For seven decades the AWM has downplayed Monash. This is in part a direct consequence of the actions and / or non-actions of CEW Bean as co-founding chairman but to be fair also a consequence of an underlying 'Tall Poppy' syndrome ever present in the Australian nation.

Bean outlived Monash by decades, living through World War Two and even the Korean War, dying in 1968 at age ninety, undeniably an outstanding journalist and historian. In later years, though he conceded that he was mistaken with his initial assessment of Monash, he did nothing to rectify a wrong. In fact Bean did nothing other than to add to the downplaying of the massive contribution of Monash to Allied victory.

The Australian War Museum is well placed today to rectify the wrongs perpetrated by its co-founding chairman. The Museum is by world standards a cut above the average and it has set a high standard generally, with Canada and others now following with their brilliant War Museum in Ottawa. The AWM in this centenary of the outbreak of the Great War will be judged by its revamp and how it portrays the AIF in general and Monash in particular.

Chapter 13

A BELATED PROMOTION TO FOUR STAR GENERAL

> 'I would name Sir John Monash as the best general on the Western Front in Europe, he possessed real creative originality, and the war might well have been over sooner, and certainly with fewer casualties, had Haig been relieved of his command and Monash appointed to command the British armies in his place.'
>
> (Field marshal and first Viscount Montgomery of Alamein.)

For colour, action and movement how could one bypass the great Lawrence of Arabia and his achievements in the Middle East in World War One? He led the capture of Aqaba from the inland and not by the expected approach from the Red Sea. He swept forward on the eastern flank of the Allenby forces as they captured Jerusalem and later Damascus. Yet he was never a general. He was eventually promoted to the rank of colonel by General Allenby of Damascus fame. (And after the Versailles Peace Conference, that Lawrence considered had dudded the Arabs, he vanished by choice into the RAF as a lowly ranked Airman.)

It is relatively easy to pick out the twenty most senior generals of two star and above rank in World War One on the Allied side, including those from Canada, India, South Africa and the USA.

What is more of a challenge is to weight them in terms of greatness. Who was most innovative? Most successful? And above all else, contributed most to ultimate victory?

Smuts from South Africa and Currie from Canada, along with two who arrived late at the top of the list, namely Foch of France and Pershing from the USA, must all rate highly. Among the British – as in true British and not from elsewhere in the Empire – you have Sir Ivor Maxse from the ranks of the lesser known and you also have Allenby, Plumer and even Wilson.

Among others from Britain of possible note are Sir John French and Sir Douglas Haig. The former was sacked early on, the latter was nearly sacked later on in the war and was still muttering about cavalry charges in the autumn of 1918. Haig did have some good points as mentioned earlier but not enough to overwhelm the negative. So those two can't be given serious consideration, let alone Rawlinson of the Somme, under whose command there were 20,000 dead on the single morning of 1 July 1916.

While Haig and Rawlinson had whatever is required to continue to command after causing so many casualties on the Allied side – a kind of black intestinal fortitude – this does not redeem them in any balanced estimation.

There are several outstanding Australian generals, all of whom learnt much at Gallipoli and went on to deliver great leadership, especially at brigade and divisional level: Blamey, Chauvel, Coates, Pompey Elliott, Howse, Morshead, Savige and Brudenell White. To these must be added the AIF Corps divisional commanders for the last 100 days in 1918: Glasgow, Rosenthal, Gellibrand, Sinclair-MacLagan (actually a Scot but with two postings to Australia before the war he was well established in the AIF) and Hobbs. As noted earlier, General Bridges, founding commandant of the Duntroon officer training college at Canberra, lost his life at Gallipoli.

Applying the criterion of 'innovation', those adjudged as having done very well from the position or positions held, there are not so many. I would nominate just Allenby, Currie, Foch, Maxse, Pershing, Plumer, Wilson, and Monash.

I have omitted King Albert I of Belgium who assumed control of the Belgium army in 1914 and delayed the lunge of the German forces across Belgium back in August 1914, later holding onto a corner of Belgium against the sea for the entire duration of the Great War. He played a difficult hand very well in the last 100 days in 1918 and was ultimately made a British field marshal after the war. As king general officer commanding of the Belgium army, he had a unique role and did his best, but is not in the top rank in terms of outstanding innovation.

To award the title of 'most innovative' you have to weigh up each general and his attributes and achievements carefully. The choice is ultimately a subjective one, just as the generals and leaders highlighted in the Imperial War Museum at Bedlam in London, with zero mention of Monash, are also subjectively chosen.

Allenby

Sir Edmund Henry Hynman, first Viscount Allenby, GCB, GCMG, GCVO was deservedly made a field marshal in July 1919 when aged fifty-eight and was a sprightly fifty-three at the start of World War One. For Allenby it was the regular path of Royal Military College, active service in India and South Africa during the Boer War and in 1914 into the British Expeditionary Force in France. After a mixed record on the Western Front, especially at Arras, in June 1917 he was promoted to general and made commander in chief of the Egyptian Expeditionary Force, and moved to Cairo. From there he planned the big drive northwards with the Middle East campaign. This major set of actions involved driving the Turks northwards past Romani, out of Beersheeba, out of Jerusalem and eventually out of Damascus.

The two standout strategies of Allenby were to facilitate an Arab revolt on his eastern flank by overlooking the many rules and regulations that Lawrence of Arabia flouted. The focus was on destroying the Turkish narrow gauge key railway line of resupply from Damascus to Medina then hitting hard the retreating Turkish units. In turn Lawrence was able to keep capturing Turkish forts and territories right up to Damascus in early October 1918, after the initial massive breakthrough of capturing the Port of Aqaba.

Secondly Allenby used the cavalry to advantage for the last time in world war history, greatly helped by the swift lateral-thinking Australian lieutenant general Sir Harry Chauvel. This led to the famous charge at sunset on 31 October 1917 from the west to capture the key wells and Turkish compound at Beersheba.

Currie

Sir Arthur William Currie GCMG KCB became commander in chief of the Canadian Army Corps on the Western Front in June 1917, one of the younger C in Cs, at age forty-one, succeeding the British-born general Sir Julian Byng. In April that year Currie had led Canadian soldiers to reach the top of Vimy Ridge in just seven hours. The planning and careful preparations were largely done by Byng but it was Currie that led their execution.

There is no doubt that Currie was innovative and always upgrading training even in the harrowing middle period of the war on the

Western Front. He was known to have a certain degree of arrogance and a bad temper, something that many, though not all, generals could be accused of.

Controversially Currie ordered – in accord with his orders – an attack on Mons on 10 and 11 November 1918, leading to the death of George Lawrence Price at 10:58 A.M. on the eleventh day of the eleventh month. Price was the last Canadian soldier killed in the war.

Upon his return to Canada after World War One, Currie was promoted to full general, about ten years – note years – ahead of Monash being so promoted by the Australian Government. Currie and Monash both had holistic strategic approaches plus a huge emphasis on general and specific training.

Foch

Ferdinand Foch GCB OM, marshal of France, field marshal of Great Britain, was not from the upper classes of France, not even the military elites with their self-perpetuating closed loops that make it hard for 'rank outsiders' down the ladder to make it through. By dint of hard work and study, Foch was steadily promoted to the point where in 1914, at sixty-three years of age, he was a lieutenant general.

After the outbreak of World War One, he was soon in battle at Morhange and after this was made head of the Ninth Army, for the first Battle of the Marne. Like so many senior military leaders, he lost family members, a son and son-in-law killed on 22 August 1914, less than three weeks into the war. It was Foch's ability to tic tac with Allied forces and his strong links with General Sir Henry Wilson that saw him catapulted to overall commander in chief in April 1918, over Haig, as discussed previously. Lloyd George had argued for a long time for an overall commander and was very happy with the selection of Foch. For George, as noted, it was a case of almost any person over Haig.

Under Foch the last big push of the Germans was resisted and commencing with the 4 July 1918 Battle of Hamel the tide turned through the last one hundred days to Armistice. Foch, by then in overall command, had a small HQ and had to bargain his way forward with the likes of Haig, Pershing and the various French marshals and generals. He did not occupy the equivalent overall command positions created in World War Two, such as held by Montgomery in the African theatre or that held by Eisenhower. However it helps to be the one at post when victory is achieved and there is complete surrender of the enemy. As he said himself, he was 'a conductor who beat time well'.

Maxse

General Sir Ivor Maxse KCB CVO DSO was so well regarded in the field and for training that in June 1918 he became inspector general of training to all of the British armies in France and the UK, at age fifty-five. He came under favourable notice when, at the Battle of the Somme, using a creeping barrage, his Eighteenth Division actually made progress on that dreadful first day of July 1916 and, later, on 16 September 1916, captured the hitherto impregnable fort of Thiepval.

There was an element of 'back to the future' with his training, bringing back as it did the four section infantry platoon, with two of these being Lewis gun sections allowing advance and cover tactics at platoon level. This meant useful capability with support fire, within the closely knit infantry platoon. Maxse appreciated how to use modern weaponry such as the improved machineguns of the era. He wrote much about the capability of Germany to recover post World War One and revert to aggressive militarism.

Pershing

John Joseph Pershing turned fifty-eight in 1918, having entered the US Army in 1886 as a Second Lieutenant at age twenty-six. In an incredible military career in various capacities including the often overlooked vital role of defence attaché, Pershing saw service in Cuba, Philippines, Mexico, the war of Japan and Russia as an observer and in 1908 the ultimate training theatre, the Balkans, but from a base in Paris. Handling the Balkans from Paris would have involved an enormous amount of time on trains and some time on ferries across the Adriatic. Pershing had the opportunity to develop a 'feel' for Europe which few US presidents and generals of more recent times have succeeded in doing.

Pershing arrived in Paris in June 1917 as a four star general and supreme commander of the US forces that had come to rescue the Allies on the Western Front.

For a period in 1918 Pershing directly commanded the US First Army but it struggled despite superior numbers, in part due to a mistaken belief of Pershing that the slow trench warfare could be overcome by fast moving accurate shooting American soldiers, in his view only requiring light artillery support. Ouch. This led to thousands of extra casualties.

It is of particular interest that Pershing called several critical shots – so as to speak – at the end of August 1918, against his broad orders from the White House but in favour of a quicker end, in 1918 and not 1919, for the war on the Western Front.

Plumer

Sir Herbert Charles Onslow, first Viscount Plumer GCB GCMG GCVO GBE, reached the age of sixty-one in 1918. He was a Yorkshire man who went to Eton College and moved through the tried and true pathway of many British World War One generals, namely India, Aden, Sudan and the Boer War, South Africa plus a stint in Rhodesia, now Zimbabwe. As a lieutenant general, Plumer went to the Western Front in January 1915 to command V Corps.

Along with one or two other leaders he was committed to a bite and hold strategy and he showed positive determination at Passchendaele but later was used to lead reinforcements to Italy. This was in the aftermath of the disastrous battle of Carporetto in the autumn of 1917 where the Italian Army was done over by a German-led drive, in fact by a young Major Rommel who later went on to become the 'Desert Fox' in World War Two.

The Italian army was made up of many peasants dragooned into service and then badly led by General Luigi Cadorna. It was Cadorna who ordered decimation of his own units as a form of discipline, one in ten of each unit judged to be not brave enough or disciplined enough being selected from the soldiers on parade at random and led out to the front and executed in front of their unit. Austrian and German forces made it to near Venice but eventually the Allies turned the tide.

Plumer showed a steady hand and was broadly successful with the tasks allocated to him. After the war, King George V made Plumer a field marshal and then in 1925 he was sent to the Middle East as high commissioner to the Palestinian British Mandate, until 1928. Already the stirrings of Arab versus Jew were emerging, some twenty years ahead of the formation of Israel, but Plumer again played a steady, stabilising and firm hand, dealing with both Balfourite Zionists and Arab nationalists.

Plumer, like Allenby before him, had to handle on the ground the impact of both the Balfour letter, issued in November 1917 and now known as the Balfour Declaration, and the knock-on of the adoption of the Sykes Picot Agreement carving up the Middle East on the wrong boundaries. In a sense Plumer's postwar success, like the success of Monash postwar in leading the Victorian State Electricity Commission, are factors that tend to elevate or at least underline their achievements in the thick of the Western Front. Others fell away at the end of the war or even in the last weeks ahead of 11 November 1918, emphasising how they had probably been over-promoted in the first place. This was not the case with Monash or Plumer.

Wilson

Sir Henry Hughes Wilson, first baronet, GCB DSO, was one of the youngest. He was fifty-four in 1918 and, due to the Wilson family employing French nursemaids, was fluent in French from a young age. Wilson, despite an Irish background, trod the familiar path of Burma via India, then the Boer War, where it helped to be noticed by Lord Frederick Roberts. A posting in 1907 as commandant of Staff College led him to meet his opposite in France, who as luck would have it was none other than Ferdinand Foch. They became close friends and working compatriots in peace then war.

For two long periods of World War One, Wilson was principal liaison officer in Paris, a position that might be denoted as British French defence attaché in chief. It was a pivotal role and, playing his cards carefully, he enhanced the power and effectiveness of it. Later in early 1918 he was made chief of the general staff for the British forces, based in London. He was one of four to be promoted to field marshal in July 1919 by King George V, together with his friend Foch and Allenby and Plumer.

After the war Wilson was involved in the Northern Ireland political cesspit and on 22 July 1922, after a trip to the Liverpool Station in London to unveil the Great Eastern Railway War Memorial, he was shot dead by two Irish nationalists in front of his own house.

So how do the magnificent seven – Allenby, Currie, Foch, Maxse, Pershing, Plumer and Wilson – stack up against Monash? There are also strong Australian commanders not to be lightly dismissed, as mentioned before, especially Chauvel and Pompey Elliott. Why might Monash be regarded as a cut above these others?

Monash was senior to all the Australian two star and three star generals of World War One and Chauvel, through no fault of his own, never made it to the Western Front, adjudged by Allenby and almost all as the critical theatre on all counts. And by 1918, on the Western Front, Monash was the greatest general when allowance is made for innovation and degree of difficulty and weighted for actual rank held.

Some suggest Monash was a coward in being reluctant to visit the very forward areas ahead of or after a battle. He argued his best place was where he could be readily contacted, where he could command based on the information gathered: 'Everybody knows where to get me, at a moment's notice, for immediate discussion or reference, and rapid decision; I can have before me, all the time, a complete and not a partial picture of what is going on, and I can, at all times, reach every possible subordinate'.

It is difficult to sustain the view that Monash was in any way a coward after being located upfront at Gallipoli, at times within earshot of the Turks. He did not miss a day of service at Gallipoli right through to the last day of evacuation and withdrawal. Further Monash personally captured two Turks as prisoners, two of the enemy duty bound to kill him if they had a chance.

It should be noted further that all of the HQs that Monash used on the Western Front were in shelling range of the German big guns or large artillery. Also they were only a few minutes' flying by a Red Baron type pilot from the German airstrips on the eastern side of the Western Front. Monash could have been killed on any and every day he was on active duty on the Western Front.

Both Allenby and Chauvel can walk tall and be proud of the Middle East campaign but at the end of the day Allenby himself regarded the Middle East as a side show and as only an indirect help to ending the war. The Western Front was in the view of Allenby and most others where the important action really was, and where the generals really had to deliver.

It is a close run thing comparing Currie and Monash. Prime Minister Lloyd George bandied around the names of both to take over from Haig, who he despised, had the world war continued into 1919. But if only because Monash had to overcome steeper odds to succeed I favour John Monash as being greater than Arthur Currie by the narrowest of margins.

Was Foch a better conductor than maestro John Monash, who also likened a perfected battle plan to a score for orchestral composition? They were both very good. However taking into account the margin of difficulty each faced, Monash was up against steeper odds, albeit on a significantly smaller scale.

Liddell Hart said of Maxse that he was one of the ablest officers of his generation: 'A man of originality and drive, and a formidable personality'. So I rely on Hart, the formidable historian, to separate Maxse and Monash. This he did when he affirmed Monash was the greatest general of World War One, in effect to the exclusion of all others.

Leaving aside the fact that Pershing disrupted the last minute preparations for the Monash led Battle of Hamel and that he air-brushed Hamel out of the highlights of the US involvement on the Western Front, Pershing was a force to be recognised but, arguably, should and could have achieved more in 1917 and 1918, with fewer casualties. He deserves the park named in his honour near the White House, with a set of World War One narrative plaques (which should, I contend again, include a mention of Hamel). But he was not as successful or innovative as Monash.

Was Plumer greater than Monash? It is hard to be definitive but those key observers of the era certainly placed Monash ahead of most if not all, including ahead of Plumer. Remembering the criteria includes innovation and contribution to overall success and victory from the position held, then again Monash is to the fore, but it is a close and eminently subjective call.

Some historians see Wilson as a conniver and deceitful operator. In any case his liaison work was vital but not to be compared with that of the generals in direct command. He was really rear echelon for most of the Great War, only briefly commanding IV Corps on the Western Front, when it played a small role in 1916.

Monash was indeed 'the maestro', all things considered: the greatest innovative general of World War One. And in all this it must be remembered that Monash was in 1918 and 1919 merely a lieutenant general, a three star, though awesome in achievements.

By 1929, however, Monash's rank was about to change.

As Australia woke up on 13 October 1929, the day after the Federal Elections, they found the centre-left, via the Australian Labor Party, had captured forty-six out of the available seventy-six seats. With this clear-cut result, the governor-general commissioned and swore in as new prime minister James Scullin. Then a few days later again, they woke up to the news from New York of the giant Wall Street share market crash, and so the scene was set for tumultuous times.

In accord with the swings and roundabouts of democracy, in 1929 Billy Hughes found himself on the back bench and SM Bruce found himself out of Parliament altogether, the first ever sitting Australian prime minister to lose his seat in Parliament.

Despite all the turmoil and in part because Scullin held a Melbourne based seat and knew personally both Sir Harry Chauvel and Sir John Monash, the new prime minister was able to give some thought to rectifying what he regarded as a wrongful omission.

It was a curious and unusual move, bringing on the promotion of two senior Army personnel. This centre-left prime minister was determined to distinguish himself early on in his term of office by promoting two establishment figures, two lieutenant generals who happened to be of religious persuasions far removed from the Irish Catholic beliefs strongly held by him.

It was part of a pattern in as much as Scullin was always prepared to take a contrarian stand. Indeed he considered both Monash and Sir Isaac Isaacs for the position of Australia's first Australian born governor-general. Due to concerns over the health of Monash and for a range of other reasons, the nomination went to former state and federal MP and minister, Chief Justice Sir Isaac Isaacs.

King George V received Scullin at Balmoral Castle in Scotland and argued against the nomination of Isaacs on the basis that he was Australian born, but Scullin stood up for his beliefs. The Irish in him was not going to be overwhelmed by an elderly British Monarch. And so Isaacs became Australia's first Australian born and Jewish governor-general.

Likewise early in Scullin's term of office, he resolved to steamroll through the promotion of both Chauvel and Monash, a decision he delivered on within a month of obtaining office and against some lingering opposition around the corridors of power.

In a clever move, Scullin decided not only to promote these two 'World War One greats' but to do so with effect from Remembrance Day, 11 November 1929. At last these devoted, dedicated and determined officers and true blue Australian leaders – with Chauvel still on active service – made it to four star full general.

Did it matter much? It was a promotion of some significance but a long time after World War One and a very long distance from either the Western Front or the Eastern Front and the Middle East.

The truth is, as stated earlier, that rank does matter, including the step from lieutenant general to general or three star to four star. It mattered for both Chauvel and Monash and also for their families. For those on active service it comes with increased pay and support staff, apart from anything else, even in peace time.

Both generals received many letters of congratulations. Both had a right to be very proud of their outstanding service. Both were giants of their time, generals of distinction, outstanding Australians.

Monash's last full year on earth, thanks to Scullin, was to be as a full or four star general.

Chapter 14

THOUGHTS ON 'DINKUM' MONASH FROM DIGGERS, COLONELS AND GENERALS

> 'My impression is that General Monash is one of the biggest and brainest (sic) men I have ever met – a big grip of his job with his ever watchful eye on everything.'
>
> (Lt Col P Abbott CMG, writing on the Western Front in his diary, Friday 15 February 1918.)

Leadership is a two way street. It cannot be successfully simply imposed from above and this is especially so during war. In this regard military command is no different and requires skilful use of rank structures, with the devising and the issue of orders, indeed with capable communication through all ranks. For Monash the basic tenets of his modus operandi did not change much throughout World War One but his strategies and tactics continually evolved, right up to Armistice Day.

Over the decades the very best political and military leaders have generally endured a severe jolt or two along the way, often leading to a kind of epiphany which has further enhanced their leadership capabilities. In many cases it has hardened and strengthened their modus operandi. Conversely those with a series of soft experiences have often gone to pieces when the pressure mounts. This cracking under pressure was despised by the diggers, considerable evidence suggests.

King George VI was an example of a stuttering introverted and sheltered person who rose above a personal difficulty, partly through his marriage to a strong willed lady, Elizabeth Bowes-Lyons. She urged the reluctant king on and gave huge morale boosting support. In addition, he had an Australian speech therapist, Lionel Logue, who helped him overcome his debilitating stutter problems. In the critical days after the resignation of Neville Chamberlain, in May 1940, his preference was to turn to Lord Halifax but instead it was Churchill he commissioned as PM and backed all the way to World War Two victory. The king received accolades all along the way.

Even Pope Francis had a jolt or two along the way, banished to Cordoba for a period and sent to Germany for another period, before being given a massive win on the second day of the 2013 Conclave to become bishop of Rome and supreme pontiff, but one very much plugged into the needs of the poor, with his feet planted firmly on the ground. In his first year he has reached popular hero status.

For Monash, his jolt and epiphany came on 8 August 1915 at Gallipoli. His completion of a turnaround came exactly three years later on 8 August 1918 when he helped create the black day for the German Army on the Western Front. By 1918 Monash and a handful of other generals, notably the Canadian Currie, had worked out what was required in twentieth century land warfare.

In turn this engendered respect and support from the troops he commanded. They were quick to say when they encountered leaders they found wanting. Soldier and field poet Sydney B Young, originally from Campsie in New South Wales, records in his diary from the Western Front during the Hamel period in July 1918 a very interesting reflection on the visit of Prime Minister WM Hughes: 'He shook hands, I walked him around to look at the men. Billy Hughes is a miserable weak looking devil with a vicious glint in his eye'.

Young then wrote of an incredible exchange between an American soldier who spoke German, who asked a German prisoner if he thought they were winning the war? The diary, recently digitised by the Mitchell Library, records that the German answered: 'Yes, God is with us'. The American GI replied: 'That's nothing, the Australians are with us'.

This tale might have been just that, another furphy from the front, but it is clearly written in Young's careful writing in his diary and the German motto was 'Gott mit uns': 'God with us'.

Sadly it was never recorded which American soldier made this utterance but it was a manifestation of the regard for the Australians at all levels, including at the highest levels. It had not been by chance that the Australians and their battlefront leader in the last 100 days of the Great War were placed on a pedestal.

To reiterate, Monash was not popular as such but revered and respected. Certainly diggers he did encounter found nothing to grumble about and many in their diaries gave him only scant mention but where they did write further, it was in praise, as per junior officer Abbott in the epigraph to this chapter stating Monash had a big grip of his job.

Lieutenant Hector Brewer of the Fifty-Fourth Battalion, part of the Fourtenth Brigade, writes in his diary for 8 August 1918 that a hot meal was served at 3:00 A.M. and then he quotes the Monash written orders issued ahead of the Battle of Amiens in absolute respectful detail. In this special message, Monash referred to this occasion as the first time the five Australian divisions had lined up together and expressed confidence that every soldier would worthily rise to the occasion.

At function after function in the 1920s that Monash attended in the community, now carefully spaced to fit in with his demanding SEC duties, he was always very well received and asked to unveil plaques and salute the fallen but overall there was scant effort to accord Monash a true and genuine, indeed a dinkum, salute.

It was not until 1924 that finally a huge effort was made to salute Lieutenant General Sir John Monash, still a three star lieutenant general five years after the war. A special Anzac Day dinner was held at the Melbourne Town Hall with over 600 people present. As was the custom of the time the ladies were admitted to the balconies for the speeches. All of the speeches were revealing and rich in praise of Monash. It was a gala occasion and the scent of hard-won victory abounded, the drumbeats of World War Two having not yet commenced.

Victorian State RSL president E Turnbull as chair set the ball rolling, questioning whether Australia really appreciated the greatness of Sir John Monash. He concluded his remarks with the observation that nobody could appreciate him more than the men who served under his command; this was greeted by sustained applause from all present, many of whom had served under Monash.

Representing the Government, as PM SM Bruce was engaged with an electorate function, was the Government Senate Whip, Senator

Edmund Drake-Brockman, who commanded the old Monash Fourth Brigade on the Western Front. To quote from his address:

> The wonderful work of this wonderful man has not been fully appreciated in Australia. I can tell you where it has been appreciated and that is by the people of Great Britain and by the general staff of the War Office. No one pays any attention to the ridiculous statement that Australia won the war but I think that we can say that it was through Sir John Monash and his men, the war finished much sooner than we thought possible.
>
> That operation that commenced on the 8th August 1918 was the sole conception of Sir John Monash. Sir John's ideas were carried forward to the commander in chief via General Rawlinson and the consent to the scheme was given in this way: Very little harm can be done, let them have a go at it! (Laughter) The Australians had a go at it and before they finished the Germans had completely cracked. (Loud applause)

From the AIF, soldier S Fowler spoke and gave perhaps the best epitaph in relation to Monash when he said that the secret of his popularity lay in the fact he possessed that rare and indefinable quality which entitled the man to be regarded in the diggers' eyes as 'dinkum'. This is at the core of what the diggers thought about the great man who did so much in the Great War.

'Dinkum' has a meaning of 'genuine', or 'real', both then and now. Monash would have been quietly cheered by that choice of word, by that descriptor, as he sat through this huge dinner in his honour. He had been called many things over his six decades of life. Dinkum was at the top end of the scale. A decade had elapsed since he had become a full-time serving colonel and head of the Fourth Brigade of the AIF. Half a decade had even elapsed since Armistice

Day, so the town hall hushed as Monash gathered his thoughts and spoke in response to the gathering.

In his formal speech in reply to the Toast and Illuminated Address, Monash said that he always remembered that the many awards he received were only as a representative of the AIF, and that all the honour was to them. Reflecting ahead of time the revisionism of the twenty-first century, Monash then went on to redefine Gallipoli in these words:

> The AIF's losses at Gallipoli were small compared with losses in later engagements. Over and over it is said that the Gallipoli campaign was a failure. It failed only in that it did not achieve its full objective. From a strategic point of view it was of great importance. Not only was the Gallipoli campaign a strategic victory, but as the builder of the AIF tradition it was alone worthwhile.

To some extent these comments might have eased the sense of loss from the defeat at Gallipoli. They certainly reflected strongly held views, of Monash and many others, that Gallipoli should be kept in perspective, especially vis-a-vis the Western Front, a view that waxes and wanes to this day. At the end of his address Monash received a huge round of applause again and made the effort to greet all and sundry. It had been another extraordinary banquet but this time in his home town with Monash granted due measure and praise, if no promotion in rank.

Anzac Day 1924, just the ninth anniversary of Anzac, had been a big day, a long day and a long overdue salute to the Australian Army Corps commander.

The Dinner speeches were well covered in the print media the next day, 26 April, including on page 16 of the *Argus*. In that era classified advertisements dominated the first few pages of the main newspapers but the *Argus* report was over 2000 words and headlined with the simple words laid out as follows across a single column:

SIR JOHN MONASH

TRIBUTE BY SOLDIERS.

PRESENTATION OF ADDRESS

Events of the War Recalled.

After years of under-acknowledgement from Bean and others, Monash had a headline or four in the *Argus* and in many other newspapers in the aftermath of this special and long overdue tribute dinner, more than five years after the end of the Great War, initiated by AIF members and not by the Government.

The comments on the night had reflected what many thoughtful writers had put down over the years. Some of the best reflections on Monash came from those who actually were under his command and were on hand on the Western Front through 1918. Frederick Morley Cutlack was born in England and grew up in Australia, meeting Breaker Morant in 1899 in Renmark just before the Breaker went to the Boer War. Cutlack was an intelligence officer in the AIF in 1917 on the Western Front but was switched to becoming 'Acting Bean' in early 1918, while Bean was on leave in London. When Bean returned he carried on as Bean's very active deputy and so saw the Battle of Hamel unfold along with the last 100 days up to and through the Hindenburg Line.

About fifteen years after World War One, Cutlack put down a lengthy essay and assessment on Monash as a foreword to the 1935 book containing the Monash war letters. His writings reflect a balance that Bean could never bring himself to achieve:

> He (Monash) never left any point veiled in ambiguity, and he could not tolerate ambiguity or carelessness in others. Understanding meant to him complete understanding, the grasping of the full detail of an event or a position and of its proper background. Never, so far as truth was humanly attainable, did he ever half know anything.
>
> He would consult with any man within his reach, high or low, in order to perfect his own understanding; and in the utmost good faith, slurring nothing, exaggerating nothing, he aimed at conveying as full an understanding to those with whom he worked. Any mere pretence of knowledge or capacity was anathema to him.
>
> No shrewder judge of men and things has ever lived.
>
> His other outstanding and most lovable trait was his humanity. These letters reveal again, what every man who worked under him learned so well – his genial kindliness, his wide-ranging and ready sympathy, his abiding love of life. Few men were rash enough to visit John Monash in anger; none, surely, could ever have left him in anger.

Cutlack did not have rose-tinted glasses as he was a true professional war-time correspondent.

Indeed he went on to canvass mistakes Monash might have made and, remember, Cutlack in various capacities had very direct contact and one on one exchanges with Monash, so was in a position to write with accuracy about him. I quote again:

> Doubtless at times he (Monash) made mistakes: if he did, they must have been fleeting, for even at this distance of time

> nobody has come forward to cite any serious mistake in the field that General Monash ever made. Certainly one of the first to admit any mistake would be the man himself. He was very proud of his work and his reputation – the letters show that – but in the daily attitude towards that work he never resented criticism.

Hardened war-time correspondents who have witnessed first-hand death and destruction, are not prone to 'bullshit writing'. They tend to call a spade a spade and Cutlack did this in clear terms. The quote above from Cutlack, an English born former serving AIF officer who then switched to the role of war correspondent at the start of 1918, therefore says a great deal.

Bean also was a great and meticulous writer but through sins mainly of omission, he created a portrait of Monash that was not completely fair or balanced.

It was obvious for those who did the fighting that Monash was a genuine hero whose personality and innovative leadership template that he continuously upgraded had done much to both shorten and win the Great War. This template and the modus operandi he embraced were very well regarded by the diggers. However, as noted, for a decade after 11 November 1918 the one bit of extra recognition that might have uplifted him further within society, in both the contemporary and traditional senses of that word – 'society' – was denied him. It was not until 1929 that he was promoted to general.

From top to bottom of big organisations, especially military ones, there exists a grapevine that rapidly transmits information and more so assessments of those who are on the way up, of who's in and who's on the way out, who can be relied on and who stuffs up, and much more. Monash had to remain well informed but was less interested in gossip as such. Since the stumble on 8 August 1915 at Gallipoli the star of Monash had continued to climb. Despite the odd sharp manoeuvre by his critics on high, notably Bean and Hughes, the Monash star was never to wane.

Chapter 15

DEVOID OF ANY VIRTUE?

Remembering the Great War

'We are assembled today to honour that day and to pledge to ourselves to keep alive the genuine spirit of ANZAC. We are not here to honour war. Those men who fought on Gallipoli hated war as we do. Because I was with them, though not privileged to be of them, I can speak with personal experience of their greatness. My role was insignificant, that of a witness. As a junior wireless operator on an Australian Naval transport which approached very close to the landing beach I witnessed the inflexible courage of those original Anzacs.

We have a duty to our fellow citizens of Australia, present and future. We have a duty to our fellowmen of other nations. We can best fulfil that twofold duty by keeping vitally alive the noble spirit of our pioneers, the spirit that actuated our servicemen and women, by living our daily life imbued with the spirit of ANZAC.'

(His Eminence, Cardinal Norman Gilroy, Archbishop of Sydney and wireless operator at Gallipoli. Anzac Day Official Service Commemorative Address, Sydney 1963.)

Flowing from the dynamics of the Great War there were major geo-political objectives obtained for the free world including two of direct substance for Australia. In addition there were many improvements with aviation and communication technology which, if they were going to happen anyhow, were accelerated by the war. It was of particular virtue and advantage for Australia, given the tyranny of distance, that these aviation and communication steps were taken more quickly.

Conversely some claim that the Great War was bereft of any virtue and elements of the broad left have over the years made a point of decrying war, even decrying Anzac Day, that 'one day of the year'. They have especially railed against the death toll of World War One, and fair enough, but that massive death toll on both sides does not mean nothing good or even virtuous took place between 1914 and 1919.

It is timely to discuss a viewpoint, bandied around again in 2013 by the former ALP prime minister (1991–1996) Paul Keating. Keating was and continues to be adroit at producing the colourful phrase and the absolute put-down. He pronounced emphatically in late 2013: 'The first world war was a war devoid of any virtue. It arose from the quagmire of European tribalism. A complex interplay of nation-state destinies overlaid by notions of cultural security peppered with racism.'

Was there not virtue in the actions of Simpson with his donkey, and others, right through to Monash ensuring maximum protection of the soldiers and care of the wounded soldiers in battle? Alternatively at the other end of the scale was there not virtue in the bolstering of Belgium and France so that they were unambiguously democratic, especially in light of the subsequent rise of fascism and communism?

The Keating statement is an ill-considered sweeping dictum that denies the small and large gains that did come about from individual and collective action in World War One for Australia and the Allies; indeed for the free world. There was considerable virtue observed in the deeds of men and women, standing in sharp contrast to the agony and brutality of the Great War but engendered in part by the very dynamic of war.

All of this is not to glorify war and all of this is notwithstanding the sacrifice of 61,000 Australian Anzac lives with many more wounded, the military death toll of ten million and the overall death toll of thirty-seven million people.

There were countless acts of enormous virtue at the individual level, including the acts detailed in the many Victoria Cross citations. There were over sixty Australian Victoria Cross recipients arising from service in World War One, and nine from Gallipoli alone. There were many other awards for bravery and valour made throughout the four long years. The Keating statement of World War One being devoid of any virtue belittles the acts of valour in the Great War and the leadership virtues of many in positions of command and government.

In any case there were other positive outcomes from World War One, as alluded to at the start of this chapter. There were gains in the area of strategic management practice on a large scale and gains in health care and health research, I accept at a cost.

Let us examine the Australian advantages gained. Germany was banished from Papua New Guinea in the first real conquest of 1914, Australia's victory and capture of Rabaul and the New Guinea German colony. In due course after the 1919 Treaty of Versailles Australian hegemony over Papua New Guinea was affirmed.

Arguably, but for World War One Japan, via its Axis liaison arrangements, would have had a huge stepping stone to Australia in eastern Papua New Guinea. It would have used this stepping stone to advantage. Kokoda would have been bypassed and the Battle of the Coral Sea would most likely have tilted towards the Japanese.

While such speculations can only be taken so far, because World War Two was in some ways a product of World War One and the treaty of Versailles, if Japan had had free and full use of the New Guinea ports and hinterland from the inception of World War Two, then it is reasonable to assume the chances of a full-on land invasion of Australia via Cooktown, Cairns and Townsville would have been very high. Due to World War One, however, New Guinea was lost to Germany forever and, as it happened, would be anything but an easy invasion stepping stone for Japan.

Brave New Zealand in the first month of World War One occupied strategic Samoa, formally lowering the German flag and raising the New Zealand flag without casualties. Again, a German-occupied Samoa in the 1930s would have greatly helped Japan.

Likewise, around the Indian Ocean, the banishment of Greater Germany from the east coast of the African continent, due to the early success of South African general and later field marshal Jan Smuts, in capturing German colonies and outposts, ensured a less perilous situation across that vital ocean in World War Two. Australia's sea channels to and from Europe were never completely safe in either world war but they were much safer than would have been the case if the huge ports of the east coast of Africa were held by Germany through the 1930s and into World War Two. The well-located port at Dar Es Salaam, now in Tanzania, would have been an extremely useful Indian Ocean base for the German 'blue water' navy.

Of course it is the case that if Germany and the kaiser and Hindenburg could have been brought to heel by diplomatic means in that uneasy month of July 1914, when many Europeans at senior levels had gone on their usual summer holidays and the big capital cities of Europe were empty, millions of lives would have been saved but, once hostilities commenced, it was necessary to follow through. Clearly the Allies had been too often inept in the early stages of the Great War but, after false starts, eventually the tide was turned.

Keating is a take-no-prisoner type of advocate, as he attacks everything from any nation-building dimension associated with Gallipoli to nation states responding to the extreme militarism of Germany. It is an arrogant Keating who announces he has never been to Gallipoli and he never will, and only Keating can answer why he wants to pour acid on the huge wounds from World War One that do continue – by degrees – to this day. Only Keating can answer why he does not recognise some true advances arising for Australia and for free-world civilisation from the defeat of the path of extreme militarism emanating from the then non-democratic Germany.

From 1919 right through to 2014 reflections and statements on the Great War have continued from prime minister after prime minister, from retired generals and even retired ambassadors and ex-deputy prime ministers. This is a good thing, that seminal events of the last century continue to be examined in detail in the next century. The writings of Monash during and after World War One helped mount this ongoing examination. The direct contribution of Monash points to the second specific dimension of Australian gain from the Great War.

Suffice to say, Australia gained a cohort of leaders who survived both Gallipoli and the Western Front, that were second to none.

There were forty-two leaders singled out at the beginning of this book, and more, who became high-achievers in so many areas where Australia desperately needed leadership, who performed and lifted productivity, boosted the economy and helped Australia remain a progressive democracy.

Take the area of aviation. Hudson Fysh was at Gallipoli and returned to Australia with a bunch of other pioneer aviators, including George Jones, Ross MacPherson Smith, Kingsford Smith and Charles Ulm. They pushed the boundaries and in the case of Hudson Fysh helped start the Qantas domestic airline serving Queensland and Northern Territory, later becoming the Australian international flag-carrying airline providing links to Africa, Asia, Europe, South and North America.

George Jones went on to become RAAF commanding officer for part of World War Two and pushed aviation and especially the RAAF along as it graduated from the fledging role of Australian Flying Corps in World War One. These were motivated people who contributed much in a creative way.

In business and politics, many Gallipoli veterans stepped up and went to the top: Lord Richard Casey as ambassador, last governor of Bengal, and Australian governor-general; SM Bruce as prime minister 1923 to 1929 and later Australian high commissioner in London during World War Two, staying for the Battle of London and the blitz, initiating many plans to assist the diggers coming through London; Hubert Anthony, William Bolton, Pompey Elliott, Harry Foll, John Gellibrand, Thomas Glasgow, Neville Howse and Granville Ryrie all served bravely at Gallipoli and through World War One, all won election to the federal parliament and most of them went on to be capable federal ministers. Arthur Blackburn and others won election to state parliaments.

Seared by Gallipoli and the experience of the Western Front or the Middle East, these people all elected to try to make a better world, to achieve and make huge contributions to the wellbeing of the fledging nation of Australia; in part no doubt as a mark of respect to their deceased colleagues. They as survivors of the slaughter fields of the Great War decided not to be whingers and layabouts but to step up and deliver.

The counter argument is that after one in five of the rising generation had been killed in action or died of wounds there were many vacancies to be filled and even a B team of leaders would have succeeded and delivered by degrees. Yet no other country had so many of the survivors of a major battle step up as pioneer aviators, ministers and senators. The Anzac spirit was imbued or embedded and it seemed to help so many to cope with the trauma of war and to deliver.

Cardinal Gilroy in his Anzac Address of 1963 reminded all of the existence of this Anzac spirit of looking after your mates and looking after your country, in part to salute those lying buried in Flanders and Gallipoli and Jerusalem.

Finally in this leadership cohort we can consider again Monash, who after being an engineer and general of genius, went on to manage the creation of the huge State Electricity Commission (SEC) in Victoria and provide a steadying influence during the dark days of turmoil at the start of the Great Depression, when Australia could have degenerated into some form of civil war (with Scullin and the feds on one side and New South Wales Premier Jack Lang on the other) and a fascist dictatorial form of government.

It was Monash and his cohort who quickly dealt with a Victorian police strike, when asked to do so in 1923, within existing laws and, in the process, quickly bringing the serious situation under control.

So Australia gained on the geo-political front, notably in New Guinea, but also gained on the leadership front, from the Great War. The free world gained from the Great War an immediate end to Prussian German militarism, at least for twenty years.

If pan-continental Europe, excepting Spain, was dominated by panzer divisions and Germany outright in 1919, following a defeat of the Allies, a one-bloc non-democratic continental Europe would have been ripe for the picking by Hitler-type fascists or Stalin's Communists. It would have been a lonely path for Great Britain and there would have been ongoing threats to the vital shipping lanes to and from Great Britain.

It was the British and US commitment to freedom for continental Europe in the Great War that set a pattern which did help ensure Belgium and France, as well as Holland and one or two others, were or became democracies. Of course this path was also helped by Australia, Canada, India, South Africa and others participating against the Axis and later the Nazis.

Poland is the standout case in this regard. Recreated under Point 13 of the Woodrow Wilson Plan taken to Versailles, it emerged as the Second Polish Republic and a nation state that sought and obtained further treaties, including the Warsaw Treaty of 1920. However Lenin sent the emerging Red Army in to invade Poland and spread communism as part of his planned World Socialist Order.

The Polish-Russian War of 1919–1921 was pivotal as Poland heavily defeated and repulsed the Red Army. It was back to the drawing board for Lenin and Poland began to develop its sheet-anchor role in Eastern Europe. This was snuffed out in 1939 by the Nazi Germans and in 1945 by Stalin's Russians but emerged again triumphantly in 1989, as the Third Polish Republic, helped along by a member of the Polish diaspora, his name Pope John Paul II.

Today Poland remains a sheet anchor of stability and progress in Eastern Europe. It is deserving of more credit and, equally, more recognition should be given to this vital building block, flowing from this one particular aspect of virtue relating to the Great War, the relaunch of Poland at a critical juncture of the twentieth century. Dare I say, had it not been relaunched immediately post Versailles, Poland may never have emerged again.

While many mistakes were made by the Allies, the Great War delivered advantage and virtuous dimensions of life to both Australia and the free or democratic world. The sheer relief that the Great War was over meant some celebration and some attempt to quickly get back to normal, but it was a new normal as the community and society were never going to be exactly the same again.

Chapter 16

A WAY OF SAYING 'THANKS'

Field Marshals, British and Otherwise

> 'On every side Field Marshals gleamed, small beer were Lords Lieutenant deemed.'
>
> (WS Gilbert from the libretto of the Gilbert and Sullivan Opera *The Gondoliers*.)

In July 1919 King George V made a very symbolic move in salute to four outstanding military leaders from World War One. That month four field marshals were created: Allenby, Plumer, Wilson and the French leader Ferdinand Foch, promoted a British field marshal. Had he been a four star general by then, it is more than possible that the king would have promoted Monash, of Jerilderie and Melbourne, Gallipoli and Hamel, one step up in rank to field marshal.

The field marshal rank had been created by King George II at the start of 1736 with the first Earl of Orkney, George Hamilton, and the second Duke of Argyll and Duke of Greenwich, John Campbell, made field marshals in January that year. The rank had started out as the fiefdom and initiative of the reigning Monarch but as the office of prime minister emerged in the UK, so the reigning Monarch's areas of absolute initiative were reduced.

Still King George V was in his stride in 1919 and able to hold sway and in consultation with Number 10 Downing Street, in the month of July 1919, he was able to promote four to the rank and with that action affirmed the use of the rank to recognise the service of non-British people to the realm of Great Britain. There was no set quota or limitation with regard to who could attain the rank of field marshal.

The creation of Marshal Ferdinand Foch as a British field marshal did not raise eyebrows, as over the centuries many leading foreigners had been created British field marshals. It was a way of saying 'thanks' for extraordinary services but also a way of conferring very special recognition for all recipients. As history unfolded in the twentieth century it became evident that some choices were not so wise. Even leaders of countries that were later to become enemies and attack Great Britain did so notwithstanding that they had been given the rank of British field marshal.

Still, for the military minded, field marshal was the ultimate rank that could be conferred in Great Britain and Commonwealth countries and was conferred as the reigning Monarch and Number 10 Downing Street saw fit.

In the first 250 years since the creation of the field marshal rank by King George II more than 10 per cent have been granted to non-British recipients but normally with some connection to the Royal family on the British throne. The rank has been used to confer honour and salute service, to build linkages in particular parts of the World, and for a period it was awarded to the most senior British military person of the day.

French and Irish born people who have effectively migrated to Britain and built their careers in the British Army were the first to break down the 'Englishness' of the position of field marshal. Perhaps the quintessential and ultimate field marshal over the centuries was born in Dublin on 1 May 1769. He was baptised Arthur Wesley but with the olde nomenclature and spelling applied, Arthur Wellesley. He was more famously known as the first Duke of Wellington, enormously popular after winning the Battle of Waterloo against Napoleon but not so popular as a somewhat distant prime minister.

Outright precedents for foreigners being made British field marshals are many: two kings of Belgium, namely Leopold I and Albert I, several Germans including Kaiser Wilhelm II himself, created by presumably his uncle, the new King Edward VII, on 27 January 1901, just a few days after the death of the kaiser's grandmother Queen Victoria.

Two kings of Nepal (Mahendra and Birenda), one king of the Netherlands (William II), two Japanese emperors and one Russian czar, the last ever czar, Nicholas II, were created field marshals by the British as part of their empire wheeling and dealing.

The two more relevant precedents are those of General Jan Smuts, OM CH, DTD, who was made a field marshal on 24 May 1941 during the dark days of World War Two. He was a giant of a man in so many ways and held in high regard in so many countries and by many key leaders of the period, including Winston Churchill.

Sir Thomas Blamey GBE, KCB, CMG, DSO, of Wagga Wagga, was born at Lake Albert on the south east side of Wagga Wagga and lived from 1884 to 1951. Blamey came from very humble circumstances, one of seven children of a small farmer and Riverina cattle drover. By dint of very hard work he drove his military career forward after a period in the school cadets, eventually being sent as a captain to Quetta Staff College where he trained for two years, over 1912 and 1913. He joined the First Division AIF and landed at Gallipoli on day one of that campaign. Later in World War One he moved to the Western Front and in May 1918 he became chief of staff to Monash.

Many historians credit Blamey with a good deal of the groundwork and staff work that led to the Monash success at Hamel on 4 July 1918 and then the follow up successes through to Armistice. Clearly Blamey played a role, especially in urging the use of artillery in a strong way at Hamel, but Monash as overall commander of the Australian Army Corps was calling the shots and making the big decisions.

After World War One, Blamey served for a period as Commissioner of the Victorian State Police Force, in which capacity he was invited each 8 August to attend dinner at 'Iona', hosted by Monash, in salute of the battle of Amiens or Greater Amiens.

Monash always thanked and praised Blamey for his support and key role and this was reciprocated though Blamey had a certain edge to his way of relating to others, not so much of steel but of jagged lead.

In World War Two he broke the Australian Government rule by having his wife Lady Olga Blamey come and live at Cairo, saying it was necessary in his role as deputy commander in chief of the Middle East, under initially Sir Archibald Wavell and later Sir Claude Auchinleck. Both Wavell and Auchinleck were made field marshals for services rendered but Blamey clashed with Auchinleck over Tobruk, where the Australians had helped to give the Nazis their first bloody nose of World War Two.

Blamey was ordered back to Australia, made commander in chief of Australian Military Forces and embarked on the tough war campaigns in Papua New Guinea. It was here that certain disparaging remarks regarding the fighting commitment of the Australian soldiers along the Kokoda Trail or Track in Papua New Guinea later created much controversy. He also had an awkward, distant relationship with the overall commander, based for a period at headquarters in Brisbane, General Douglas MacArthur. Eventually after a career in two world wars Blamey retired from military service in early 1946 and, as mentioned, was made a field marshal in mid-1950, backdated to 1 January that year.

The rank lives on as in mid-2012 a retired UK chief of the defence staff was made an honorary field marshal, namely Field Marshal Charles Ronald Llewelyn Guthrie, Baron Guthrie of Craigiebank GCB LVO OBE DLI. At the time of writing he continues to be an outspoken member of the House of Lords and, on occasion, wears his field marshal uniform.

Here I pose the question: If Monash is posthumously made a field marshal, what then would become of the standing of Field Marshal Blamey? The Blamey critics would say 'No harm done', as if the Monash award was backdated to 11 November 1930 then Blamey would remain a field marshal but in fact would be Australia's second field marshal.

Most historians would concede that Monash was by far the superior general for the period he was on deck than Blamey ever was, so I say also, 'No harm done'.

Blamey was a solid staff officer but it has to be said he was never an innovative general of the calibre of Monash.

As can be seen, precedents abound with regard to 'foreign' personnel of various standing receiving the rank of field marshal. Arguably if in fact the posthumous Monash promotion went ahead it would be as an Australian field marshal, following changes made in 1972, but it could be denoted a British field marshal with approval from London or it could in fact be both. I favour it being denoted as: Australian Field Marshal Sir John Monash, recommended by the prime minister or passed by Parliament, announced and implemented formally by the governor-general and commander in chief, representing the queen of Australia.

Over the centuries, various armies have promoted dead soldiers and officers with an increase in rank, along with awarding dead soldiers and officers various awards for heroism and valour, including the greatest bravery award of them all in the British and Australian context, the Victoria Cross. In short there is absolute precedent for action by Commonwealth governments to provide both one step in rank promotion and the formal recognition for outstanding bravery, posthumously.

To reiterate, there are two issues here: posthumous rank promotion and posthumous valour recognition. For the record at no stage do I commend Monash for any kind of valour recognition, although in any fair surmise, Monash must have gone very close to winning a Military Cross or a heroic award around that level.

I simply do not contend that there is sufficient evidence to say Monash was cheated out of a Military Cross or other bravery award, but he was certainly kept one step in rank below where he should have been immediately after World War One. This view is firmly based on all that is known to have transpired post Armistice Day 1918. Monash was wronged by both Bean and Hughes.

The question of making awards and promotions posthumously and distinguishing the question of rank from valour is straightforward. Now if a person is alive when the decision is made to grant rank promotion or a heroic award but by the time the news and application of the promotion or award reaches the recipient, he or she is dead, then it becomes obviously posthumous.

This is all the more so if the person is already dead at the moment of formulating and granting the promotion, back at HQ, as well as actually when the news is received in the field. As mentioned, in the case of George Washington, he had been dead for over 150 years when the White House decided and effected the promotion of one step in rank in 1976, on the 200th anniversary of the US Declaration of Independence and the related War of Independence between Great Britain and the USA. Congress and the White House ensured that in making the promotion in 1976, George Washington could never ever be outranked.

So in 1976, some 176 years after his death, George Washington became officially a 'General of the Armies' or field marshal equivalent, when previously he had been merely a general and of course president of the USA.

This is a clear-cut precedent and a deliberate promotion in salute of outstanding long ago service to the cause and to the fledging nation of the USA.

The French had a system entrenching posthumous rank promotion, by way of the granting of the promotion and title of marshal, on death. It is a concept that might have grown out of the French Foreign Legion but it is a system that continues to this day. However France also has some very specific examples of posthumous promotion, seven in total including two rising from the first Battle of the Marne in World War One. Marshals Joseph Galliene and Michel-Joseph Maunoury were promoted to the rank of marshal after their deaths, though it should be noted that marshal in France is not so much a rank as an award for 'National dignity and honour'.

The British and other armies have a more sparing application of posthumous rank promotion. In the 1760s British major Thomas Adams, who gave outstanding service in putting down a rebellion in and around Calcutta, or more recently Kolkata, was knowingly by the powers that be in London at the time, posthumously promoted to brigadier.

In all of this there was no huge jump in rank but in the main just one step in rank. Through thick and thin, rank was always applied through the well ordained one step stages that have existed for centuries, with few exceptions. Of course one area of exception relates to Monarchs and Royal consorts often being promoted to field marshal on the death of the previous ruler and so their ascent to the throne. It can and has applied also to consorts on their spouse ascending to the throne.

On valour more often the decision to award was done further up the chain and sometimes it took a long period for the award to become known in the battle field. One classic example is from the Zulu Wars in South Africa when a poor young Irishman lieutenant, Neville Coghill, had been dead twenty-eight years before his Victoria Cross award was announced and given.

The truth of the matter is posthumous bravery awards and posthumous promotions have been around for decades, on both sides of the Atlantic Ocean.

Promote Monash and you add further cement to the fact his actions were not in vain and were not bereft of virtue. This is not a driving argument in favour of posthumously promoting Monash but it is a useful bonus from doing so, a bonus that would answer those who would rip up the very real achievements on the Western front that added to the fabric of many nations, including Australia, Belgium, Canada, South Africa and the USA as well as Great Britain.

Rank matters. The ranking of nations matters as well. And in essence it was countries with a deep commitment to democracy that did over the Axis powers. As Monash wrote to a relative at the outset, Australia had 'to help the Empire to crush a peril which may mean the end of Australia as a free country'. If the then militaristic Germany had won World War One who knows how Australia and New Zealand would have emerged.

At the end of the day, a nation is only as good as the care it provides for its citizens, especially the less well-off citizens, as has been said elsewhere. In another sense, citizens past, present and future deserve the best the 'Magna Carta' and the nation's democracy can deliver.

Dreyfus was cheated upon by France, resulting in bitter divisions that echo to this day. Brilliant US secretary of defence under Kennedy and Johnson, namely Robert McNamara, cheated upon Vietnam veterans generally, as he admitted in his autobiography, by extending that war and he also cheated upon the thirty-four sailors of the USS *Liberty*, killed on the fourth day of the Six-Day War in 1967, as mentioned.

One hundred years ago, John Monash was cheated upon by several powerful individuals in the hierarchy of Australia and robbed of rank. Now is the time to ponder the very best way this might be rectified.

Chapter 17

THE FIELD MARSHAL RANK

Giving John Monash His Due

'He should be a field marshal.'

(Hon Joe Hockey, future federal treasurer, speaking in the House of Representatives about John Monash, 24 November 2008.)

It is not possible to examine all those who might have been improperly overlooked for promotion within the Australian army, let alone other Allied armies, within one book. However, all things considered, there was an overwhelming case for Monash to be promoted to the rank of general from the rank of lieutenant general in December 1918, or at the latest in the first quarter of 1919 when he had become established in the pivotal position of director-general of Repatriation and Demobilisation, based in London.

In turn had he been a general prior to July 1919 there was a good chance that King George V might have promoted Monash to field marshal when he promoted four others in that month, some seven months after the Armistice Day and the end of World War One. If not, then as we learnt in a previous chapter, new prime minister

James Scullin was determined to promote Monash, along with Chauvel, clearly as a kind of general salute, so Monash would have almost certainly become a field marshal on 11 November 1929.

Foch and many others were promoted in the immediate aftermath of World War One, in the case of Foch within France but as mentioned also to the rank of British field marshal. It was a clear exception to the general rule that Monash remained frozen at lieutenant general for a full ten years after the fighting ceased on Armistice Day 1918. No other leading Western Front general was treated that way and some of those already field marshals were given cash payments and promotion to the House of Lords.

In making this statement, I do so not to advance any argument that Monash should have been promoted throughout the end phases of World War One. While in the first half of Gallipoli, Monash had been commanding a brigade as a full colonel and not a brigadier, this had no impact on his deserved promotions on the Western Front. These promotions were in accord with the size of units Monash was formally commanding. But in the final push towards the Hindenburg Line, as mentioned, he was commanding very large numbers.

However to make it clear and in order that the purist military historian brigade and the successors to the Bean Club of history do not have an easy target, I reiterate that Monash on the morning of 11 November 1918 held – broadly speaking – the correct rank (lieutenant general) as he drove eastwards towards the border between France and Germany.

And at no stage would I ever support posthumous promotion of more than one step in rank. This in a sense precludes opening the floodgates and knocks on the head potential campaigns for others that come to mind, such as Lawrence of Arabia. To give an idea of what a mighty brake the one step in rank limitation constitutes, lifting Lawrence from colonel to field marshal would be no less than five steps in rank. This will likely never be done by the British Government or Buckingham Palace, and certainly not while Prince Philip, the Duke of Edinburgh and field marshal of six decades, is still around.

The British Government has gradually reduced the use of the rank of field marshal since World War Two and since pulling out of operations east of Suez. At one stage the chief of the imperial general staff and the chief of the defence staff would both receive promotion to five star for the last period of their term as the overall UK Army commander. By 1961 the great General Festing received promotion to field marshal for a year or so while CIGS before retirement.

Monash is deserving of the field marshal rank for a host of negative reasons – correcting the discrimination he suffered, as canvassed – but also for two very clear-cut positive reasons. Firstly it would be a salute indirectly to every member of the AIF who went to World War One, with 61,000 of them never to return. Yes it is a kind of symbolism and reflected glory but as Monash said time and time again, his knighthoods and all other accolades and awards he owed to the members of the AIF. In further saluting Monash as ultimate commander of the Australian Army Corps the great work of the men and women of the AIF would be acknowledged by a grateful nation, on the occasion of the centenary of Gallipoli and many aspects of World War One.

This would also help make up for the hundreds of occasions when the brave exploits of the Anzac diggers were tucked away in reports that simply led with the terminology 'British Expeditionary

Force' and made no mention whatsoever that any Australians or New Zealanders were ever involved. The long lists of killed in action (KIA) and wounded in action (WIA), usually published on the front pages of country newspapers and in the capital city newspapers, were the stark reminder that the diggers were there.

It would also help crack open and expose the tilt associated with much of the early-written history of World War One that underplays the heavy lifting of Australia, New Zealand and Canada on the Western Front, especially throughout 1918. The version laid down by American and British historians and governmental leaders of the era too often simply overlooked the role of the colonial forces.

Secondly, this posthumous award would be a properly appropriate recognition of one truly great Australian, namely John Monash of Jerilderie and Melbourne, Gallipoli and Hamel. Most who study military history in detail, including the purists, concede that Monash was our greatest general to date.

Prime Minister Tony Abbott spoke at the Melbourne Shrine of Remembrance on 17 April 2014 when presenting the Monash Scholarships for 2014 and stated that Monash was our greatest genius general and a man of substance who changed the world. He added that as the centenary of World War One approached, it was desirable and necessary to recognise our victories on the Western Front as well as our defeat at Gallipoli.

Recognising Monash by posthumous promotion would salute all that he did for Australia, including his decisive stand in 1931 to decline to lead a coup against the governments and parliaments of the day and set up a kind of fascist or limited dictatorship. Yes you could build a decent monument for Monash in Jerilderie, in Melbourne and Hamel, if not on top of Mont St Quentin, however it is the bold step of posthumous promotion that would ensure all Australians took another look at this incredible person.

For the record a few years ago, just near Hamel, a large image of Monash was erected. It lasted less than a decade and was pulled down as it had deteriorated rapidly in the harsh winter climate of the area, to the extent that some thought Monash in the statue bore a resemblance to Hitler. So the Australian Government and relevant Departments, having failed to recognise Monash in a meaningful way after 11 November 1918, added insult to injury when they made an attempt to do so on French soil.

There will be those who say this is all about war mongering and worshipping those generals of yesteryear who were involved in bloody battles that merely ended up a dress rehearsal for World War Two, really gaining nothing long-term for the world. In the case of Monash, this is patently unfair as he had consciously declined to step up for the Boer War, he was a citizen or militia soldier/officer and he did not have any sway at Versailles. It was the political class of the era on the Allied side that made a mess of things at Versailles.

The fact that World War One did have some virtue is dealt with elsewhere. Meanwhile having stated the two overall positive reasons, it is also worth reviewing the several key wrongs that would be reversed in posthumously promoting Monash.

Firstly the years of discrimination directed at Monash as a Jew of Prussian descent, the subtle and not so subtle criticisms and put downs that Monash had to bear, would be corrected in one decisive stroke. The extraordinary Indigenous Lovett family, that had four brothers serve in the world wars, was hugely discriminated against upon their return, essentially because they were blacks. Moves are now being made to better recognise this family in Canberra and elsewhere. Likewise Monash was discriminated against because he was a Jew and this is overdue for correction.

Secondly there were the derogatory references to him being too old, a form of age discrimination. Thirdly there was also the fact he was a colonial, a militia soldier and officer and of course not Duntroon or Sandhurst at any stage in his training, as mentioned. Again posthumous promotion in one sweep would rectify and as much as is possible reverse all of this.

Monash deserves this extra salute, inexpensive but absolutely timely and, when it happens, twelve field marshal replica batons might be produced and numbered. These would be best allocated one each to the Jerilderie Council, Melbourne's Shrine of Remembrance, the Australian War Memorial Canberra (to help them make up for lost decades in the portrayal of Monash), one for Hamel, France, Parliament House Victoria and Parliament House Canberra, the General Sir John Monash Scholarship Foundation HQ, Monash's secondary schooling alma mater Scotch College, the Bennett family of Monash descendants, Melbourne University and Monash University, and finally the twelfth should be held in readiness for the re-opening of the Mt Buffalo Chalet, the location that Monash loved and in a sense from which he departed to the Great War. This last might be held in the meantime at the Bright Railway Station Museum.

The original baton should be the preserve of the Australian Army. It should do the rounds of the various training units and otherwise be held at Army HQ or the various Victoria Barracks on rotation. I reiterate there should be twelve only numbered replicas, as a mark of respect perhaps for the twelve decades since Monash gained serious command in the Army and later sailed from Melbourne and Albany into the Great War and the history books forever more.

On 11 November 2013, Field Marshal Prince Philip attended the 2013 Armistice Day service at Menin Gate in Ypres, Belgium, wearing military uniform and with a huge overcoat. Prince Philip was as ever very sprightly in his saluting and commitment, at age ninety-two and in his sixtieth year of being a field marshal. He had clearly fully recovered from some recent illnesses.

In the antipodes on the same day, the newly elected prime minister Tony Abbott along with most MPs and senators attended Remembrance Day services around Australia, prior to going to Canberra for the opening of the new forty-fourth Parliament after the 7 September federal elections. The new prime minister laid a wreath at the huge shrine in Melbourne which Monash had created. The Victorian state governor gave an uplifting speech on the occasion, along the lines of 'Lest we forget'.

The media covering Armistice Day or Remembrance Day in both Australia and Europe had a major focus on World War One, reflecting the fact that the centenaries of World War One are, at the time of writing, drawing near. There were also a number of op-ed articles and interviews relating to World War One, including one by Prime Minister Tony Abbott, who suggested that the 'genius' of General Sir John Monash was under recognised. This accords with recent endeavours of many to boost the focus on the Western Front and not just have a focus on Gallipoli with regard to World War One.

Earlier in the year, on Anzac Day 2013, an article appeared in *The Australian* by Josh Frydenberg, Liberal MP for Kooyong. It was a well-argued treatise that effectively relaunched the idea of posthumous promotion of Monash, four years after I had originally floated the idea in a lecture at the Sydney Institute on Remembrance

Day, 2008. I am not aware of any other detailed propositions for key posthumous promotions in the Australian context.

On the Sydney Institute occasion I had gone head to head with a historian, Professor Jeffrey Grey, who described the idea, as I recall vividly, as being 'somewhat silly'. His arguments were centred on Monash holding more or less the correct rank for the units he was commanding, especially in 1918. He also argued that history cannot be altered retrospectively. On the first argument there was no argument as I agreed and have previously stated: Monash did hold the correct rank through to 11 November 1918.

I would interpose though that for periods of the second half of 1918, as Peter Pedersen and a few discerning military historians have highlighted, Monash was commanding numbers way above his then rank of lieutenant general in his role as head of the Australian Army Corps. Many extra units had been placed under his command, including for the Battle of Amiens on 8 August 1918.

On the second argument, again I agree that history cannot be altered but you can alter the designation and portrayal of history and specific events. There are many examples of ferocious onward debate over the portrayal of well documented events. To cite just one, the debate goes on and on with regard to the designation of the Armenian slaughter by Turkey after World War One. It is an explosive issue to this day.

As mentioned earlier there is also the little known USS *Liberty* saga. In 1967 Israeli forces attacked the USS *Liberty*, killing thirty-four US sailors. Israel apologised and did the right thing, paying reparations, but it was the USA that restricted the official investigation as demonstrated by the statements of Official Investigator Ward Boston Junior. There was a cover up, the USS *Liberty* story was airbrushed out of history, and brave sailors were virtually ignored by Washington. The USS *Liberty*, with gaping holes in its hull above surface level, limped back to Malta, where it was hidden away and shrouded in secrecy.

This has ramifications to this day in the Middle East policy imbalance of the USA. In short, the USA would have been more even-handed in dealing with the Middle East if every US college student over the last four decades knew, as a matter of course, that thirty-four US sailors had been killed by the Israeli Defence Force, deliberately in the view of Dean Rusk (US secretary of state 1961–1969), accidentally in the view of Robert McNamara (US secretary of defence, 1961–1968).

The accurate portrayal of history is an ongoing quest. While the facts of history cannot be altered, key players can have their roles reviewed and designations recalibrated. In the interests of accuracy and understanding, it is a powerful quest that should never be overlooked. Google 'Ward Boston Junior' and you will read the truth about the USS *Liberty*. Google 'World War One casualties' and absorb the shocking statistics.

However recalibrating the portrayal of events in history cannot be simply imposed from above and is best driven from the bottom up and so this is the chance for you to be involved, should you wish to be, in the cause of recalibrating the designation of Monash. This would best be through the implementation of an official posthumous promotion to the rank of field marshal. If you agree with the proposition then step up for the cause and help make it happen. (See Appendix A.)

One last question: Would old man John Monash, of Jerilderie and Melbourne, Gallipoli and Hamel, agree with the proposition of his posthumous promotion? As a salute to all members of the AIF then

I think he would agree, but I leave the last word to Monash himself. He wrote about this subject indirectly on the Anzac Cove beach at Gallipoli on 20 May 1915:

> I desire to bring under special notice, for favour of transmission to the proper authority, the case of Private Simpson, stated to belong to C section of the 3rd Field ambulance. This man has been working in this valley since April 26th, in collecting the wounded, and carrying them to the dressing station – he had a small donkey which he uses to carry all cases unable to walk.
>
> Private Simpson and his little beast earned the admiration of everyone at the upper end of the valley. Simpson knew no fear, and moved unconcernedly amid shrapnel and rifle fire, steadily carrying out his self-imposed task day by day, and he frequently earned the applause of the personnel for his many fearless rescues of wounded men. Simpson and his donkey were yesterday killed by a shrapnel shell.

Monash was seeking some form of posthumous recognition with this nomination and salute to the very brave Simpson and his donkey to which I would conclude: Amen.

Meanwhile, the legend and memory of 'Maestro John Monash' stands tall today, as it did in 1929 when he was eventually made a full four star general, but the genius of Monash would stand even taller if he was deservedly posthumously promoted one step in rank to field marshal.

POSTSCRIPT AND CONCLUDING COMMENTS

'This is not peace, it is an armistice for twenty years'.

(Ferdinand Foch commenting presciently, in mid-1919, on the terms of the Versailles Peace Treaty.)

As the decades rolled on after World War One, Foch and Clemenceau were to become revered heroes in the pantheon of French twentieth-century history, failed French commanders Joffre and Nivelle were downplayed, and Pétain went on to head Vichy France in World War Two before being tried for treason and sentenced to death in 1945. This sentence was commuted by post World War Two French president Charles de Gaulle, to life imprisonment.

Woodrow Wilson departed the White House as a crushed person, broken in spirit and broken physically after failing to persuade Congress to adopt the terms of the Versailles Peace Treaty and after Congress failed to support the League of Nations.

Pershing went on to receive many awards and lived a long life but steered clear of advising on World War Two. He died in June 1948 at the age of eighty-eight.

Lloyd George was to hold office as Liberal leader and British prime minister until 17 October 1922. In late 1918 and in 1919 he was hugely popular but gradually day-to-day politics undid him and the Liberal-Conservative coalition split. The Liberals did not return to power for decades: today Nick Clegg is Liberal leader and UK deputy prime minister in coalition with the Conservative government led by David Cameron.

Haig and Rawlinson were damned and praised over the decades. In more recent times there has been some revisionism along the lines that the 1916 Battle of the Somme was a necessary engagement despite the heavy casualties. Rawlinson remained in praise of the Australian Western Front efforts, writing in 1918 about Amiens and the black day: 'The 8th of August was as fine a feat of arms as any that this war can produce, the Canadians have done splendidly and the Aussies even better.'

Allenby, Plumer and Wilson all stood tall but, as mentioned, Wilson was cut down by assassin bullets in front of his London home in 1922. In July 1919 King George V made the quartet of Allenby, Foch, Plumer and Wilson field marshals, also as mentioned. This was a pointer to those that mattered in bringing World War One to an end in 1918 rather than letting it drift into 1919.

In this regard the decisive factor was Foch persuading Pershing to go for a 1918 victory. Needless to say Currie and Monash needed no persuading.

Some went on to play critical roles in World War Two, especially Smuts, prime minister of South Africa (twice) and field marshal, and Churchill, first lord of the admiralty (twice), prime minister and colonel. The man who grew up in New Zealand and served in many capacities, including as governor-general of New Zealand 1946 to 1952, Bernard Freyberg VC, was ultimately elevated to the House of Lords.

There was a special father and son day for Freyberg after the Allies captured Rome in June 1944. The Canadians, New Zealanders and Polish had done much of the heavy lifting but the US arrived first to take possession of the Eternal City, the Germans having fled the day before. Freyberg knew that his son, Lieutenant Paul Freyberg, had been held as a German POW south of Rome, however Paul had escaped and crept past many German guards to gain entry to the Pope's Summer Palace at Castel Gandolfo, where he was offered food and shelter.

The Rome 'Rat Line' or escape line swung into action and the famous Monsignor Hugh O'Flaherty drove up to Castel Gandolfo and entered the courtyard, hidden from the German guards outside. Paul was placed in the boot of the car and safely driven to the Vatican where he was held until Rome was freed. His father drove through Porta St Anna and collected his son from the Vatican before they repaired to the Hotel Quirinale for deserved refreshments.

Monash lived long enough to see Hughes bundled out of prime ministerial office in 1923, received promotion finally in 1929, and died in 1931. He enjoyed his grandchildren a great deal but suffered enormously when one grandson died at an early age. The Bennett family continue in Melbourne today as third-, fourth- and fifth-generation direct descendants of John and Vic Monash.

Bean was to outlive Monash by more than three decades, dying in 1968 at the age of eighty-eight. As co-foundation chair of the Australian War Memorial he did much good work but inadvertently or otherwise saw to the downplaying of the contribution of Monash. Even Chauvel received greater attention and display of his nomenclature. As noted, all eyes of those concerned for Monash's place in history will be on the new and revamped AWM World War One Gallery, due to open soon in Canberra.

Over the decades many plaques unveiled by Monash were shifted or were on buildings that later were replaced.

In November 1915 Monash sent some acorn seeds home from the Palestine Oaks at Gallipoli and this led to two oak trees growing at Hamilton and two at Geelong in the grounds of Geelong Grammar. Under a brilliant project led by Peter Whitelaw and involving the National Trust of Victoria, schools are signing up for the acorns descended from the Gallipoli oaks to be planted as part of the Anzac 100 set of initiatives. This is separate from the Lone Pine at Gallipoli and various plantings made from it.

I had the privilege of unveiling a plaque in north-east France at Le Mouquet farm, while I was deputy prime minister. The plaque was part of a number brilliantly created by Dr Ross Bastiaan, acting largely on a voluntary basis. These are narrative plaques explaining various battles on the Western Front. It was a great privilege to do the unveiling and led me to studying the Western Front in more detail. To date Monash does not feature greatly in any of these wonderful narrative plaques, even at Hamel.

The Melbourne Rotary Club remains intensely proud of its second president and on or about 8 August each year salutes Monash at a special luncheon, generally held in the Windsor Hotel. Scotch College is proud of their old boy Monash, equal dux of 1881, and have named major entrance gates 'The Monash Gates'. Both Melbourne and Monash universities remain active with regard to their Monash linkages. At Monash University there are advanced plans for a life-sized Monash statue.

Alas the Gippsland town created by Monash, Yallourn, no longer exists, due to coal mining developments, but other towns are proud of their Monash connections, including Yallourn North and most notably Jerilderie, which now has an annual Monash public lecture.

Narrandera is giving consideration to a 'National Crossroads' project that might be allocated the name 'John Monash National Crossroads', but do not hold your breath, even though for 500 metres the Sturt and Newell highways are on the same roadway. All Brisbane-Melbourne traffic and all Adelaide-Sydney traffic using those highways are joined for half a kilometre among nice river gums just south of the Murrumbidgee River but to date no flag pole can be sighted near this section of joint thoroughfare.

When former Victorian State Premier Ted Baillieu was asked to launch in Melbourne the new three-volume *Cambridge History of The First World War*, in Anzac week 2014, he was forced to choke on his words as he highlighted that in the three large volumes and some seventy chapters there was not one mention of John Monash and barely a mention of Canadian Arthur Currie.

On this absence alone it would be possible to rest my case.

Finally, while momentum in the media builds for a more balanced consideration of all aspects of World War One, including the contribution of Monash, it is the prime minister and the Commonwealth Government of Australia, as well as the Australian Federal Parliament, that together are the key to the question of posthumous promotion of Monash, one step in rank to field marshal. Watch this space.

APPENDICES

APPENDIX A

How to Secure Posthumous Promotion of Sir John Monash

If you seek to support the proposition of posthumous promotion of John Monash, the best approach is to make contact with your local federal MP and also with senators from your State or Territory. This is the chance for you to be involved in the cause of recalibrating the designation of Monash. This would best be through the implementation of official posthumous promotion to the rank of field marshal. If you agree with the proposition then step up for the cause and help make it happen.

Nothing will happen unless there is movement at the station, so to speak: a widespread taking up of the cause by electors across Australia and not just by particular organisations with specific interests. In a crowded public square dominated by a raft of agenda items of more immediate currency – the economy, infrastructure, national security and so forth – a somewhat abstract issue will be hard pressed to receive priority.

The need exists to seize this period to mount a campaign and override the naysayers. If ever the rank of Monash is to be upgraded then 2015 through to 2018 represents the obvious period to get it done, as it goes to the core fabric of the nation, righting a wrong for both positive and negative reasons already detailed.

Bringing this about is in your hands as readers of this book and as members of the voting public. You will need to become engaged if you want to see this happen and do so with focus and strategy. All available elements should be activated and with a sequencing that would make the 'Maestro General' himself proud.

The proposal needs to be honed and stated repeatedly along simple lines that will cut through and head-off inevitable criticisms that it will open floodgates for posthumous promotions. The proposal and objective is really all about the following and best stated with these words:

> As a salute to all members of the AIF in World War One and as a salute to Australia's greatest general and an extraordinary citizen, steps be taken to provide for the posthumous promotion of General Sir John Monash one step in rank to the rank of field marshal, effective 11 November 1930, exactly one year after he eventually became a general, in accord with the Blamey precedent, where Blamey was placed on active service for one day to allow his field marshal promotion to proceed.

In turn this should be conveyed to local federal members of the House of Representatives and to senators on both sides. This can be done by letters, emails, delegations of small groups or simply by politely accosting every MP on every occasion encountered. Emails and letters should definitely not take the form of a circularised letter but be individually drafted and reflect your own angle and thoughts on the matter.

This action detailed above will not be enough in itself so an attempt should be made to concentrate the fire so as to speak, to hit-up MPs and senators in particular months, notably early February at the start of the parliamentary sitting year, April as in the month of Anzac, July as in the month of the anniversary of the Battle of Hamel, and November as in the month of Remembrance or Armistice Day. A small group of say ten electors seeking a fifteen-minute only appointment with their local federal MP will be rarely turned down, especially if the topic of Monash is clearly stated and the request asks specifically for just fifteen minutes. MPs appreciate delegations that have focus as they are genuinely busy with much ground to cover.

Further, local RSL sub-branches or other community organisations can convene community conferences and forums and such like to discuss the issue of AIF recognition and the particular promotion proposal with regard to Monash. All this type of activity would be best done not under the umbrella of any particular political party but with a more broadly based approach.

In 2014 the South Australian Branch of the RSL unanimously passed a resolution in support of the posthumous promotion of John Monash, one step in rank to that of field marshal.

Over the decades, members of the public have turned out in large numbers for all sorts of issues, from politically loaded St Patrick's Day parades opposing conscription to rallies on climate change. Indeed on Boxing Day 1919 thousands turned out to welcome home Monash and his family. Surely then nearly 100 years on at least hundreds will step up in consideration of the Monash posthumous promotion proposal.

The other avenue for building momentum is of course via the media and in recent years there has been a renewed interest in both Monash and the Western Front, as well as the treasure trove of articles, published essays and books with regard to Gallipoli and the Anzac legend. Back on 11 November 2008, after I had spoken at the

Sydney Institute, *The Australian* published an editorial, 'Lest we ever forget', that read in part as follows:

> Prominent amongst the heroes … has been the Western Front commander of the Australians … General Sir John Monash. As Mr Fischer and others are seeking, it would do well for the … Government to promote Monash posthumously in recognition of his achievements and sheer humanity.

In federal parliament that month, in a Question Time exchange, then veterans affairs minister Alan Griffin agreed with then shadow minister Joe Hockey that Monash 'Should be a field marshal'.

This coverage sparked long-serving executive director of the Australian Defence Association, Neil James, to come out publicly against the idea, using the old argument that Monash had the correct rank through to the end of World War One, a matter about which I concur. The focus regarding Monash and rank should be as I have mentioned – repeatedly – on what happened or failed to happen, post 11 November 1918.

In 2008, the late Rusty Priest, a strong president of the NSW sub-branch of the RSL, then came forward publicly supporting posthumous promotion of Monash, arguing further that had Monash been promoted earlier on the Western Front that many Allied soldiers' lives would have been saved.

From these reports of media coverage pertaining to Monash and the Western Front at the time of the ninetieth anniversary of Remembrance Day, it is clear media interest will further build as the centenaries of the start of World War One, key battles and eventually Armistice Day 100 years on, take place or draw near.

So those interested in supporting the Monash promotion proposal should think of ways of getting traction in the media to build community interest and more positive understanding of what is involved. We live in a democracy with a 'free press' and of course now with many more avenues available, including via social media.

The tools are there to mount a campaign and go about achieving a bottom-up commitment for this long overdue promotion. Equally the naysayers will fight back for the status quo and leaving Monash at four star general. It is useful to highlight the main points that can be expected to be raised against, and reflect on them.

Firstly it will be contended the rank is effectively dormant and Australia has not had a field marshal appointed since Blamey on 1 January 1950, and even in the UK there has only been a handful in the last two decades. This is true but they do continue, including one on the Ides of March, 15 March 1994, when then CGS Sir Peter Inge was promoted to chief of the defence staff (CDS) with the five star rank, and recently Lord Guthrie in 2012. The rank has never been formally abolished.

Further the consort of the queen of Australia, namely Prince Philip, Duke of Edinburgh, remains a field marshal and will do so for the entirety of his life. The rank exists, there are people alive with the rank and in any event Charles, the Prince of Wales and or his son Prince William, in succeeding to the throne one day, will be made a field marshal. This will also be the case for Prince George (Junior), down the track, and properly so.

Secondly the contention will be that it will open the floodgates and corporals will be made colonels, and gunners will be made generals and so forth. One key limiting factor to this happening is to highlight that only one step in rank is sought and posthumous promotion should be one step in rank only. This is critical to preventing a deluge of dubious promotions. A one step in rank precedent effectively blocks such a deluge.

The temptation to break this down will be when various key centenaries associated with Winston Spencer Churchill comes around but we are already through several of these, for example the North West Frontier campaign in India, the Khartoum retaliatory raid and the Boer War when he jumped over a wall in downtown Pretoria and made it to freedom. Nobody has gained traction with the suggestion that Churchill be made a field marshal. Nevertheless a case may be made for Churchill to be made a posthumous field marshal in 2045, but it is a matter for Great Britain.

General Sir Harry Chauvel is also a possibility for consideration of field marshal rank down the track but I feel the claims for the Monash promotion are stronger. I have not finalised a view about the possible one step in rank posthumous promotion of Chauvel of Gallipoli and Palestine but he has an impressive record. It will be for others to decide in due course and one more does not constitute a stampede.

Thirdly some would argue it would be too costly but the cost would be minimal, especially if the brains trusts in charge of running the business programs of both Houses of federal parliament were cunning in scheduling debate on any 'Monash Bill' towards the end of a sitting session, such as the last sitting week in March. The lower House often has to fill in time waiting on legislation from the senate and, earlier on, vice versa.

The fourth set of objections would centre on the assertion that you cannot rewrite history or change history but you most certainly can recalibrate the portrayal of history, especially the fast and furious history generated by World War One and World War Two. I have mentioned repeatedly that I do not argue that Monash was under his correct rank or argue for any alteration of the rank of Monash during World War One, but for a symbolic and overdue gesture relating to the period post World War One.

Nothing would do more to obtain a more balanced coverage of World War One than to posthumously promote Monash. It would greatly help in the recognition of the 'genius' of Monash, a term and objective favoured by Prime Minister Tony Abbott. But it would also help put perspective into the Gallipoli-versus-the-Western Front question.

The knockers and naysayers will be plentiful but they should be challenged in polite debate and their arguments dissected and ultimately destroyed.

Again it is over to you, the reader who has read this far and finds agreement in support of the Monash proposal. Do not hesitate to be engaged and actively involved in the interests of fairness and in the interests of boosting the core fabric of the nation of Australia. The best window for completion of this posthumous promotion would be between Anzac Day eve 2015 and Anzac Day eve 2018, 2018 being the centenary year of the Battle of Hamel and the centenary of Armistice Day or Remembrance Day, to which Monash contributed so much.

At Government level there are two ways to proceed. Implementation, once agreed, could be done by simple government decree, signed off at Executive Council by the commander in chief, the governor-general of Australia, and then published in the *Government Gazette*. It would then be announced on an appropriate day, for instance high noon on Anzac eve of 2015; certainly no later than 4 July 2018. This last date would be the centenary of the battle of Hamel.

Alternatively a private member's Bill could be presented to federal parliament and passed. Again this should not be embarked on until there is a good understanding of the proposal at large and momentum has built accordingly. The proposed legislation logically would have just four simple clauses.

The first clause would be an enabling clause that so much of the Defence Act and related provisions be suspended as would preclude the provision for posthumous one step in rank promotion. This removes any objections and possible legal challenges to the validity of the proposal when enacted.

The second clause would declare that General Sir John Monash be deemed to be on active service on 11 November 1930, one year to the day after Monash had been finally promoted general. This follows closely the approach adopted by then prime minister Sir Robert Menzies in relation to Sir Thomas Blamey in 1950, after some resistance from the British War Office at that time.

The third clause would declare that Monash be promoted field marshal as of 11 November 1930. This date is chosen to emphasise the fact that it is one step in rank only and after Monash had done one full year in a sense as a four star general.

The last clause would be the standard clause that the legislation takes effect on assent of the governor-general. It is a relatively simple Bill but I affirm again it is best driven from the bottom up, hopefully with widespread support.

The title of such a private member's Bill would be something along the lines of the 'Field Marshal Sir John Monash Bill' and on its passage it would become the Field Marshal Sir John Monash Act of Parliament. The final part of implementation – if passed by both Houses of parliament – would be the signing of assent by the governor-general of the day and this would usually be at Government House, Yarralumla, but could be at a Special Meeting of the Executive Council, at the Australian War Memorial or at the Shrine of Remembrance in Melbourne.

Amongst others who might be invited to attend is one David Burke, now living in Kiama, who attended and watched the huge funeral parade of John Monash through the streets of Melbourne to Brighton Cemetry. He recently recalled that it was an unforgettable first memory; the crowds were in their thousands and in silent salute as the cortege passed to the beat of a muffled drum. Dare I conclude, it is time to unmuffle that drumbeat.

APPENDIX B

Letter from Buckingham Palace, February 2014

BUCKINGHAM PALACE

HIGH COMMISSIONERS OFFICE 20 FEB 2014

18th February, 2014.

Dear Mike,

Thank you for your letter of 6th February to Christopher Geidt regarding a request from former Deputy Prime Minister of Australia, the Hon Tim Fischer AC, to include a Buckingham Palace menu and seating plan in a book that he is writing about Field Marshal John Monash.

I am pleased to enclose copies of both the menu and seating plan from this event, which took place on 27th December 1918, and can confirm that The Queen would be content for them to be published as detailed in your letter.

With all good wishes,

Yours sincerely,

Edward

Edward Young
The Deputy Private Secretary to The Queen

H.E. the High Commissioner of Australia.

Addressed to then Australian high commissioner Mike Rann

APPENDIX C

Seating Plan Buckingham Palace Banquet, 27 December 1918

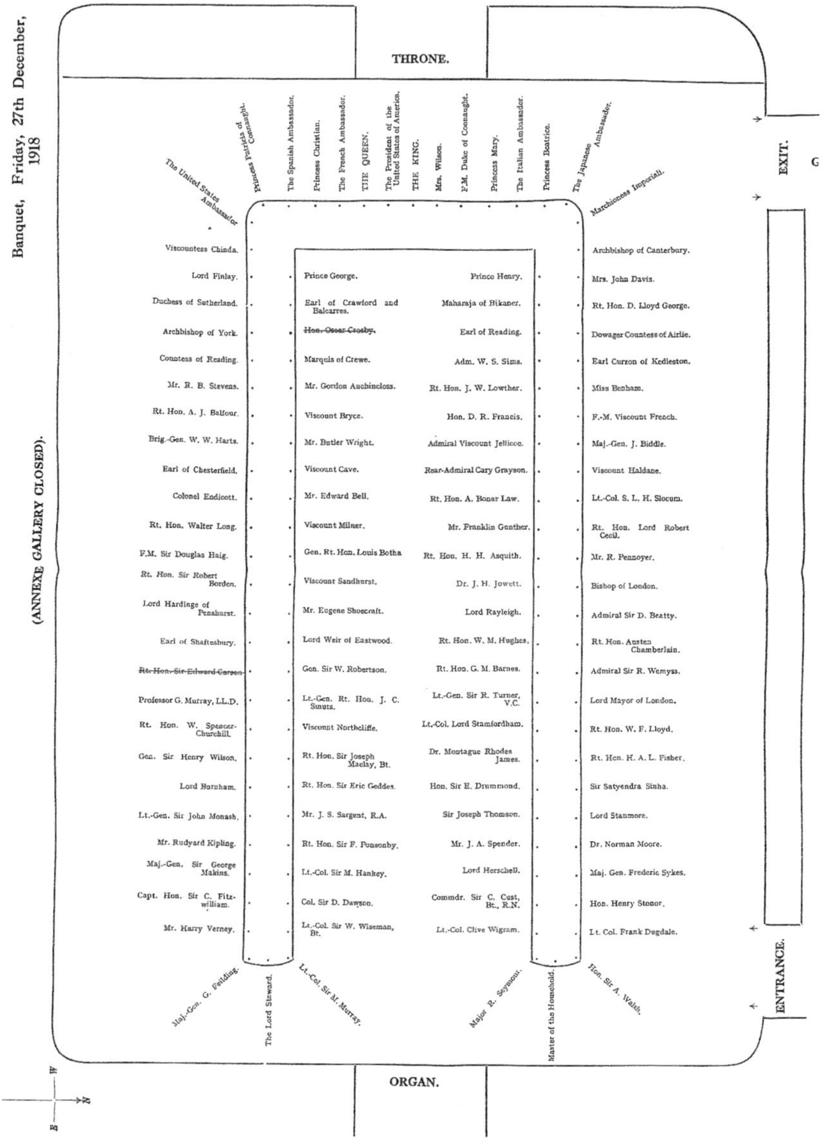

REFERENCES

A Note on Sources

My initial interest in and knowledge of the Great War sprang from studies which led to matriculation with honours in History, too many years ago, at Xavier College in Melbourne. This led to research over several decades into the Australian Imperial Force and particularly the role of General Sir John Monash. Just when I might push the subject area to one side, something would happen, such as a new book or film, that brought it all back to centre stage.

I conducted field inspections at Gallipoli and on the ground along parts of the Western Front. Nothing is better than seeing first-hand the ground and terrain that the AIF had to operate on and this I did in some detail, for example walking from the Start Line of the Battle of Hamel right through to the other side of Vaire Wood and Hamel village. Alongside I had a professional, thoughtful guide in Vic Puik, who knew exactly where the key locations were. These inspections added greatly to my formal knowledge and writings about the Great War.

I have been able to draw on my own three year stint in the Australian Army as a junior officer, serving mainly with the First Battalion, Royal Australian Regiment, 1 RAR, in Australia and Vietnam. This led to me attending various useful military history lectures but also gave me a direct understanding of Army rank structures.

Many ambassadors I encountered as Australian Rome resident ambassador to the Holy See were fountains of knowledge on twentieth-century history. There were about eighty Rome resident ambassadors in the diplomatic corps of the Holy See, or Vatican; a large number of these were from European nations and had what were for me insightful views on events of yesteryear (safer ground to canvass than asking about the current standing of particular presidents and prime ministers).

The Polish ambassador to the Holy See for over a decade in Rome, Hannah Suchocka, was a particularly sharp observer of events past, present and future. I valued her comments and responses to my queries as I came to a better understanding of Europe and especially the role of Poland over the last one hundred years.

Of the many works of reference I have drawn upon, the major biographies of Monash by Perry and Serle have been especially important.

Select Reference List

Anthony, Doug, and Margot Anthony (eds). *Letters Home: To Mother from Gallipoli and Beyond,* Allen and Unwin, St Leonards, 2009.

Australia, House of Representatives 1918–1931, *Debates.*

Bean, C.E.W. *Anzac to Amiens: A Shorter History of the Australian Fighting Services in the First World War*, Australian War Memorial Publishing, Canberra, 1952.

Beaumont, Joan. *Broken Nation: Australians in the Great War,* Allen and Unwin, Sydney, 2013.

Billett, Bill. *Mont St Quentin: A Soldier's Battle,* Rosenberg Publishing Pty Ltd, Dural, 2009.

Braga, Stuart. *Anzac Doctor: The Life of Sir Neville Howse, VC*, Hale & Iremonger, Sydney, 2000.

Churchill, Winston. *The World Crisis 1911– 1918,* Odhams Press Limited, London, 1939.

Davies, Will. *In the Footsteps of Private Lynch,* Vintage Books, New South Wales, 2008.

Davies, Will. *The Boy Colonel: Lieutenant Colonel Douglas Marks, the Youngest Battalion Commander in the AIF,* Vintage Books, New South Wales, 2013.

Dennis, Peter and Jeffrey Grey (eds), *Defining 1918 Victory: Proceedings of the Chief of Army's History Conference Held at the National Convention Centre, Canberra, 29 September 1998*, Army History Unit, Canberra, 1999.

Everitt, Nicholas. *British Secret Service during the Great War,* Hutchinson and Co., London, 1920.

Fidge, Major A.C. 'Sir John Monash – An Effective and Competent Commander?', *Geddes Papers*, Australian Command and Staff College, 2003, pp.28–35.
Fromkin, David. *Europe's Last Summer: Who Started the Great War in 1914?*, Vintage Books, New South Wales, 2005.
Faulkner, Andrew. *Arthur Blackburn VC: An Australian Hero, His Men, and their Two World Wars*, Wakefield Press, South Australia, 2008.
George, David Lloyd. *War Memoirs of David Lloyd George*, Odhams Press Limited, London 1938.
Gilbert, Martin. *Churchill,* Chancellor Press, Sydney, 1980.
Gladwin, Michael. *Captains of the Soul: A History of Australian Army Chaplains*, Big Sky Publishing, New South Wales, 2013.
Grattan, Michelle. *Back on the Wool Track,* Random House, New South Wales, 2004.
Harries, Meirion and Susie Harries. *The Last Days of Innocence: America at War 1917–1918*, Vintage, London, 1998.
Hart, Basil Lidell. *Europe in Arms*, Faber and Faber Ltd, 1937.
Hart, Basil Lidell. *Foch: Man of Orleans*, vols.1 & 2, Penguin, London, 1937.
Hart, Basil Lidell. *Reputations*, John Murray, 1928.
Hart, Basil Lidell. *The Current of War*, Hutchinson, 1941.
Hart, Basil Lidell. *The Defence of Britain*, Faber and Faber Ltd, 1939.
Hart, Basil Lidell. *The Ghost of Napoleon*, Faber and Faber Ltd, 1933.
Hart, Basil Lidell. *The Other Side of the Hill: Germany's Generals, their Rise and Fall, with their own Account of Military Events, 1939–1945*, Cassell, 1951.
Hart, Basil Lidell. *The Strategy of Indirect Approach*, Faber and Faber Ltd, 1967.
Hart, Basil Lidell. *This Expanding war*, Faber and Faber Ltd, 1962.
Hart, Basil Lidell. *Thoughts on War*, Faber and Faber Ltd, 1944.
Hart, Basil Lidell. *When Britain Goes to War: Adaptability and Mobility*, Faber and Faber Ltd, 1935.
Hart, Basil Lidell. *Why Don't we Learn from History?*, Allen and Unwin, 1972.
Heathcote, T.A. *The British Field Marshals, 1736–1997: A Biographical Dictionary*, Leo Cooper, London, 1999.
King, Jonathan. *The Western Front: The ANZACs' Own Story, Battle by Battle,* Simon and Schuster, Pymble, 2010.
Levi, John S. *Rabbi Jacob Dangelow: 'The uncrowned monarch of Australian Jews',* Melbourne University Press, Victoria, 1995.
Macdougall A. K. (ed.), *War Letters of General Monash*, Halstead Printing Company Sydney, 2002.
Oldham, Peter. *Messines Ridge*, Pen and Sword Military, United Kingdom, 1998.
Pedersen, Peter. *Fromelles,* Pen & Sword Books Ltd, United Kingdom, 2004.
Pederson, Peter. *Hamel,* Pen & Sword Books Ltd, United Kingdom, 2002.
Pedersen, Peter. *The Anzacs: Gallipoli to the Western Front*, Penguin, Ringwood, 2007.
Pedersen, Peter. *Villers-Bretonneux,* Pen & Sword Ltd, United Kingdom, 2004.
Pedersen, Peter, with Chris Roberts. *Anzacs on the Western Front: The Australian War Memorial Battlefield Guide*, John Miley and Sons, Queensland, 2012.

Perry, Roland. *Monash: The Outsider Who Won a War*, Random House, Milson's Point, 2004.
Rosenthal, Newman. *The Albert Coates Story: The Will that Found the Way*, Hyland House, Victoria, 1997.
Ryan, M.J. *A Most Unusual Regiment: A History of Melbourne University Regiment*, Australian Military History Publications, 2008.
Serle, Geoffrey. *John Monash: A Biography* , Melbourne University Press, 1982.
Singleton-Gates, Peter. *General Lord Freyberg VC: An Unofficial Biography,* Michael Joseph, United States, 1963.
Smithers, A.J. *Sir John Monash,* Lee Cooper Ltd, London, 1973.
Snelling, Stephen. *VCs of the First World War: Gallipoli,* Sutton Publishing, England, 1995.
Thomson, Alistair. *Anzac Memories: Living with the Legend*, Monash University Publishing, Melbourne, 2013.
Younger, R.M. *Keith Murdoch: Founder of a Media Empire*, Harper Collins, New South Wales, 2003.

INDEX

INDEX